©Master Key
to the GRE

Volume 5

Geometry

Made by
Sherpa Prep

Master Key to the GRE: Geometry.

ISBN: 978-0-9966225-1-6

© 2018 Sherpa Prep.

Register Your Book!

To access the online videos that come with this book, please go to:

www.sherpaprep.com/videos

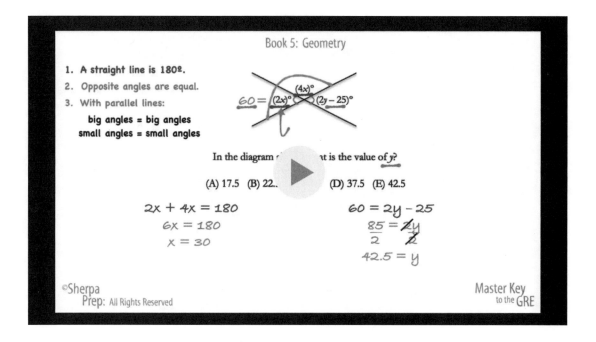

When registering:

Be sure to provide the **same** email address that you used to purchase this book or to enroll in your GRE course with Sherpa Prep!

Register @ www.sherpaprep.com/videos

Master Key by
Sherpa Prep

Dear Student,

Thank you for purchasing Sherpa Prep's guide to <u>Geometry</u>. We know that preparing for the GRE can be a grueling and intimidating process. The fact that you've chosen us to assist you is deeply appreciated.

This series of books is the culmination of nearly three decades of experience teaching the GRE on a daily basis. We think you'll find that experience and expertise reflected in the pages that follow.

As with any undertaking of this size, there are a number of people who deserve special recognition. First among them is Nasheed Amin, who critiqued <u>Master Key to the GRE</u> in its entirety and whose insightful recommendations significantly enhanced all five volumes. We would also like to recognize the contributions of Seth Alcorn, Shawn Magnuson, Bronwyn Bruton, and Jessica Rider Amin. Without their assistance, this project would not have been possible. Finally, we would like to extend our gratitude to the students and instructors of Sherpa Prep, whose feedback, questions, and experiences lie at the heart of these materials.

Good luck with your preparation! If we can be of further assistance, please reach out to us at **jay@sherpaprep.com** or **nafeez@sherpaprep.com**. We'd love to hear from you.

On behalf of everyone at Sherpa Prep,

Jay

Nafeez

Jay Friedman
Founder
Sherpa Prep

Nafeez Amin
President
Sherpa Prep

Table of Contents

Volume 5

Geometry

Introduction to the GRE

Introduction

To be discussed:

Master Key to the GRE

Get a sense of how to use our books, how to study properly for the GRE, and how to access our online video content.

1	Choosing the Right Guide	**4**	Proper Study Habits
2	Why Master Key is Special	**5**	The App
3	How to Use Our Guides	**6**	Register Your Book!

The Structure & Scoring System

Read about the structure and scoring system of the GRE. Learn how to sign up for the exam and report your scores.

7	The Structure of the GRE	**9**	Registering for the GRE
8	The Scoring System	**10**	Reporting & Canceling Scores

Navigating the Exam

Get an in-depth sense of how the GRE's scoring system works and what you can do to maximize your performance on test day.

11	How the Exam Works	**13**	Strategy & Time Management
12	The Scoring Algorithm	**14**	Practice Tests

Intro to Quantitative Reasoning

Before you get started, educate yourself about the sort of math you'll find on the GRE and the four ways in which the exam formats its math questions.

15	Content Overview	**18**	Numeric Entry Questions
16	Problem Solving Questions	**19**	Quantitative Comparisons
17	"Select One or More" Questions	**20**	Before You Get Started

Master Key to the GRE

(1) Choosing the Right Guide – If you're like most people preparing to take the GRE, you probably have little sense of what differentiates one GRE guide from another.

• You may think that all GRE guides are more or less the same, or that the guides you see in bookstores are the most comprehensive on the market.

> ➤ The basic story is that most guides fall into one of two categories: "strategy-based" or "content-based".

• **The guides that you find in bookstores are almost always strategy-based.** In general, strategy-based guides provide:

1. A brief discussion of each question type that you find on the GRE.
2. A small set of suggestions for approaching these question types.
3. A collection of one hundred or so practice questions with some brief solutions.

• You also tend to find instructions on how to register for the GRE and report your scores; advice for the test day experience; and a few appendices that review vocabulary and elementary math principles.

> ➤ You won't find a lot of "know-how", however, in strategy-based guides. **The focus of such books is test-taking advice, not education**.

• The latest "premier" guide of one well-known test-prep provider, for example, devotes just nineteen pages to explaining math concepts.

• This said, you will find some useful ideas for taking the exam strategically, among them: ways to use the answer choices to your advantage; advice on how to pace yourself; and recommendations on how to read.

> ➤ In our experience, learning these sorts of strategies is helpful for most test-takers. Unfortunately, **they will not help you attain a strong GRE score, on their own**.

• If you do not know how to solve the problems you find on your exam, you will not do well, regardless of how well you can eliminate irrational answers, pace yourself, or otherwise "game" the exam.

> ➤ In contrast, **content-based guides teach the "know-how" you need** to solve exam questions without guessing.

• Such guides generally devote several pages of discussion to most of the major topics tested by the GRE.

• At the end of each discussion, you tend to find a set of section-ending exercises that allow you to practice what you've studied. As a result, content-based guides almost always have far more practice questions than their strategy-based counterparts.

> ➤ In our view, **this sort of approach is critical to success on the GRE**. It may not be the only thing you need to succeed, but it is the most important.

• Think about it logically for a moment. Is there any other exam you would dare take without learning its content beforehand?

• Of course not. Yet students regularly "prep" for the GRE using books that do not review the content of the exam. It takes years to graduate from college, and some admissions committees weigh GRE scores more heavily than grade point averages. Isn't an exam that means so much worth preparing for properly?

> ➤ Unfortunately, there a number of drawbacks to the content-based guides currently available for the GRE.

• For starters, **these guides almost always ignore the tactics recommended by strategy-based guides,** tactics that we believe are an asset to any test taker.

• What's more, such guides rarely tell you how frequently a particular topic is tested. Knowing which topics to study is important if you only have limited time to prepare for the GRE!

> ➤ Most importantly, none of the guides actually teach you EVERYTHING tested by the GRE.

• While most cover the major topics found on a typical exam, **none cover the vast array of rare and advanced concepts that you need to grasp if you're hoping to score <u>above</u> the 90th percentile.**

(2) Why Master Key Is Special – <u>Master Key to the GRE</u> is the only guide to the GRE that will teach you everything you need to attain a perfect score.

• Whether you're looking for help with advanced concepts, or are starting from scratch, our materials will have what you need.

> ➤ **We start by assuming you know NOTHING.** Everything is laid out for you as if you haven't done math in years.

• Each chapter focuses on a specific topic, such as Fractions, Rates, or Triangles, and opens with a thorough discussion of its simplest, most fundamental concepts.

• Bit by bit, we gradually explore ALL the wrinkles associated with that topic, so that you can solve problems involving sophisticated nuances, not just easy problems.

> ➤ At the ends of our chapters, you'll find a treatment of **every RARE and ADVANCED concept tested by the GRE.**

• You won't find these topics discussed anywhere else. <u>Master Key to the GRE</u> is the only resource that covers them.

• We know that some of you only need help solving the most difficult questions — the questions that determine who scores ABOVE the 90th percentile. We've made sure that our guides teach <u>everything</u>, so that students in your position get all the support they need.

> ➤ To keep things simple, we discuss math in **language that's EASY to understand** and focus on **SMART strategies for every level of material**.

• In writing <u>Master Key to the GRE</u>, we were determined to make our guides helpful for everyone, not just math geeks.

• We are GRE specialists who have spent our entire professional careers making math ACCESSIBLE to students who hate it. **These books are the culmination of over three decades of daily classroom instruction.** No matter how difficult a topic may be, we walk you through each concept, step by step, to ensure that everything makes sense.

> ➤ Along the way, **we sprinkle in hundreds of SHORTCUTS and TRICKS** that you won't find in any other guide.

• We know that TIME is a major concern for many test-takers, so we've included every time-saving strategy out there to help you "beat the clock".

Chapter 1: Introduction

- We don't care how well you think you know math. These shortcuts will save you valuable minutes, no matter what your current skill level may be.

  ➢ To complement our content-oriented approach, the first volume of <u>Master Key to the GRE</u> devotes **an entire chapter to something we call "Plan B" strategies**.

- A "Plan B" strategy is a strategy that can help you deduce a correct answer when you don't know how to solve a problem.

- Such "tricks of the trade" are sometimes encountered in mainstream strategy-based guides. No other guide, however, features a collection like the one we've put together here. We've got all of the tricks, not just a few.

  ➢ We also complement our content-oriented approach by telling you **how FREQUENTLY the GRE tests every concept** — something no other guide does.

- We know that most people don't have the time to study everything and aren't looking for a perfect score — just a score that's good enough to get them into the school of their choice.

- So, we let you know which topics are <u>commonly tested</u> and which ones are not so that you can determine for yourself which topics are worth your time.

  ➢ Additionally, **we organize our discussions by level of DIFFICULTY**, as well as by topic.

- As we see it, test-takers deserve to know which topics they need to master in order to get elite scores and which topics they can afford to skip if they're only looking for above average scores.

- Our hope is that by organizing our material in this way, you'll be able to limit your efforts to material that is right for you.

  ➢ In total, <u>Master Key to the GRE</u> includes **nearly ONE THOUSAND practice questions**. That's more than any other resource out there.

- Like our teaching sections, our practice questions are sorted by difficulty, as well as by topic, so that you can focus on any level of material and on any topic that you like.

- Moreover, nearly a quarter of these questions involve the most rare or advanced topics tested by the GRE. So if you're looking for a lot of help with diabolical fare, you'll find it here.

➢ Most of the solutions to these questions come in the form of **ANIMATED VIDEOS, which you can play on any computer, tablet, or smart phone**.

• We understand that the short, written explanations found in other GRE handbooks are often insufficient for students who find math challenging.

• By providing you with video solutions, we are able to talk you through our practice problems, every step of the way, so that you can follow along easily and see where your solution went wrong.

➢ In many cases, you'll find that our animated videos discuss **multiple ways to solve a question**.

• In math, there is often more than one way to solve a problem. Not all of these approaches, however, are equally efficient.

• Our videos discuss the best of these approaches to ensure that you're exposed to a solution that's not only fast and simple, but also works well with your way of thinking.

➢ We know that <u>Master Key to the GRE</u> is the most expensive GRE guide on the market.

• It's anywhere from $60 to $100 dollars more expensive than most of the alternatives out there. That's a lot of money.

• But let us ask you this. Which would rather have: an extra $60 to $100 dollars or the GRE scores that you need?

➢ Remember, it took you years to graduate from college, and many admissions committees weigh GRE scores more heavily than your grade point average.

• Isn't an exam that means so much worth the cost of a college textbook? Of course it is.

• If you're still not certain, **we encourage you to compare our materials to anything else** that you can find. Whether you're looking for help with advanced material or something a little less extreme, we have no doubt that you'll see why <u>Master Key to the GRE</u> is worth the difference.

(3) How to Use Our Guides – As mentioned, <u>Master Key to the GRE</u> has been designed to help you solve EVERY question on the GRE.

• It explains ALL of the TOUGH concepts that no other GRE prep book attempts to cover, not just the easy ones.

> ➤ Depending on your goals, however, you may NOT need to master everything. Not every program requires a perfect score. In fact, most don't require anything close.

• If you've yet to do so, we strongly encourage you to contact the programs you're interested in to see what sort of scores they require.

• Knowing "how high" to set the bar will give you a sense of whether you need to cover everything or just the core material. (Remember, we'll tell you how frequently each topic is tested!)

> ➤ Every volume of <u>Master Key to the GRE</u> has been designed to help someone starting from SCRATCH to build, step by step, to the most challenging material.

• Thus, Chapter 1 is intended to precede Chapter 2, and the same is true for each volume: <u>Arithmetic & "Plan B" Strategies</u> (Vol. 1) is intended to precede <u>Number Properties & Algebra</u> (Vol. 2).

• The chapters, however, are largely independent of one another, as are the books, so you're welcome to skip around if you only need help with a few key topics or are short on time.

> ➤ As you study, bear in mind that you DON'T have to master one topic before studying another.

• If you have a hard time with something, put it aside for a day or two. It can take one or two "exposures" for a concept to "click" – especially if it's new or tricky.

• You also don't need to solve all 1,000 of our practice problems. If you're comfortable with a topic, feel free to skip the questions marked "fundamental" to save time.

> ➤ Finally, remember that our ADVANCED materials are intended for students in need of PERFECT scores.

• If that's not you, don't waste your time! Questions involving advanced topics are generally rare for the GRE, so if you'd be thrilled with a score around the 90th percentile, you're more likely to achieve it by focusing on questions and materials involving core concepts.

(4) Proper Study Habits – Whatever your goals may be for the GRE, it's important that you work consistently.

• Studying a little EVERY DAY is the best way to retain what you're learning and to avoid the burn out that comes with studying too intensely for too long.

> ➢ In a perfect world, we'd have you study about an hour a day during the workweek and one to two hours a day on the weekends.

• Unfortunately, we know that such a schedule is unrealistic for some people. If you can't find an hour each day, at least DO SOMETHING!

• Even 5 minutes a day can help you stave off rust and prevent the cycle of guilt and procrastination that comes from not studying.

> ➢ If you can, do your best to AVOID CRAMMING. Much of what you'll be studying is boring and technical. It will take "elbow grease" to master.

• We truly question how much of this information can be absorbed in a few short weeks or in study sessions that last three or four hours.

• In our experience, most students who do too much too rapidly either burnout or fail to absorb the material properly.

> ➢ To avoid "study fatigue", SWITCH things up. Spend part of each day studying for the math portion of the exam and part for the verbal portion.

• And do your best to incorporate at least part of your study routine into your daily life.

• If you can study 30 minutes out of every lunch break and a few minutes out of every snack break, we think you'll find that you have more time to prepare than you might believe. We also think you'll find the shorter study sessions more beneficial.

> ➢ As you study, be sure to bear in mind that QUALITY is just as important as QUANTITY.

• Many test-takers believe that the key to success is to work through thousands of practice questions and to take dozens of exams. This simply isn't true.

Chapter 1: Introduction

- While working through practice questions and taking exams are important parts of preparing for the GRE, doing so does not mean that you are LEARNING the material.

  ➤ It is equally important that you LEARN from your MISTAKES. Whenever you miss a practice question, be sure to watch the video explanation that we've provided.

- Then, redo the problem yourself. Once you feel that you've "got it", come back to the problem two days later.

- If you still get it wrong, add the problem to your "LOG of ERRORS" and redo it every few weeks. Keeping track of tricky problems and redoing them MORE THAN ONCE is a great way to learn from your mistakes and to avoid similar difficulties on your actual exam.

  ➤ As you prepare, keep the REAL exam in mind. The GRE tests your ability to recognize concepts under TIMED conditions. Your study habits should reflect this.

- If it takes you 3 minutes to solve a problem, you may as well have missed that problem. 3 minutes is too much time to spend on a problem during an actual exam. Be sure to watch the video solutions for such problems and to redo them until you can solve them quickly.

- Likewise, bear in mind that you will take the GRE on a COMPUTER, unless you opt to take the paper-based version that is administered only three times a year.

  ➤ So adopt GOOD HABITS now. Whenever you practice, avoid doing things you can't do on a computer, such as writing atop problems or underlining key words.

- And make a NOTECARD whenever you learn something. The cards don't have to be complicated – even a sample problem that illustrates the concept will do.

- As your studying progresses, it can be easy to forget concepts that you learned at the beginning of your preparation. Notecards will help you retain what you've learned and make it easy for you to review that material whenever you have a few, spare minutes.

  ➤ Finally, do your best to keep your emotions in check. It's easy to become overconfident when a practice exam goes well or to get down when one goes poorly.

- The GRE is a tough exam and improvement, for most students, takes time.

- In our experience, however, test-takers who prepare like PROFESSIONALS — who keep an even keel, who put in the time to do their assignments properly, and who commit to identifying their weaknesses and improving them – ALWAYS achieve their goals in the end.

(5) The App – <u>Master Key to the GRE</u> is available in print through Amazon or through our website at **www.sherpaprep.com/masterkey**.

• It's also available as an app for iPhones and iPads through Apple's App Store under the title <u>GRE Math by Sherpa Prep</u>.

> ➤ Like the printed edition, the app comes with access to all of our LESSONS, practice QUESTIONS, and VIDEOS.

• And, like any book, it allows you to BOOKMARK pages, UNDERLINE text, and TAKE NOTES.

• Unlike a book, however, it also allows you to design practice quizzes, create study lists, make error logs, and keep statistics on just about everything.

> ➤ The ⟨**DESIGN a PRACTICE QUIZ**⟩ feature lets you make quizzes in which you select the TOPICS, the NUMBER of questions, and the DIFFICULTY.

• It also allows you to SHUFFLE the questions by topic and difficulty and to SET a TIMER for any length of time.

• For example, you can make a 30-minute quiz comprised of fifteen intermingled Ratio, Rate, and Overlapping Sets questions, in which all the questions are advanced. Or you can make a 10-minute quiz with just ten Probability questions, of which some are easy and others are intermediate. You can pretty much make any sort of quiz that you like.

> ➢ AFTER each quiz, you get to REVIEW your performance, question by question, and to view video solutions.

• You also get to see the difficultly level of your quiz questions, as well as the time it took you to answer each of them.

• You even get to COMPARE your performance to that of other users. You see how frequently other users were able to solve the questions on your quiz and how long it took them, on average, to do so.

> ➢ As you read through our lessons, the $\boxed{\textbf{MAKE a STUDY LIST}}$ feature allows you to form a personalized study list.

• With the tap of a button, you can add any topic that you read about to an automated "to do" list, which organizes the topics you've selected by chapter and subject.

• From your study list, you can then access these topics instantly to revisit them whenever you need to.

> ➢ Similarly, the $\boxed{\textbf{CREATE an ERROR LOG}}$ feature allows you to compile a list of practice problems you wish to redo for further practice.

• Every time you answer a question, you can add it to this log, regardless of whether you got the question right or wrong, or left it blank.

• By doing so, you can keep track of every problem that you find challenging and redo them until they no longer pose a challenge.

> ➢ Finally, the app $\boxed{\textbf{TRACKS your PERFORMANCE}}$ at every turn to help you identify your strengths and weaknesses.

• In addition to the data from your practice quizzes, the app provides key information on how you're performing, by TOPIC and across DIFFICUTLY LEVELS.

• So if you want to know what percentage of advanced level Algebra questions you're answering correctly, the app can tell you. Likewise, if you want to know what percentage of intermediate level Triangle questions you're answering correctly, the app can tell you that too.

> ➢ The app offers the first volume of <u>Master Key to the GRE</u> for $\boxed{\textbf{FREE}}$. The other four volumes retail for $9.99 apiece.

(6) Register Your Book! – Every volume of <u>Master Key to the GRE</u> comes with six months of free access to our collection of video solutions.

- If you have a print edition of <u>Master Key</u>, you'll need to $\boxed{\textbf{Register}}$ your book(s) to access these videos.

  ➢ To do so, please go to **www.sherpaprep.com/videos** and enter your email address.

- **Be sure to provide the SAME email address that you used to purchase your copy of <u>Master Key to the GRE</u>.**

- If you received your books upon enrolling in a GRE prep course with $\boxed{\textbf{Sherpa Prep}}$, be sure to enter the same email address that you used to enroll.

  ➢ If your registration is $\boxed{\textbf{Unsuccessful}}$, please send your last name and shipping address to **sales@sherpaprep.com**.

- We will confirm your purchase manually and create a login account for you.

- In most cases, this process will take no more than a few hours. Please note, however, that requests can take up to 24 hours to fulfill if you submit your request on a U.S. federal holiday or if we are experiencing extremely heavy demand.

  ➢ Six months after your date of registration, your video access to <u>Master Key to the GRE</u> will come to an end.

- An additional six months of access can be purchased at a rate of $9.99 per book. To do so, simply login at **www.sherpaprep.com/videos** and follow the directions.

Chapter 1: Introduction

About the GRE

(7) The Structure of the GRE – Before examining the content of the GRE, let's take a moment to discuss how the exam is structured and administered.

- The GRE is a computer-based exam that is offered world-wide on a daily basis.

  ➢ The test consists of six sections and takes around 3 hours and 45 minutes to complete (not including breaks).

- These sections are as follows:

  I. An Analytical Writing section containing two essays.
  II. Two Verbal Reasoning sections.
  III. Two Quantitative Reasoning sections.
  IV. One Unidentified Research section.

- The Analytical Writing section is always first, while **the other five sections may appear in ANY order**. You get a 10-minute break between the third and fourth sections, and a 1-minute break between the other test sections.

  ➢ The Unidentified Research section **does NOT count towards your score** and is either a Verbal Reasoning section or a Quantitative Reasoning section.

- Unfortunately, the Unidentified Research section is designed to look exactly like the other sections — there is no way to spot it.

- As such, you must take all five sections seriously. Even though one of them will not count towards your score, there is no way of knowing which section that is.

  ➢ Finally, some exams have an **Identified Research section** in place of the Unidentified Research section.

- This section is marked "For Research Purposes" and does not count towards your score. If your exam has an Identified Research section, it will appear at the end of the test.

- On the following page, you'll find a breakdown of all six sections. Notice that every Quantitative Reasoning section has 20 questions and is 35 minutes long.

• Similarly, notice that every Verbal Reasoning section also has 20 questions but is only 30 minutes long.

➢ When viewing the table below, remember that **the order of sections 2 through 6 is RANDOM**. These sections can occur in any order.

• This means that the Unidentified Research section can be ANY section after the first and that you might get two Quantitative sections in a row (or two Verbal sections)!

Section	Task	Number of Questions	Time	Note
1	Analytical Writing	Two Essays	30 minutes per essay	
2	Verbal Reasoning	20	30 minutes	
3	Quantitative Reasoning	20	35 minutes	
10-minute break				
4	Verbal Reasoning	20	30 minutes	
5	Quantitative Reasoning	20	35 minutes	
6	Unidentified Research	20	30 or 35 minutes	Not scored

• Also remember that that Unidentified Research section may be replaced with an Identified Research section. If so, the Identified Research section will appear at the end of the test.

(8) The Scoring System – After your GRE has been completed and graded, you will receive three scores:

1. A Verbal Reasoning score.
2. A Quantitative Reasoning score.
3. An Analytical Writing score.

• **Both the Verbal Reasoning and Quantitative Reasoning scores are reported on a scale from 130 to 170, in one-point increments**.

➢ The Analytical Writing score is reported on a scale from 0 to 6, in half-point increments.

• A score of NS (no score) is given for any measure in which no questions (or essay prompts) are answered.

• In addition to these scaled scores, you will also receive percentile rankings, which compare your scores to those of other GRE test-takers.

➢ Before applying to graduate school or business school, you should have a basic sense of what constitutes a good score and what constitutes a bad score.

• Currently, **an average Verbal Reasoning score is 151, an average Quantitative Reasoning score is 152, and an average Analytical Writing score is approximately 3.5**.

• Roughly two-thirds of all test-takers receive a score within the following ranges:

1. Verbal Reasoning: 142 to 159
2. Quantitative Reasoning: 143 to 161
3. Analytical Writing: 3 to 4.5

➢ As a loose guideline, these ranges suggest that any score in the 160s is fairly exceptional and that any score in the 130s may raise a red flag with an admissions committee.

• The same goes for Analytical Writing scores higher than 4.5 or lower than 3. In fact, only 7 percent of test-takers receive a score above 4.5 and only 9 percent receive a score below 3.

• You can find a complete concordance of GRE scores and their percentile equivalents on page 23 of this document: **http://www.ets.org/s/gre/pdf/gre_guide.pdf**.

➢ As you prepare for the GRE, we strongly encourage you to research the programs to which you plan to apply.

• Get a general sense of what sorts of scores your programs are looking for. See whether they have "cutoff" scores below which they no longer consider applicants.

• Knowing what you need to achieve is important. If your program needs an elite math score, it's best to know immediately so that you can make time to prepare properly!

➢ In some cases, you'll find the information you need online. In many cases, however, you'll need to contact your program directly.

• If you are reluctant to do so, bear this in mind: many programs are more forthcoming about scores in person or over the phone than they are by email or on the internet.

• Moreover, it never hurts to make contact with a prospective program. Saying "hi" gives you a chance to ask important questions and — if you can present yourself intelligently and professionally — to make a good impression on a potential committee member.

➢ If a school tells you they are looking for applicants with an average score of 160 per section, remember that such quotes are only averages!

• Some applicants will be accepted with scores below those averages and some will be turned down with scores above them.

• An average is simply a "ballpark" figure that you want to shoot for. Coming up short doesn't guarantee rejection (particularly if the rest of your application is strong), and achieving it doesn't ensure admission.

➢ Unfortunately, not all programs are willing to divulge average or "cutoff" GRE scores to the public.

• If that's the case with a program you're interested, here are some general pointers to keep in mind:

1. Engineering, Economics, and Hard Sciences programs are likely to place far more emphasis on your Quantitative Reasoning score than your other scores.

2. The more prestigious a university it is, the more likely its programs will demand higher scores than comparable programs at other schools.

3. Public Health, Public Policy, and International Affairs programs likely require very strong scores for all three portions of the GRE.

4. Education, Sociology, and Nursing programs are less likely to require outstanding scores.

➤ Should you wish to get a sense of average GRE scores, by intended field of study, you can do so here: **http://www.ets.org/s/gre/pdf/gre_guide_table4.pdf**.

• When viewing these scores, remember that these are the scores of INTENDED applicants!

• The average score of ACCEPTED applicants is likely to be higher for many programs — in some cases, much higher.

➤ Finally, it's worth noting that many programs use GRE scores to determine which applicants will receive SCHOLARSHIPS.

• When contacting programs, be sure to ask them about the averages or "cutoffs" for scholarship recipients.

• And if you find it difficult to study for an exam that has little to do with your intended field of study, just remember: strong GRE scores = $$$!

(9) Registering for the GRE – The GRE is administered via computer in over 160 countries on a near daily basis.

- This means that you can that you take the GRE almost ANY day of the year.

  ➢ To register, you must create a personalized GRE account, which you can do online at **http://www.ets.org/gre/revised_general/register/**.

- When creating your account, the NAME you use must MATCH the name you use to register for the GRE.

- **It must also match the name on your official identification EXACTLY**! If it doesn't, you may be prohibited from taking the exam (without refund).

  ➢ We encourage you to schedule a date that gives you ample time to prepare properly. Don't choose a random date just to get it over with!

- If possible, wait until you score a few points higher than your target score at least TWO TIMES in a row on practice exams. Doing so will ensure that you're ready to take the exam.

- When scheduling the time of day, **don't schedule an 8 a.m. exam if you are not accustomed to waking up at 6:30 a.m. or earlier**. The exam is challenging enough. Don't take it when you're likely to be groggy or weary!

  ➢ If you plan to take the exam on a specific date, register at least one month in advance. Exam centers have limited capacity, so dates can fill up quickly, especially in the fall.

- On the day of the test, be sure to bring your official identification and your GRE admission ticket.

- Once you register for the exam, your admission ticket can be printed out at any time through your personalized GRE account online.

  ➢ Finally, if you need to reschedule or cancel your exam date, you must do so no later than FOUR days before your test date. (Ten days for individuals in mainland China.)

- This means that a Saturday test date must be canceled by Tuesday and that an April 18th test date must be canceled by April 14th.

- You can find more information on canceling or rescheduling a test date here: **http://www.ets.org/gre/revised_general/register/change**.

(10) Reporting & Canceling Scores – Immediately upon completing your exam, you will be given the opportunity to cancel your scores or to report them.

• If you choose to cancel your scores, they will be deleted irreversibly.

> ➤ Neither you nor the programs to which you're applying will see the numbers. Your official score report, however, will indicate a canceled test.

• In general, there's almost no reason to cancel your scores.

• **The GRE has a Score Select option that allows you to decide which scores to send if you've taken the GRE more than once**. Thus, if you take the exam a second time (or a third time), you can simply choose which set of scores to report.

> ➤ If you choose to report your scores, you will immediately see your unofficial Quantitative Reasoning and Verbal Reasoning scores.

• Roughly 10 to 15 days after your test date, you will receive an email notifying you that your official scores and your Analytical Writing score are available.

• To view them, simply go to the personalized GRE account you created to register for the exam.

> ➤ You won't need to memorize any school CODES to send your scores while at the test center.

• Such codes will be accessible by computer, should you wish to report your scores when you're there. To get the code for a particular program, you'll need:

1. The name of the college (e.g. College of Arts & Sciences).
2. The name of the university.
3. The city and state of its location.

• As long as you have this information for each of your programs, you'll have everything you need to send out your score reports on the spot.

> ➤ **Your OFFICIAL and UNOFFICIAL scores are unlikely to differ**. If they do, the difference will almost surely be a single point.

• For example, your Verbal Reasoning score may rise from a 157 to a 158 or your Quantitative Reasoning score may dip from a 162 to a 161.

• The scores you receive on test day are an estimate comparing your performance with previous data. The official scores compare your performance with those of everyone who took that particular exam – hence the potential discrepancy.

> **Your official scores will be valid for FIVE years**. For example, a test taken on August 2nd, 2015 will be valid until August 1st, 2020.

• Over the course of those five years, your scaled scores will never change. The percentiles, however, may shift marginally.

• Thus, a scaled Verbal Reasoning score of 162 may equate to the 89th percentile in 2015. Come 2018, however, that 162 may equate to a 91st percentile.

> On test day, after viewing your unofficial scores, you will be given a choice at the test center.

• You can choose NOT to send your scores at that time or to send **free score reports** to as many as FOUR graduate programs or fellowship sponsors.

• If you choose to send out score reports at the test center, you will be given two further options:

1. The **Most Recent** option – send your scores from the test you've just completed.
2. The **All** option – send the scores from all the GREs you've taken in the last five years.

> After your test date, you can send additional score reports for a fee. **For each report**, you will be given the options above.

• **You will also be given the option to send your scores from just one exam OR from ANY exams you've taken over the last five years.**

• You cannot, however, choose your best Quantitative Reasoning score from one exam and your best Verbal Reasoning score from another. When sending scores, you must send all the scores you receive on a particular exam date.

> ➤ Given all of these options, **here's our advice**. First, NEVER cancel your scores. There's no point.

• Even if you believe you've had a bad performance, you may as well learn how you did. You never know — you might even be pleasantly surprised.

• If your scores are great, you're done. Send out your scores on test day to take advantage of the four free score reports.

> ➤ If you feel you can do better, retake the exam as soon as possible. Don't let your hard work go to waste.

• Anyone can have a bad day, misplay their time, or make an uncharacteristic number of careless errors.

• **You can retake the exam every 21 days** and up to 5 times within any 12-month period, so you won't have to wait long.

> ➤ Upon receiving your second set of scores, use the Score Select option on test day to determine which set of scores to send for free (or to send both sets).

• In the unpleasant event that you take the exam more than twice, consider utilizing the Score Select option the day after your last exam.

• This will allow you to send the single set of scores (or pair of scores) that puts you in the best possible light. Of course, if that last score is awesome, use the four free score reports to send out your most recent scores while you're at the test center!

Navigating the Exam

(11) How the Exam Works – Although the GRE is administered on computer, the exam has been designed to mimic the experience of a traditional, paper-based standardized test.

- This means that you can:

  - ☑ Skip questions and return to them later.
  - ☑ Leave questions blank.
  - ☑ Change or edit an answer.

- You can even "flag" questions with a check mark as a reminder to revisit them before time expires. (As with a paper-based exam, however, you cannot return to a section once that section ends.)

  ➢ If you took the GRE before 2011, you'll notice that this format differs dramatically from the one you remember.

- **The exam is no longer adaptive on a question-by-question basis**, so the problems don't get harder if you answer a prior problem correctly.

- In fact, you can now preview every question within a section the moment that section begins. (If you like, you can even do the problems in reverse order.)

  ➢ There are, however, a few differences between the way the GRE works and that of most paper-based standardized tests.

- First, the questions in each section do NOT get progressively harder.

- Unlike, say, the SAT, where the first questions within a section are generally easy and the last questions within a section are generally hard, **the difficulty of GRE questions varies throughout a particular section**. In other words, a section might start with a hard question and end with an easy question.

  ➢ Furthermore, the GRE has a "Review Screen" that allows you to see which questions you've answered and which ones you haven't.

- The Review Screen can also be used to see which questions you've flagged for further review. (A very helpful feature!)

> ➤ **Finally, the GRE adapts on a section-by-section basis**. If you perform well on your first quantitative section, your second quantitative section will be harder.

• Likewise, if you do not perform well on your first quantitative section, your second quantitative section will be easier.

• The verbal sections work this way, too. The quantitative and verbal sections, however, are independent of one another. A strong performance on a verbal section will not result in more difficult quantitative sections, or vice versa.

> ➤ According to our experiments with the GRE's official test software, **how you perform on your first quantitative section can produce 1 of 3 results.**

• The same is true of your performance on the first verbal section:

Approximate # of Correct Questions on First Section	Difficulty Level of Second Section
0 to 6	Easy
7 to 13	Medium
14 to 20	Hard

• In some exams, it might take 15 correct answers to end up with a hard second section. In others, it might take 13. The correlation between the number of questions you get right and the difficulty level of your second section, however, generally matches the chart above.

> ➤ Our experiments also indicate that **the difficulty of the questions that you get right has no bearing on the difficulty level of the second section.**

• In other words, getting any 14 (or so) questions correct will give you a hard second section — it doesn't matter whether those questions are the hardest 14 or the easiest 14.

• It also doesn't matter how quickly you answer anything. There are no bonus points for solving problems quickly.

> ➤ It should, however, be noted that **a hard second section is not comprised entirely of hard questions**, nor an easy second section entirely of easy questions.

• The questions in ANY section span a range of difficulties. A hard second section simply has a greater number of hard questions than an easy one. Thus, if you receive easy questions in your second quantitative section, it does not mean that you've done poorly!

(12) The Scoring Algorithm – Exactly how the GRE is scored is a closely guarded secret.

• From the official practice test software, however, it's clear that Quantitative Reasoning and Verbal Reasoning scores are essentially the byproducts of two factors:

1. How many questions you answer correctly.
2. Whether your second sections are easy, medium, or hard.

• As you may recall from our discussion of the structure of the GRE, every exam has two Quantitative Reasoning sections and two Verbal Reasoning sections that count.

➢ Since each of these sections has 20 questions, every GRE has 40 Quantitative Reasoning questions and 40 Verbal Reasoning questions.

• As you may also recall, each of these measures is scored on a 41-point scale (from 130 to 170). This means, that **each question is essentially worth 1 point**.

• Thus, to get a Quantitative Reasoning score of 170, you likely need to answer all 40 questions correctly. Each question that you get wrong more or less subtracts 1 point from your score.

➢ In analyzing the practice test software, however, it's also apparent that there are deductions for failing to achieve a hard or medium second section.

• In general, these deductions range from 1 to 3 points.

• For example, if you were to get 11 questions correct on your first Quantitative Reasoning section, your score would be lowered 9 points on account of the 9 questions you got wrong or left blank since the exam treats blank and incorrect answers equally. (**There is NO PENALTY for getting problems wrong, so always GUESS when you're stuck!**)

➢ Your 11 correct answers, however, would also result in a second section of medium difficulty.

• Thus, your score would be lowered an additional 1 to 3 points for failing to make it to the hard section.

• Likewise, if you were to answer only 4 questions correctly in your first Quantitative Reasoning section, your score would be lowered 16 points for the blank or incorrect answers, 1 to 3 points for failing to make it to the hard section, and another 1 to 3 points for failing to make it to the medium section.

➤ Thus, a test taker who gets 10 questions right in each of his or her Quantitative Reasoning sections would likely receive a score from 147 to 149.

• The 20 questions left blank or answered incorrectly would deduct 20 points from the total score.

• Failing to make it to the hard section would deduct an additional 1 to 3 points. Subtracted from 170 (a perfect score), this would leave a final score of 147 to 149:

170	A perfect score
10	10 missed questions in section 1
10	10 missed questions in section 2
− 1 to 3	The penalty for not reaching the hard section
147 to 149	

➤ In all likelihood, the scoring algorithm considers a few other factors as well.

• For example, when exam-makers opt to include a greater number of difficult questions on a particular exam, they likely slide the scale for that exam 1 to 2 points in order to normalize its data with past exams that contain fewer difficult questions.

• From what we've seen, however, the dynamics described above will predict your score perfectly in most instances.

(13) Strategy & Time Management – Given the factors we've just discussed, there are several tactics that we recommend when taking the GRE.

1. SKIP around.

• It doesn't matter which questions you get right, so you may as well work on the questions that are easiest for you first.

> ➢ **Don't waste your time on a question that you don't understand or that confuses you.**

• Engaging such questions will only take time from questions that may be easier for you. If you come across something that makes you nauseous, FLAG IT and double back after you've solved the questions that you know how to solve.

2. FOCUS on your FAVORITE 15.

• As we've seen, there are potentially harsh deductions for failing to achieve a hard or medium second section.

> ➢ Since reaching the hard second section generally demands a minimum of 13 to 15 correct responses, we encourage you to focus your efforts on the 15 easiest questions.

• You shouldn't ignore the hardest 5 questions, but you should save them for last. **If you don't think you can answer 15 questions correctly, focus your efforts on the easiest 10 questions.** Landing in the lowest tier can devastate your score.

3. GUESS on questions that you don't understand.

• We've also seen that an incorrect answer is no worse than a blank answer, so you may as well <u>guess</u> on anything that you don't understand and flag it for further review. Remember, there's no penalty for guessing!

> ➢ As you'll see, **there's either a 1 in 5 chance or a 1 in 4 chance of guessing most GRE questions correctly.**

• Those chances increase if you can eliminate a couple of answer choices through logic. If you have time left over, you can return to the questions you've flagged after you've answered everything else.

4.   REMEMBER the $\boxed{\text{"Two-and-a-Half Minute Rule"}}$.

• Over the years at Sherpa Prep, we've noticed that test-takers who take more than 2.5 minutes to solve a question do so correctly only 25% of the time.

➢ Given that there are usually five answers to choose from, the odds of guessing correctly are 20%. If you can eliminate bad answer choices, those odds rise further!

• We know that it's tempting to battle questions to the end, especially if you "think" you can solve them. **Stubbornly hanging on, however, is a sure way to MANGLE your score**.

• Doing so wastes time (time that could be used to solve other problems) and is no more likely to result in a correct answer than guessing.

➢ So, if you find yourself stuck on a particular question, do yourself a favor: flag the question, then guess.

• If you can eliminate answer choices before doing so, great. Obeying the "2.5 minute rule" will help you save time for the questions at the end of the exam and avoid the debilitating panic that comes upon realizing that you've squandered your time.

5.   Don't work TOO QUICKLY.

• We know that time is a critical factor on the GRE and that the exam-makers don't give you much of it.

➢ **Working at a frenzied pace, however, will only result in one thing — careless errors. A lot of them.**

• The key to saving time is obeying the "2.5 minute rule" and learning the right way to solve each type of problem – not working at breakneck speeds.

• If you know how to solve a problem, take the time to do so properly. You may not have time to triple check your work, but you do have time to work through any problem with care.

➢ **Watch out, however, for any question that you can solve in 10 seconds or fewer.**

• While there are plenty of GRE problems that can be solved in 10 seconds, exam-makers often design questions to take advantage of quick assumptions. Taking an extra 10 seconds to ensure that you haven't missed something is a great way to catch potential traps!

(14) Practice Tests – As you work through <u>Master Key to the GRE</u>, we strongly encourage you to take a practice exam every week or two.

• Success on the GRE is not just the byproduct of mastering its content — it also demands good test-taking skills.

   ➢ **Taking practice exams will help you build stamina and improve your time management.**

• Remember, the GRE takes nearly four hours to complete. Learning how to deal with the fatigue you'll encounter is part of the battle!

• The same is true of the pacing of the exam. If you don't master the speed at which you need to work, you can easily sabotage your score by working too quickly or too leisurely.

   ➢ Before you take the GRE, we encourage you to **take a minimum of SIX practice exams**.

• If you're like most test-takers, you'll need anywhere from six to eight practice exams to properly familiarize yourself with the GRE.

• For the first few — don't bother with the essays. As you begin your preparation, your time is better spent studying new material and reviewing what you've learned. Towards the end of your preparation, however, your practice exams should be full-blown dress rehearsals.

   ➢ **There are a number of different practice exams available online. Of these, only two are produced by the ETS, the company that designs the GRE.**

• At no cost, you can download the software that runs these exams from the following address: **http://www.ets.org/gre/revised_general/prepare/powerprep2/**.

• These exams have been designed to work on both Macs and PCs. As long as your computer's operating system and software are reasonably up to date, you should be able to use them on any computer.

   ➢ For additional exams, almost any of the available options will do. While they all have issues of one sort or another, most are reasonable facsimiles of the GRE.

• When taking such exams, however, please bear in mind that they are NOT the real thing. Some of their questions are unrealistic and their score predictions, though roughly accurate, are best taken with a grain of salt.

➢ Whenever you take a practice exam, it's important that you **make the experience as REALISTIC as possible**.

• Doing things you can't do on test day will only corrupt your practice results and prevent you from adopting helpful habits.

• If you can, take each exam in one sitting and resist the urge to pause the test or to use outside help. Likewise, refrain from drinking or eating during your tests. No coffee, no water, no snacks. Save these things for your 10-minute break between sections 3 and 4.

➢ Remember, you're preparing for a stressful "brain marathon" that's essentially 4-hours long. You'll need STAMINA to be successful.

• Figure out how much you need to eat and drink before your test. Figure out what to eat during your break. Identify the kind of foods that suit you best.

• The same goes for your bathroom habits. At the exam center, you can't pause the test to go to the bathroom. So, use your practice exams to learn how your eating habits affect your bodily needs! "Holding it in" for over an hour is a brutal way to take this test.

➢ As you take your practice exams, do your best to **stay off the "emotional rollercoaster"**. Don't get too high when things go well.

• And don't get too down if your scores don't shoot up instantly. Improving GRE scores is hard work.

• For some people, progress is a slow, steady crawl. For others, it's an uneven process, filled with periods of stagnation, occasional drops, and dramatic increases.

➢ However your exams may be going, keep grinding away! Stay focused on your goals and keep up the hard work.

• Test-takers who prepare like professionals — who keep an even keel, who do their assignments properly, and who commit to improving their weaknesses — ALWAYS achieve their goals in the end.

• As we tell our students, preparing for the GRE is like going to the gym. It may take you a while to get in shape, but ANYONE can do so if they put in the time and train properly.

➤ **After you complete each practice exam, go through it carefully and learn from your mistakes.**

• See whether you can identify any trends in your performance. Are you working too quickly and making careless errors? Are you struggling with the same topics repeatedly?

• Are you running out of time because you're violating the "2.5 minute rule"? Do you start off strong and then taper off as the test goes along? Does it take you half an hour to get "locked in" and then get better as you go?

➤ A lot of people believe they are "bad test-takers". This is nonsense. The reality is that people get questions wrong for tangible reasons.

• Analyzing your mistakes when the "game is real" will allow you to PINPOINT those reasons so you can ADDRESS them.

• To help you become a more "self-aware" test-taker, we encourage you to fill out the following table every time you complete an exam:

	Knew How to Solve	Didn't Know How to Solve
Correct	Bravo!	Luck
Incorrect	Carelessness?	**Expected**

➤ If you get a question wrong because you don't know how to solve it, see whether you can identify its TOPIC or notice any TRENDS.

• For example, you might notice that a lot of your mistakes involve Algebra. If so, that's a clear indication that you need to improve your Algebra skills.

• If you get a question wrong despite knowing how to solve it, see whether you can figure out how it happened. Did you misread the question?   Did you write down information incorrectly? Did you make a silly math error?

➤ Mistakes such as these are often the result of RUSHING, which in turn is generally the byproduct of poor time management elsewhere.

• So keep track, to the best of your abilities, of whether you are finishing your sections too quickly or are making frantic efforts to finish because you're violating the "2.5 minute rule" too frequently. Both scenarios generally lead to a host of careless mistakes that will sabotage your progress.

Chapter 1: Introduction

> Intro to Quantitative Reasoning

(15) Content Overview – The quantitative portion of the GRE is designed to measure your ability to think <u>smartly</u> about math — to find simple solutions to problems that seem complicated.

• The problems that you'll encounter may appear difficult or time-consuming, but there's ALWAYS a straightforward way to solve them.

> ➢ In terms of content, the GRE solely tests concepts that you learned in high school or use in everyday life.

• These concepts fall into four categories:

> 1. Arithmetic, Algebra, and Number Properties
> 2. Word Problems
> 3. Data Interpretation
> 4. Geometry

> ➢ You won't find any Calculus or Trigonometry on the GRE, nor will you find some of the more sophisticated forms of Algebra typically taught in an Algebra II course.

• That's because the emphasis of this exam is on your ability to reason.

• By limiting the content to the topics listed above, the GRE becomes less about "what you know" (everyone studied those topics in high school) and more about your ability to APPLY commonly known information and to think logically.

> ➢ This said, don't be fooled into thinking that GRE math can't be sophisticated. The exam demands that you know these topics EXTREMELY well.

• To be successful on the GRE, you'll need to relearn everything you learned about them (or were supposed to learn) back in high school.

• And, if you want to solve the most advanced questions, you'll need to learn a few intricacies that you almost surely were never taught.

➤ Based on our analysis of the official exam materials released to the public, roughly one-third of GRE questions focus on Arithmetic, Algebra, and Number Properties.

• Approximately 33% are Word Problems and a little more than a third involve Geometry or the interpretation of Charts and Graphs:

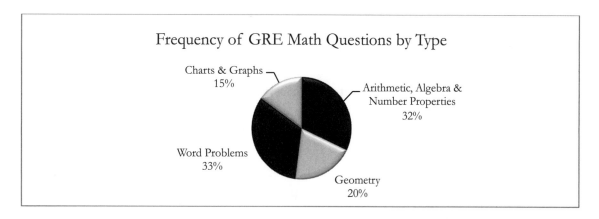

• When viewing the diagram above, bear in mind that Word Problems and problems involving Geometry or Charts and Graphs often demand the use of Algebra and Arithmetic. Thus, in many ways, Algebra and Arithmetic are even more critical to your success than the diagram above suggests.

➤ Volume 1 of <u>Master Key to the GRE</u> is devoted to **Arithmetic & "Plan B" Strategies**.

• Here, you'll find discussion of such topics as:

Arithmetic Shortcuts	Strategies for "Smart Math"
Essential Number Lists	Strategies for Using the Answer Choices
Fractions	Number Picking Strategies
Decimals	Strategies for Guessing
Digit Problems	

➤ Volume 2 is dedicated to **Number Properties & Algebra**. Among the topics you'll find covered are:

Factors & Multiples	Exponents & Roots
Prime Factorization	The Properties of Evens & Odds
Number Line Problems	Algebra
Absolute Value	Functions, Sequences & Symbolism
Remainder Problems	

Chapter 1: Introduction

> ➤ Our discussion of **Word Problems** is divided between Volumes 3 and 4. Volume 3 focuses on topics such as:

Percents	Algebraic Word Problems
Mixtures	Age Problems
Alterations	Overlapping Sets
Ratios & Proportions	Exponential & Linear Growth
Rate Problems	

- Volume 4 examines **Statistics & Data Interpretation**.

> ➤ Among the various chapters of Volume 4, you'll find discussions of a wide range of topics, including:

Means, Medians & Modes	Probability
Weighed Averages	Combinatorics
Standard Deviation	Bar Graphs & Line Graphs
Quartiles & Boxplots	Pie Charts & Data Tables
Normal Distributions	Multi-Figure Data Sets
Equally Spaced Number Sets	

- Finally, Volume 5 is devoted to **Geometry**.

> ➤ Here, you'll find a detailed treatment of everything you may have been taught in high-school but have probably forgotten.

- The major topics include:

Lines & Angles	Rectangular Solids
Triangles	Cylinders
Quadrilaterals	Coordinate Geometry
Polygons	
Circles	

- If all of this seems intimidating, don't worry! We promise you: <u>Master Key to the GRE</u> will show you just how simple these concepts can be.

(16) Problem Solving Questions – Before we get started, let's take a few pages to discuss the ways in which the GRE formats its math questions.

• As you may recall, every GRE has two Quantitative Reasoning sections. Since each of these sections has 20 questions, your exam will feature a total of 40 math questions (that actually count).

> ➤ 25 of these will be "Problem Solving" questions and 15 will be "Quantitative Comparison" questions.

• If you've taken standardized tests before, Problem Solving questions will be familiar to you. Here's an example:

If $x + y > 14$ and $x = 2y + 8$, then which of the following must be true?

(A) $y < -3$ **(B)** $y < -2$ **(C)** $y = 0$ **(D)** $y > 2$ **(E)** $y > 4$

Answer. D. To answer questions in this format, you simply need to select the answer choice that represents the correct answer.

> ➤ Here, for example, we've been told that $x = 2y + 8$. Thus, we can rewrite $x + y > 14$ as follows, by substituting $2y + 8$ for x:

Replace x with $2y + 8$

$\longrightarrow (2y + 8) + y > 14$

• To simplify the Algebra, we can drop the parentheses and subtract 8 from both sides of the inequality. Doing so proves that the correct is (D), since:

$2y + 8 + y > 14$	Drop the parentheses.
$2y + y > 6$	Subtract 8 from both sides.
$3y > 6$	Add $2y + y$.
$y > 2$	Divide both sides by 3.

• If the math doesn't make sense here, don't worry! This question is simply intended to show you what a Problem Solving question looks like. The math behind it is covered in our book on Number Properties & Algebra.

(17) "Select One or More" Questions – From time to time, Problem Solving questions will prompt you to select one or more answer choices.

• On a typical exam, each quantitative section will contain (at most) one or two of these questions.

> ➤ "Select One or More" questions are easy to spot — they always ask you to "indicate <u>all</u> such values".

• What's more, **the answer choices are always in square boxes.** In regular Problem Solving questions, the answer choices are circled.

• According to the Official Guide to the GRE revised General Test, the directions for such questions are always as follows:

> <u>Directions</u>: **Select ONE or MORE answer choices according to the specific directions.**

• If the question does not specify how many answer choices to select, you must select ALL that apply. The correct answer may be just one of the choices or as many as all of the choices. **There must, however, be at least one correct answer.**

> ➤ The exam-makers further specify that no credit is given unless you select all of the correct answers and no others. In other words, there is NO PARTIAL credit.

• Thus, if there are two correct answers, and you only select one, the GRE gives you zero credit. The same is true if there are three correct answers and you select four.

• Let's take a look at a sample question:

> **If $-2 \leq x \leq 8$ and $-4 \leq y \leq 3$, which of the following could represent the value of xy?**
>
> **Indicate <u>all</u> such values.**
>
> **$\boxed{A}$ –40 $\boxed{B}$ –32 $\boxed{C}$ 7 $\boxed{D}$ 15 $\boxed{E}$ 32**

Answer: B, C, and D. Notice that there are two clues indicating that we may need to select more than one answer here.

- First, the question asks us to "indicate <u>all</u> such values". **Additionally, the answer choices are in boxes.**

  ➤ To answer this question, we first need to determine the range of possible values for xy.

- We can do so by identifying the greatest and smallest possible values for x and y.

- According to the problem, $-2 \leq x \leq 8$ and $-4 \leq y \leq 3$. Thus, the greatest and smallest values for each variable are:

$$x = -2 \text{ and } 8 \qquad\qquad y = -4 \text{ and } 3$$

  ➤ Next, we can **test all four combinations** of x times y to determine the largest and smallest values of xy.

- If x can be as small as -2 and as large as 8, and y can be as small as -3 and as large as 4, then those combinations would be:

Combo #1	Combo #2	Combo #3	Combo #4
$(-2)(-4) = 8$	$(-2)(3) = -6$	$(8)(-4) = -32$	$(8)(3) = 24$

  ➤ As we can see from these combinations, the greatest possible value of x times y is 24 and the smallest possible value is -32.

- Thus, the range of values for xy extends from -32 to 24. Algebraically, this can be stated as $-32 \leq xy \leq 24$.

- Since -32, 7, and 15 all fall within the range of value from -32 to 24, **we must select** $\boxed{\text{B}}$, $\boxed{\text{C}}$, **and** $\boxed{\text{D}}$, **and nothing more, to get credit for this question.** If we fail to select all three answer choices, or select a fourth, our response would be considered incorrect.

  ➤ Again, if the math doesn't make sense here, don't worry! This question is simply intended to show you what a "Select One or More" question looks like.

- The math behind it is covered in our book on Number Properties & Algebra.

(18) Numeric Entry Questions – On each of your quantitative sections, anywhere from one to three of your Problem Solving questions will ask you for a "Numeric Entry".

• Numeric Entry questions prompt you to **type a numeric answer into a box** below the problem.

> ➤ Such questions tend to be more difficult than other Problem Solving questions since you can't use the answer choices to determine whether you're on the right track.

• Further, it's almost impossible to guess the correct answer. With regular Problem Solving questions, you at least have a 1 in 5 chance of getting lucky.

• Let's take a look at a sample question:

When walking, a person takes 24 complete steps in 15 seconds. At this rate, how many steps does this person take in 5 seconds?

• There are several ways to solve a problem like this. Perhaps the easiest way is to set up a proportion:

$$\frac{24 \text{ steps}}{15 \text{ seconds}} = \frac{x \text{ steps}}{5 \text{ seconds}}$$

• When comparing the bottoms of the two fractions, notice that "15 seconds" is exactly three times as large as "5 seconds".

> ➤ With proportions, the relationship between the tops of the fractions is the same as that between the bottoms.

• In other words, "24 steps" must be three times as large as "x steps", since "15 seconds" is three times as large as "5 seconds".

• Thus, $x = 8$, because 24 is three times as large as 8. To solve this problem, therefore, **we would need to type 8 into the numeric entry box** beneath the question.

> ➤ As with the previous sections, don't worry if the math doesn't make sense here! This question is simply intended to show you what a Numeric Entry question looks like.

• The math behind it is covered properly in our book on Word Problems.

(19) Quantitative Comparisons – The rest of your math questions will prompt you to compare two quantities.

• Such questions, commonly known as "Quantitative Comparisons", consist of two quantities, labeled Quantity A and Quantity B, and, in many cases, some additional information.

> ➢ Beneath the two quantities you'll find four answer choices, asking which of the two quantities is LARGER. The answer choices are always the SAME.

• **MEMORIZE them IMMEDIATELY**. 15 of your 40 math questions will be in this format. If you spend 10 seconds wading through the answer choices on each of these questions, you'll be wasting 2.5 minutes of your exam!

• Let's take a look at a sample problem:

$$xy \geq 1$$

Quantity A	**Quantity B**
xy	$(xy)^3$

(A) **Quantity A is greater.**
(B) **Quantity B is greater.**
(C) **The quantities are equal.**
(D) **The relationship cannot be determined from the information given.**

Answer: D. At the top of the problem, we are told that $xy \geq 1$. This means that xy can be any value equal to or greater than one.

> ➢ If $xy = 1$, notice that the quantities are equal, since $(1)^3 = 1 \times 1 \times 1 = 1$. If $xy = 2$, however, notice that Quantity B is greater than Quantity A, since $(2)^3 = 2 \times 2 \times 2 = 8$.

• Because the two quantities can be equal or can be different, we cannot determine which quantity is larger from the given information. The correct answer is therefore (D).

• Any time two quantities have an INCONSISTENT RELATIONSHIP — i.e. any time that A can be greater than or equal to B or that B can be greater than or equal to A — the relationship between the two quantities CANNOT be determined.

__(20) Before You Get Started__ – If you've read through the preceding pages, you're ready to get started.

• Before you do, we'd like to offer you a last few bits of advice. We know that many people who take the GRE are not very comfortable with math.

➢ If you're one of them, you may have been told at an early age that you weren't a "math person" or that your brain "doesn't work that way".

• That's total nonsense. The truth is that EVERYONE can learn the sort of math required by the GRE.

• Yes, it may require hard work — especially if you haven't done math in over a decade. But you CAN do it. Don't let the idiotic assessment of a bad teacher or a misogynist prevent you from attaining your goals.

➢ As you begin to practice, __DON'T try to do everything in your head__. Scratch work is an IMPORTANT part of the problem solving process.

• Taking notes will SPEED you up and help you avoid careless errors.

• Make sure, however, that your writing is organized and legible. Sloppy handwriting is a sure path to careless errors. Writing the work for one problem atop the work for another problem is even worse. (Yes, some people do this.)

➢ Likewise, __make sure that your handwriting is appropriately sized__. If you can solve twenty problems on a single sheet of paper, your writing is too small.

• Yes, the GRE only provides you with a few sheets of unlined scratch paper, but you can always raise your hand to trade for new sheets BEFORE you run out.

• Conversely, if you're using one sheet of paper per question, write smaller. You shouldn't need to request paper frequently. Divide your sheets of scratch paper into six equal sections. With proper penmanship, you should be able to fit the work for any problem in one of the sections.

➢ When solving problems, __beware of crazy decimals or fractions__. If your scratch work involves something like $0.123 \times \frac{7}{13}$, you're doing something wrong.

• In general, the GRE tends to use "smart numbers" — numbers that are designed to yield simple results under the proper analysis.

• When the GRE uses exotic numbers, the exam is almost always testing your ability to identify patterns or relationships (e.g. $0.\overline{54} = \frac{5}{9}$) or to approximate.

➢ If you're worried about anxiety, preparing THOROUGHLY for the GRE is the best way to beat test-taking jitters.

• Nothing calms unsteady nerves more than seeing problems you KNOW how to solve because the content is EASY for you.

• You should also **set up a test date that allows you enough time to schedule a retake**, if necessary. (Remember, you can take the GRE every 21 days and up to 5 times a year.) Knowing that you'll have a second shot at the GRE can take the pressure off your first exam.

➢ On test day, bring food and water with you to the exam center. You'll be there for nearly five hours.

• Doing anything for that length of time is fatiguing. Eating a few nuts and a piece of fruit before your exam (and during your break) will help keep you sharp.

• Just be sure to steer clear of drinking too much water or consuming too much sugar or caffeine. You don't want to take multiple bathroom breaks while your exam is running or to crash during the final hour of your test.

➢ If you can, **get to the test center early**. Taking the GRE is stressful enough. You don't want to exacerbate that stress by running late.

• Plan to get there a half hour in advance. If you're commuting to an unfamiliar area, research the commute carefully and allot an additional 15 minutes (in case you get lost).

• Once inside (don't forget your ID and admissions ticket!), use the extra time to warm up with a few practice problems or to review your notes. Doing so will help get your brain "in gear" before your exam.

➢ Finally, **brace yourself for broken air-conditioners, sniffling neighbors, and unfriendly staffers**.

• Although test centers are generally well run, it's important to remember that there can be problems.

• As long as you dress in layers, however, and make use of the headphones or earplugs that are supplied with your exam, these issues shouldn't pose you any problems.

Chapter 2

Lines & Angles

Lines & Angles

To be discussed:

Fundamental Concepts

Whether you're aiming for a perfect score or a score closer to average, mastery of the following concepts is essential.

Strategy Concepts

Geometry is more than a collection of facts and formulas. To solve the most difficult questions, you need to complement the essential concepts with the following tactics.

Practice Questions

There's no substitute for elbow grease. Practice your new skills to ensure that you internalize what you've studied.

Fundamental Concepts

(1) Introduction – If you're like most people who take the GRE, it's been years since you last studied Geometry.

• You probably recall that it's got a lot of formulas, and that circles involve something called "pie", but not a lot else.

> ➤ If this sounds like you, there's no need to worry. The following pages will cover EVERYTHING you need to know about Geometry.

• Whether you need a simple discussion of the CORE ideas or a detailed treatment of the most ADVANCED wrinkles, you will find it in the sections to come.

• Before we delve into that material, however, let's take a moment to discuss a few background matters.

> ➤ As you might guess from the length of this work, Geometry is an important topic on the GRE. On a typical exam, roughly 20 percent of the questions involve Geometry.

• That's 8 out of 40 questions. So, this is not a topic you can afford to avoid.

• Whether you hate Geometry or find that it comes easily to you, we encourage you to LEARN the formulas BEFORE solving the practice questions. If you practice the questions without understanding the formulas, you'll struggle to solve anything.

> ➤ We also encourage you to REVISIT concepts you find challenging. The material here is CUMULATIVE. Each section builds upon those before it.

• If you only "sort of" get something, and press on without returning, you may run into problems with concepts that follow.

• Go back and rework the material another day. Come back to it with a fresh mind. Redoing things you find difficult will clarify the material and make new concepts easier to digest.

> ➤ Finally, we urge you to sample as many practice problems as you can. Geometry questions come with a lot of wrinkles.

• The best way to brace yourself for these wrinkles is to work through as many of them as possible. EXPERIENCE is crucial if you want to be properly prepared on test day.

<u>**(2) Straight Lines & Opposing Angles**</u> – If you haven't done Geometry in years, you may not recall much about lines and angles.

- So let's start with the basics.

  ➤ The term LINE refers to a collection of points that stretch without end in both directions.

- In some cases, the GRE will indicate that a line extends indefinitely by marking both ends with little arrows. In most cases, however, the GRE does NOT put arrows on the ends of its lines.

These LINES run indefinitely   … and so do these LINES

  ➤ A line differs from a LINE SEGMENT in that a line segment TERMINATES at both ends.

- A line also differs from a RAY in that a ray extends indefinitely at ONE end, but terminates at the OTHER.

This is a LINE SEGMENT   … and this is a RAY

- The distinction between a line, a line segment, and a ray is rarely important on the GRE, but it is a distinction that you should be aware of.

  ➤ When lines, line segments, or rays meet, they form ANGLES. Angles can be LABELED in one of two ways.

- The most common way is with a number or a variable, as in the diagram below:

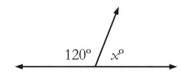

Sherpa
Prep

➤ From time to time, however, the GRE will identify an angle through its VERTEX, or point of intersection.

• In the figure below, the angle to the LEFT can be referred to as ∠ *DCA*, since the vertex *C* is flanked by rays *D* and *A*.

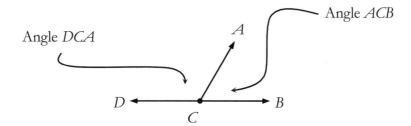

• Likewise, the angle to the RIGHT can be referred to as ∠ *ACB*, since the vertex *C* is flanked by rays *A* and *B*.

➤ When it comes to lines and angles, there are two properties that you need to know. The FIRST is that **the ANGLE of a LINE is always 180°.**

• It doesn't matter whether the line is vertical, horizontal, or diagonal. The measure is always 180° since there are 360° in a CIRCLE and every line cuts <u>some</u> circle in HALF:

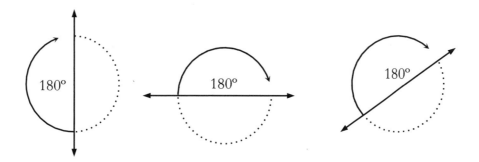

• Thus, in the diagram below, angles *x* and *y* add to 180°, since together they form a line. The same is also true for *y* + *z*, *z* + *w*, and *w* + *x*, since they too make lines. Of course, since *x* + *y* = 180° and *z* + *w* = 180°, the sum of all 4 angles is therefore 360°:

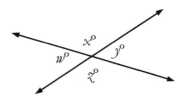

➢ Note that it doesn't matter how you DIVIDE a line. As long as the divisions form a line, the sum of their angles will be 180°.

• Thus, in the diagram below, the sum of angles w, x, y, and z is 180°, since together they form a line:

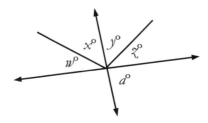

• The same is also true of angles y, z, and a.

➢ The SECOND property of lines and angles is that <u>directly</u> OPPOSITE angles are always EQUAL.

• To understand why, consider the diagram below. Notice that 80° + x form a line, as do 80° + z.

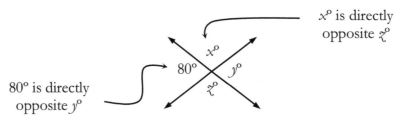

$x°$ is directly opposite $z°$

80° is directly opposite $y°$

• Since the angle of a line is always 180°, x must therefore equal 100°. The same is true of z. Further, if $x = 100°$, then $y = 80°$, since $x + y$ form a line. Thus, both pairs of opposite angles are equal: $x = z$ and 80° = y.

➢ This rule is ALSO true if more than two lines intersect at a SINGLE point, as in the figure below.

• Here, $a = d$, $b = e$, and $c = f$, since these angles are directly opposite one another:

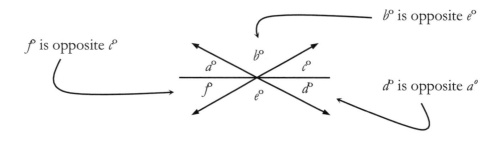

$b°$ is opposite $e°$

f is opposite $c°$

$d°$ is opposite $a°$

• To give you a better feel for straight lines and opposing angles, let's work through a practice problem together:

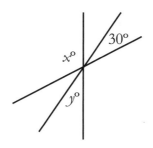

In the figure above, if $x = 4y$, then $x - y =$

(A) 90° (B) 100° (C) 120° (D) 125° (E) 130°

Answer. A. Because opposite angles are equal, the angle directly across from the 30° angle must also have a measure of 30°, as shown in the diagram below.

In this diagram, x, 30°, and y form a line. Since the angle of a line is always 180°, we therefore know that $x + 30° + y = 180°$. Subtracting 30 from both sides proves that $x + y = 150°$.

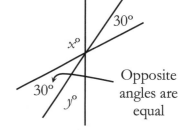

According to the problem, $x = 4y$. If we insert this into the equation $x + y = 150$, we get:

Let $x = 4y$

$\longrightarrow 4y + y = 150°$

Because $5y = 150°$, we therefore know that $y = 30°$. As mentioned above, the problem states that $x = 4y$. Thus, $x = 120°$, since:

$x = 4y$ According to the problem.
$x = 4(30°)$ Substitute $y = 30°$.
$x = 120°$

If $x = 120°$ and $y = 30°$, then the answer to the question must be (A), since:

$$x - y \ \rightarrow \ 120° - 30° = 90°$$

(3) Perpendicular & Parallel Lines – Lines that intersect at a 90° angle (often referred to as a RIGHT angle) are known as PERPENDICULAR lines.

• On the GRE, exam-makers can indicate that two lines are perpendicular in several ways.

➢ In some diagrams, they use the symbol ⊥, which means "perpendicular". In others, they simply tell you that one line is vertical and the other is horizontal.

• In most cases, however, they draw a small SQUARE at the point of intersection, as in the diagram below:

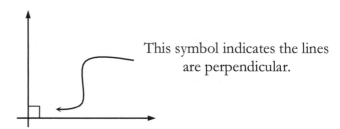

This symbol indicates the lines are perpendicular.

➢ Lines that lie in the same plane but NEVER intersect or touch one another are known as PARALLEL lines.

• Parallel lines are typically demarcated with the symbol ‖. For example, in the diagram below, lines l_1 and l_2 are parallel, since the diagram indicates that $l_1 \parallel l_2$:

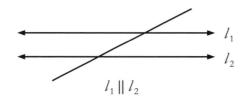

$l_1 \parallel l_2$

➢ When parallel lines are intersected by a third line, called a TRANSVERSAL, the angles in MATCHING CORNERS are referred to as CORRESPONDING angles.

• Because the transversal crosses both parallel lines at the same angle, all corresponding angles are equal:

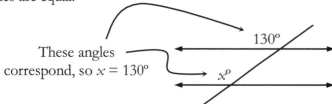

These angles correspond, so $x = 130°$

130°

$x°$

➤ Notice that a transversal creates eight angles, four of which are BIG and four of which are SMALL.

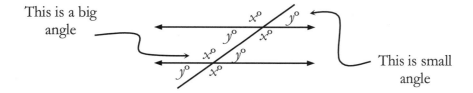

• BIG angles are bigger than 90° and SMALL angles are smaller than 90°. In the diagram above, all four angles marked $x°$ are BIG, since they are greater than 90°. Likewise, all four angles marked $y°$ are SMALL, since they are smaller than 90°.

➤ When working with parallel lines cut by a transversal, there are TWO relationships that you ought to keep in mind.

• The ⎡**First**⎤ is that all four big angles are EQUAL and that all four small angles are EQUAL. The ⎡**Second**⎤ is that any BIG angle + any SMALL angle = 180°.

• To get a sense of why these relationships are helpful, consider the following:

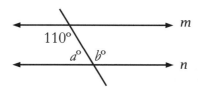

In the diagram above, lines _m_ and _n_ are parallel.

Quantity A	Quantity B
$b - a$	40°

Answer. C. According to the problem, lines _m_ and _n_ are parallel. When parallel lines are intersected by a transversal, the following is always true: all 4 big angles are equal, all 4 small angles are equal, and any big angle + any small angle = 180°.

Since 110° and b are both big angles, $b = 110°$. Likewise, since 110° is a big angle and a is a small angle, $110° + a = 180°$. Thus, if $b = 110°$ and $a = 70°$, then $b - a = 40°$. The correct answer is therefore (C), since the two quantities are equal.

• If you don't remember how the answer choices work for Quantitative Comparison questions, be sure to visit section ⎡19⎤ of our Introduction!

➢ Finally, be aware that exam-makers sometimes CONCEAL parallel lines in ways that make them harder to work with.

• If you come across a diagram with parallel lines, LENGTHEN the parallel lines and the line cutting them. Expanding the lines will help you recognize relationships that the GRE is trying to obscure.

• Consider the following:

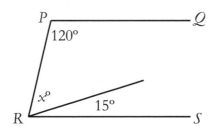

In the figure above, if $PQ \parallel RS$, then $x =$

(A) 35   (B) 37.5   (C) 40   (D) 45   (E) 55

Answer. D. In the diagram above, lines PQ and RS are parallel, and line PR cuts them. If we extend these lines, we get:

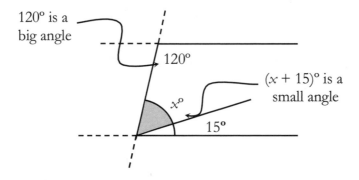

From this diagram, we can see that 120° is a big angle and $(x + 15)°$ is a small angle. The sum of these two angles must therefore equal 180°:

$$120° + (x + 15)° = 180°$$

If we subtract 120° from both sides of this equation, we get $x + 15° = 60°$. Since $60° - 15° = 45°$, the correct answer is (D).

(4) Bisectors & Midpoints – Any line that splits something into two EQUAL parts is known as a BISECTOR.

- That "something" can be an angle, a line, or a line segment:

ANGLE Bisector   LINE Bisector

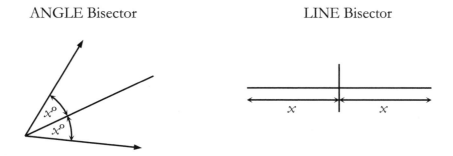

➢ The KEY to solving problems involving bisectors is to assign the SAME variable to the two EQUAL halves, as in the diagrams above.

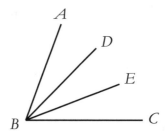

The measure of ∠ABD is 25°. If BD bisects ∠ABE and BE bisects ∠DBC, what is the measure of ∠ABC?

(A) 65° (B) 70° (C) 75° (D) 80° (E) 85°

Answer. C. According to the problem, angle *ABD* has a measure of 25°. Since line segment *BD* bisects angle *ABE*, angle *DBE* must also have a measure of 25°.

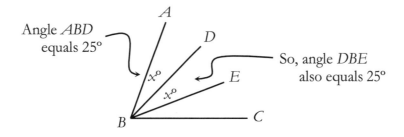

Likewise, if angle *DBE* has a measure of 25°, then angle *EBC* must also have a measure of 25°, since *BE* bisects angle *DBC*. Thus, angle *ABC* must have a measure of 75°, since ∠*ABD* + ∠*DBE* + ∠*EBC* = 25° + 25° + 25° = 75°.

➢ Any point that lies in the MIDDLE of a line (or a line segment) is known as a MIDPOINT.

• Like bisectors, midpoints split a line into two EQUAL parts. Thus, the key to solving problems involving midpoints is to set the two halves equal to one another.

• Consider the following:

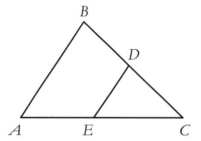

In triangle *ABC* above, point *E* is the midpoint of *AC* and *DE* is the bisector of *BC*. If triangle *DEC* has a perimeter of length 12 and *BD* and *AE* have lengths of 4 and 5, respectively, what is the length of *DE*?

(A) 1   (B) 3   (C) 4   (D) 5   (E) 7

Answer. B. According to the problem, line segment *BD* has a length of 4. Since line segment *DE* is the bisector of side *BC*, line segment *DC* must also have a length of 4, as shown below.

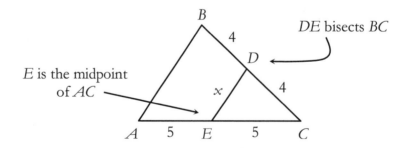

Likewise, if line segment *AE* has a length of 5, then line segment *EC* must also have a length of 5, since point *E* is the midpoint of side *AC*.

The problem also states that triangle *DEC* has a perimeter of 12. Since line segments *DC* and *EC* have lengths of 4 and 5, respectively, the length of line segment *DE* must therefore be 3, since $3 + 4 + 5 = 12$.

(5) Polygons – When three or more line segments form an enclosed figure, that figure is known as a polygon.

• The line segments of a polygon are known as SIDES. Each side intersects with exactly two other sides at their ENDPOINTS.

> ➤ A point of intersection between two sides is known as a VERTEX. Two or more points of intersection are known as VERTICES.

• A polygon with three sides is known as a triangle, and a polygon with four sides is known as quadrilateral:

TRIANGLE   QUADRILATERAL
(3 sides)   (4 sides)

> ➤ Exam-makers rarely refer to other polygons by name, but they can do so every now and then.

• You should also be familiar with the following polygons:

PENTAGON   HEXAGON   OCTAGON
(5 sides)   (6 sides)   (8 sides)

> ➤ In a REGULAR polygon, every side has the SAME length, and every angle has the SAME measure.

• Be aware that polygons do NOT have to be regular:

This hexagon is NOT regular

➤ The distance around a polygon is known as the PERIMETER, and the space enclosed by the sides of a polygon is known as the AREA.

• The perimeter of any polygon can be determined by TOTALING the lengths of its sides. Thus, in the diagram below, if regular pentagon *ABCDE* has a side length of 6 inches, its perimeter is 30 inches, since 5×6 inches $= 30$ inches:

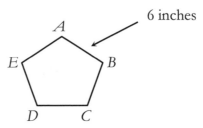

➤ The area of a polygon is measured in terms of SQUARE UNITS such as square feet (feet^2) or square meters (meters^2).

• The areas of standard polygons such as triangles, squares, rectangles, parallelograms, rhombuses and trapezoids must be determined through the area formulas associated with those shapes.

• We will discuss those formulas in the sections to come.

➤ The areas of COMPLEX polygons must be determined by CARVING the polygon into simple shapes such as right triangles, rectangles and squares.

• For example, in the diagrams below, polygon *ABCD* can be broken down into four right triangles and a rectangle, while regular octagon *ABCDEFGH* can be split into 8 equal triangles.

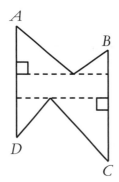 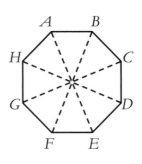

(6) Interior Angles – Any angle located INSIDE a polygon is known as an interior angle.

A TRIANGLE has 3 interior angles   … and a QUADRILATERAL has 4

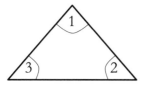   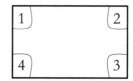

• The SUM of the interior angles of a polygon depends on the number of sides that the polygon contains.

➢ The simplest polygon is a TRIANGLE. The interior angles of ANY triangle add to 180°, regardless of its size or shape.

• Thus:

These angles add to 180°   These also add to 180°

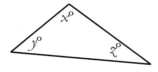   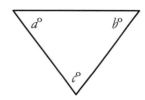

➢ Every quadrilateral (4 sides) is made up of TWO triangles, so the interior angles of ANY quadrilateral add to 180° + 180° = 360°.

• Likewise, every pentagon (5 sides) is made up of THREE triangles, so the interior angles of ANY pentagon add to 180° + 180° + 180 ° = 540°:

These 4 angles add to 360°   These 5 angles add to 540°

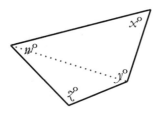   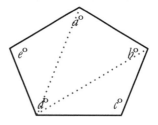

➢ The TABLE below lists the SUM of the interior angles for several common polygons.

• Notice that the sum of the angles of each polygon is exactly 180° greater than the polygon before it:

Polygon	Total Angles
Triangle	180°
Quadrilateral	360°
Pentagon	540°
Hexagon	720°

• The reason that each polygon adds 180° to the shape before it is that each ADDITIONAL side adds ANOTHER triangle to the interior of the shape. Thus, a 4-sided shape contains 2 triangles, a 5-sided shape contains 3 triangles, a 6-sided shape contains 4 triangles, and so forth.

➢ In other words, a polygon with n sides always contains a total of $n - 2$ triangles.

• Therefore, since the interior angles of any triangle add to 180°, you can determine the sum of the interior angles of any polygon through the following FORMULA, where n = the number of sides:

Sum of the Interior Angles of any Polygon = $(n - 2)180°$

• For example, the interior angles of a 7-sided polygon add to 900°, since:

$$(7 - 2)180° = 5(180°) = 900°$$

• Likewise, the interior angles of an 8-sided polygon (an octagon) add to 1,080°, and those of a 12-sided polygon add to 1,800°, since:

The interior angles of an 8-sided polygon:	The interior angles of a 12-sided polygon:
$(8 - 2)180° = 6(180°) = 1,080°$	$(12 - 2)180° = 10(180°) = 1,800°$

➢ To give you a better feel for interior angles, let's work through a practice problem together.

• Consider the following:

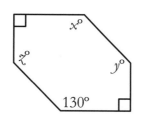

Quantity A	**Quantity B**
$x + y + z$	$360°$

Answer. A. The figure above contains 6 sides. Therefore the sum of its interior angles equals 720°, since $(6 − 2)180° = 4(180°) = 720°$. Because two of these interior angles equal 90°, and a third equals 130°, we know that:

$$90° + 90° + 130° + x + y + z = 720°$$
$$310° + x + y + z = 720°$$
$$x + y + z = 410°$$

Thus, the correct answer is (A), since 410° is greater than 360°.

(7) Exterior Angles – Any angle formed by extending the side of a polygon is known as an exterior angle.

• In the diagram below, angles *a* and *x* are EXTERIOR angles, since each is formed by extending a side of the polygon.

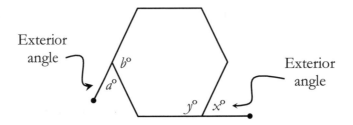

➤ The SUM of an EXTERIOR angle and the INTERIOR angle beside it is ALWAYS 180°, since together the two angles form a line.

• Thus, in the following figures, $p + q = 180°$ because exterior angle *p* and interior angle *q* form a straight line. The same is true of angles *r* and *s*:

➤ In every polygon, there are an EQUAL number of interior and exterior angles. For example, a TRIANGLE only has 3 exterior angles, since it also has 3 interior angles.

• Likewise, a QUADRILATERAL only has 4 exterior angles, since it also has 4 interior angles:

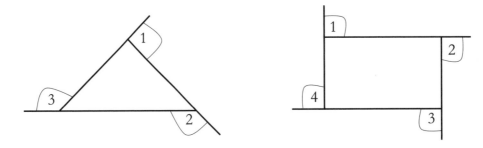

➤ It's important to note, however, that for EACH interior angle within a polygon, the exterior angle beside it can be VISUALIZED in one of TWO ways.

• For example, in the diagram below, the exterior angle to interior angle *x* can be visualized either as angle *y* or as angle *z*:

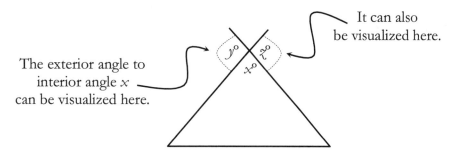

• Angles *y* and *z*, however, are NOT considered distinct exterior angles. This is because every interior angle ONLY has ONE exterior angle, regardless of how we visualize it.

➤ Similarly, in the diagram below, we see a triangle that appears to have SIX exterior angles.

• Like all triangles, however, it only has THREE exterior angles. Hence, the exterior angle to interior angle *a* can be visualized in either position #1 OR position #2:

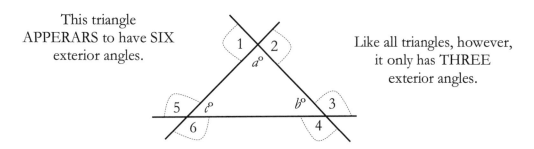

• Likewise, the exterior angle to interior angle *b* can be visualized in EITHER position #3 OR position #4. Finally, the exterior angle to interior angle *c* can be visualized in EITHER position #5 OR position #6.

➢ Many GRE questions involving exterior angles will test your knowledge of the following axiom:

The SUM of the exterior angles of ANY polygon is always 360°.

• This law may seem odd, since we just saw that the interior angles of any shape increase as the number of sides increase.

• With exterior angles, however, the sum is CONSTANT.

➢ It doesn't matter whether the polygon has 3, 4, or 10 sides. The sum of the exterior angles is ALWAYS 360°.

• To prove it, consider a triangle whose interior angles are 55°, 55°, and 75°, and a quadrilateral whose interior angles are all 90°:

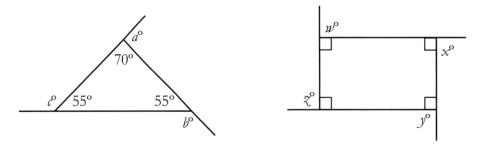

➢ Since an exterior angle and the interior angle beside it add to 180°, we know that $a = 110°$, $b = 125°$, and $c = 125°$.

• Thus, the sum of the exterior angles of the triangle equals 110° + 125° + 125° = 360°.

• Likewise, if the interior angles of the quadrilateral are all 90°, we know that $w° = 90$, $x = 90°$, $y = 90°$, and $z = 90°$. Therefore, the sum of the exterior angles of the quadrilateral also equals 360°, since 90° + 90° + 90° + 90° = 360°.

➢ To give you a sense of how the GRE might test your knowledge of exterior angles, let's work through a practice problem together.

• Consider the following:

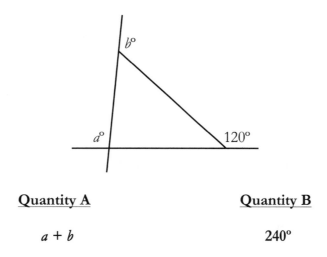

Quantity A	Quantity B
$a + b$	240°

Answer: C. In the diagram above, angles $a°$, $b°$, and 120° are all exterior angles, since each forms a line with the interior angles of the triangle.

The exterior angles of any polygon add to 360°, so $a + b + 120° = 360°$. If we subtract 120° from both sides of this equation, we get $a + b = 240°$. Therefore the correct answer is (C), since the two quantities are equal.

• Here's a second example for you:

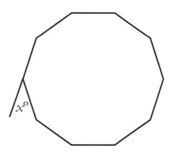

The figure above shows a regular 10-sided polygon. What is the value of x?

$$x = \boxed{}$$

Answer: 36°. Because this polygon has 10 sides, it also has 10 interior angles and 10 exterior angles. In a regular polygon, every side has the same length and every angle has the same measure. Since the exterior angles of any polygon add to 360°, each of these 10 angles must equal 36°, as:

$$\frac{\text{exterior angles of any polygon}}{\text{number of exterior angles}} = \frac{360°}{10} = 36°$$

(8) The Exterior Angles of A Triangle – As we saw in the preceding section, an exterior angle of a polygon forms a 180° angle with the interior angle beside it.

• In TRIANGLES, exterior angles have a special relationship with the OTHER interior angles, too. This relationship can be stated as follows:

➢ An EXTERIOR angle of a triangle is always equal to the SUM of the NON-ADJACENT interior angles.

• Thus, in the diagram to the left, $a = c + d$, since a is the exterior angle and $c + d$ are the non-adjacent interior angles:

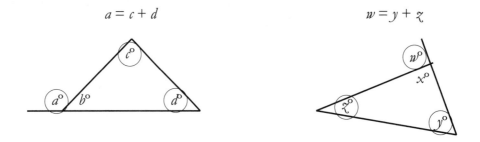

$$a = c + d \qquad\qquad w = y + z$$

• Likewise, in the diagram to the right $w = y + z$, since w is the exterior angle and $y + z$ are the non-adjacent interior angles.

➢ To understand the basis for this rule, consider the triangle below. Notice that $a + 30°$ form a straight line, so $a = 150°$.

• Similarly, notice that $30° + b + c$ are the interior angles of the triangle. The interior angles of a triangle always add to 180°, so $b + c = 150°$.

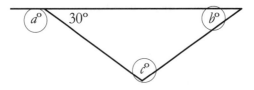

• Since $a = 150°$ and $b + c = 150°$, we therefore know that $a = b + c$. This is why an exterior angle of a triangle equals the sum of the two non-adjacent interior angles.

> ➤ In some cases, you may need to RELABEL the angles of a diagram to give a triangle one exterior angle and two interior angles that are non-adjacent.

• Here's an example:

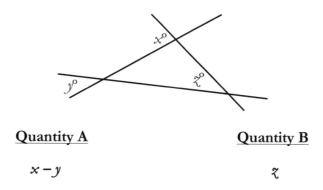

Quantity A	**Quantity B**
$x - y$	z

Answer. C. In the diagram above, x is an exterior angle and z is an interior angle. **Angle y is NOT an exterior angle because it does not form a STRAIGHT line with an interior angle**. It is simply an angle outside the triangle.

> ➤ Because there is no rule that relates one exterior angle, one interior angle, and one angle outside a triangle, let's label the angle opposite y as follows:

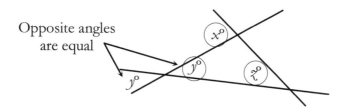

Opposite angles are equal

• In doing so, our triangle now has 1 exterior angle and 2 interior angles.

> ➤ Since an exterior angle of a triangle always equals the sum of the two interior angles that are non-adjacent, we know that $x = y + z$.

• If $x = y + z$, we simply need to subtract y from both sides of the equation to determine the value of Quantity A:

$$x = y + z \qquad \text{According to the diagram.}$$
$$x - y = z \qquad \text{Subtract } y \text{ from both sides.}$$

• Since $x - y = z$, the two quantities are therefore equal. Thus, the correct answer is (C).

(9) Shapes Within Shapes – In many cases, Geometry questions often involve shapes composed of smaller shapes. Here's an example:

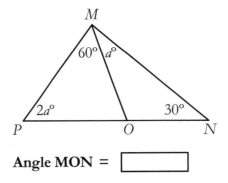

Angle MON = [   ]

• When working with "shapes within shapes", it is important to VISUALIZE ALL the POSSIBLE shapes, since you never know which shape will be critical to the solution.

> ➤ For example, in the problem above, there are THREE triangles: large triangle *MNP*, and the two smaller triangles, *MOP* and *MON*, that comprise it.

• In most problems, the shape that has ALL of its angles LABELED will be the KEY to solving the problem. Of the triangles above, only triangle *MNP* has all of its angles labeled:

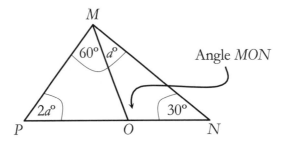

Angle *MON*

> ➤ The angles of triangle *MNP* are $2a$, $60° + a$, and $30°$. The measure of angle a must therefore be $30°$, since the interior angles of a triangle always add to $180°$:

$$2a + (60° + a) + 30° = 180°$$
$$3a + 90° = 180°$$
$$3a = 90°$$

• If $a = 30°$, then the measure of $\angle MON$ must be $120°$, since the interior angles of triangle *MON* add to $180°$:

$$a + 30° + \angle MON = 180°$$
$$30° + 30° + \angle MON = 180°$$
$$\angle MON = 120°$$

(10) Can You Trust the Diagrams? – If you're like most people preparing to take the GRE, you may be wondering how much can you trust the diagrams.

• In MOST cases, the GRE draws its diagrams APPROXIMATELY to scale. This is particularly true of its angle measurements.

➤ For example, if an angle equals 45°, the exam roughly draws it as 45°. If one angle doubles another, the exam roughly draws the two angles as such.

• However, the diagrams are NOT always to scale, so you **NEVER** want to use the look of a diagram as the basis for a solution.

• For example, in the question below, you might be tempted to assume that angle p is greater than 90° since it's been drawn that way:

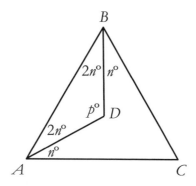

In the figure above, if the measure of ∠ C is 30°, then p =

(A) 60° (B) 80° (C) 100° (D) 120° (E) 140°

➤ The correct answer, however, is LESS than 90°. Since the sum of angles A, B, C add to 180°, the measure of $n = 25$°:

$$(2n + n) + (2n + n) + 30° = 180°$$
$$6n = 150°$$
$$n = 25°$$

• Likewise, if $n = 25$°, the measure of $p = 80$°, since the interior angles of triangle ABD also add to 180°. Thus, the answer is (B):

$$2n + 2n + p = 180°$$
$$50° + 50° + p = 180°$$
$$p = 80°$$

➢ There are also TWO ways in which the exam uses diagrams to MISLEAD test-takers.

• We call the most common of these ways the ⟨**"LOOKS Like" trap**⟩. Exam-makers love to draw angles that LOOK like 90° angles, quadrilaterals that LOOK like squares, lines that LOOK like they're parallel, and so forth.

• Unless you are TOLD, however, that the angle equals 90°, the shape is a square, or the lines are parallel, you CANNOT assume that they are.

➢ Although most diagrams are ROUGHLY drawn to scale, this does not mean that they are EXACTLY drawn so.

• For example, in the diagram below, you might assume that the correct answer is (C), since the corresponding angles of parallel lines are always equal:

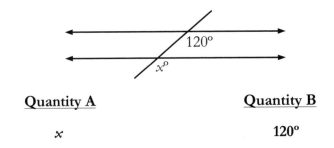

Quantity A	**Quantity B**
x	120°

• The correct answer, however, is (D), since we have NO proof that the lines are parallel. For all we know, the lines are slanting towards one another at a grade too subtle to be seen.

➢ The exam also misleads test-takers with diagrams that are intentionally DISTORTED.

• This is particularly true of diagrams in which the LENGTHS of the lines are critical to the problem. As mentioned earlier, in most diagrams, the angle measurements are usually drawn to scale. This is generally less true of the lengths of lines.

• When you're lucky, distorted diagrams are labeled "not drawn to scale". In most cases, however, the GRE gives no warning.

➤ If a diagram does not match its description, you may find it helpful to REDRAW the diagram so that you're not misled by the version you've been given.

- Consider the following:

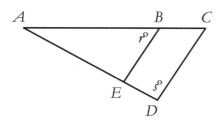

In the figure above, if $BE \parallel CD$, $AE = BE$, and $r = 40°$, then $s =$

(A) 40° (B) 50° (C) 100° (D) 110° (E) 140°

Answer: C. Although the problem states that $AE = BE$, the diagram has not been drawn accordingly. Given that $BE \parallel CD$, a more accurate diagram would look as follows:

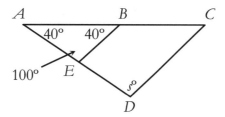

As we'll discuss in our chapter on Triangles, any triangle with two sides of equal length is known as an isosceles triangle. In an isosceles triangle, the angles OPPOSITE the equal sides are always equal.

According to the problem $AE = BE$, so triangle ABE is an isosceles triangle. Thus, if $r = 40°$, then angle $EAB = 40°$ too, since angles r and EAB are opposite the equal legs.

Because the interior angles of a triangle add 180°, we know that angle $AEB = 100°$. $BE \parallel CD$ and the corresponding angles of parallel lines are always equal, so angle s must therefore equal 100°. Thus, the correct answer is (C).

Strategy Concepts

---

(11) Strategy 101 – Sometimes, you need more than facts and formulas to solve a Geometry problem.

• You also need a bit of strategy.

➢ This is particularly true of difficult problems. As questions become more demanding, the path to the solution generally requires some creative thinking.

• Consider the following:

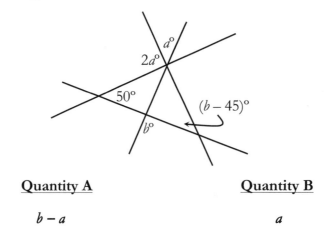

Quantity A	**Quantity B**
$b - a$	a

• If you're like many test-takers, your reaction to a question like this ranges from "where do I even begin?" to "I hate the GRE".

➢ We get it. Even if you like Geometry, the sort of Geometry questions you find on the GRE can be a real challenge.

• To start, **DON'T try to solve the problem all at once.** This is a common mistake on the part of many test-takers. It's often quite difficult to solve a Geometry question immediately upon reading it.

• Geometry questions are a lot like murder mysteries. They've got a number of clues, and it usually takes some careful sleuthing to see how they fit together.

➢ As you look over the question, **DRAW the diagram and LABEL everything** that you can. Doing so will allow you to add your insights as you find them.

• Remember, Geometry is a VISUAL subject. Adding those insights atop the original problem will help you SEE RELATIONSHIPS that you might otherwise miss.

Sherpa
Prep

➢ Once you've drawn the diagram and labeled whatever you could, **LOOK for relationships that YOU KNOW.**

• Are there opposite angles that you can label? Do any angles form a line? Does your triangle have an exterior angle? Can the interior angles of a polygon be labeled?

• Every problem involving Lines and Angles boils down to the properties discussed in the preceding sections. Look for them ACTIVELY.

➢ For example, in the problem above, you might begin by labeling the OPPOSITE angles, such as the one opposite angle a.

• You might also take note of any EXTERIOR angles within the diagram, such as angle b:

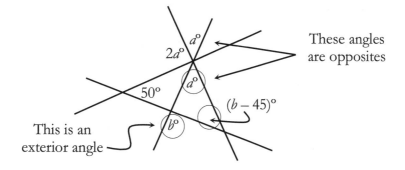

• Notice how these two simple steps prove that $b = a + (b - 45°)$. We know this is so because an exterior angle of a triangle equals the sum of the two interior angles that are not adjacent.

➢ From time to time, **exam-makers DISGUISE basic relationships** in complex diagrams.

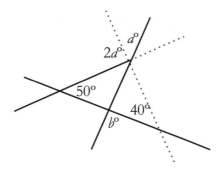

• If your diagram has a LOT of lines, **don't be afraid to REMOVE or IGNORE some of them** temporarily. Doing so can help you catch HIDDEN relationships that are difficult to see.

➤ For example, in the problem above, if we "tune out" the dotted lines, notice how angles $2a$ and a form an EXTERIOR angle to the triangle beneath them:

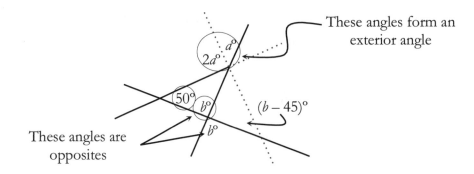

These angles form an exterior angle

These angles are opposites

• Thus, if we LABEL the angle opposite angle b, we know that $2a + a = 50° + b$, since an exterior angle of a triangle equals the sum of the interior angles that are not adjacent.

➤ If you can establish more than one equation, **don't forget to COMBINE the equations** through substitution or elimination.

• Earlier, we saw that $b = a + (b - 45)°$. This statement can be simplified to $0 = a - 45°$ by subtracting b from both sides. It can then be simplified to $45° = a$ by adding $45°$ to both sides.

• If we plug this information into $2a + a = 50° + b$, we learn that $b = 85°$:

$90° + 45° = 50° + b$	Substitute $a = 45°$.
$90° = 5° + b$	Subtract $45°$ from both sides.
$85° = b$	Subtract $5°$ from both sides.

➤ Finally, **LOOK BACK at the problem** to check whether **your solutions MAKE SENSE.**

• Remember, most diagrams on the GRE are approximately accurate, unless they are marked "not drawn to scale". A quick glance at our diagram shows that b and $2a$ are roughly the same size. Our values for a and b suggest the same, so it appears that we're on the right track.

• The question compares:

<u>Quantity A</u>   <u>Quantity B</u>

$b - a$ a

• Since $b = 85°$ and $a = 45°$, the correct answer is therefore (B), as $85° - 45° = 40°$.

(12) The "180° – _x_" Trick – A simple but effective strategy for solving tricky Lines and Angles problems is something we call the "180° – _x_" trick.

• As you know, the angle of a line is 180°. Thus, if two adjacent angles form a line, and the first angle equals _x_, the OTHER angle must equal 180° – _x_, as in the diagram below:

$x°$ \ $180° – x$

• The basis for this conclusion, of course, is simple arithmetic. If added, _x_ and 180° – _x_ have a sum of 180°:

$$x + (180° - x) = 180°$$

➤ When working with a polygon formed by crossing lines, it can be extremely useful to **label ALL of the interior (or exterior) angles of that polygon.**

• Because the interior (and exterior) angles of every polygon add to a fixed sum, labeling all the angles can often establish a helpful equation.

• For example, if the interior angles of a triangle are 30°, _a_, and 180° – _b_, then we know that $30° + a + (180° - b) = 180°$.

➤ When polygons are formed by crossing lines, however, one or more of the interior (or exterior) angles is typically UNMARKED.

• In such cases the "180° – _x_" trick can prove invaluable. To use the trick, simply rewrite any UNMARKED angle as "180° – its adjacent angle". Like this:

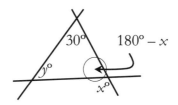

• Just be sure that the two angles form a STRAIGHT line. The "180° – _x_" trick only works if the two angles add to 180°!

• To get a sense of why the "180° – *x*" trick can be so helpful, consider the following problem:

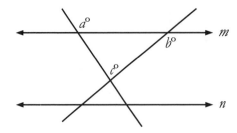

Lines *m* and *n* are parallel.

Quantity A	**Quantity B**
a + *b*	180° + *c*

Answer: C. Given the diagram above, we can use the "180° – *x*" trick to label all 3 interior angles of the triangle or all 3 exterior angles.

➢ Since 2 of the 3 angles given above are exterior angles, let's rewrite the exterior angle adjacent to angle *c* as 180° – *c* to minimize the work:

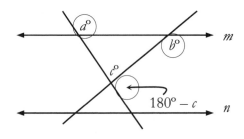

• Because the exterior angles of any polygon add to 360°, we therefore know that:

$$a + b + (180° - c) = 360°$$
$$a + b - c = 180°$$

• To determine the value of Quantity A, we can add *c* to both sides of this equation. Doing so proves that *a* + *b* = 180° + *c*. Thus, the correct answer is (C).

(13) Picking Numbers – Picking numbers is also a great way to attack tricky Geometry problems.

- Consider the following:

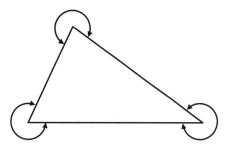

In the triangle above, the sum of the measures of the three marked angles is

(A) 630°   (B) 720°   (C) 810°   (D) 900°   (E) 990°

- As discussed in section **8** of the "Plan B" chapter of our book on <u>Arithmetic & "Plan B" Strategies</u>, any problem without CONCRETE values can be solved by PICKING NUMBERS.

  ➤ When picking, be sure to choose numbers that are SMALL and EASY to work with, and respect any constraints, should your problem have them.

- In the problem above, there are no concrete values and only two constraints: the interior angles of a triangle must add to 180° and there are 360° degrees within a circle.

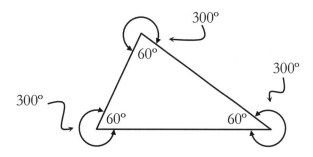

  ➤ To make the arithmetic simple, let's pick 60° for all three angles. Doing so makes the measure of each marked angle 300°, since in all three cases 360° – 60° = 300°.

- Thus, the correct answer must be (D), since the sum of 300° + 300° + 300° = 900°.

- Note that we get the same answer, regardless of the values we choose. Thus, if we had picked 40°, 60°, and 80° for the three angles, the measure of their marked counterparts would have been 320°, 300°, and 280°. These measures also add to 900°.

> ➤ As you'll see in the sections to come, picking numbers is a VITAL tool for solving Geometry problems.

• We cannot overemphasize its importance. To ensure that you're comfortable doing so, let's pick numbers to solve a second sample problem:

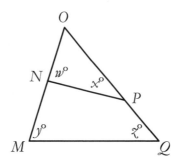

Quantity A

$w + x$

Quantity B

$y + z$

• In the problem above, there are no concrete values and only one constraint: the interior angles of a triangle must add to 180°.

> ➤ To solve it, therefore, we can pick numbers. Notice that if we let the angle at point $O = 30°$, then $w + x = 150°$, since the interior angles of triangle NOP add to 180°.

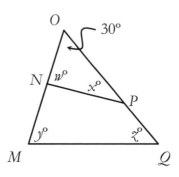

• Likewise, if $O = 30°$, then $y + z = 150°$, since the interior angles of triangle MOQ also add to 180°.

• Thus, the $w + x = y + z$. Since this relationship is true regardless of what value of we choose for angle O (try picking other values for O), the correct answer must be (C).

(14) Problem Sets – The following questions have been arranged into three groups: fundamental, intermediate, and rare or advanced.

• Whether you're aiming for a perfect score or a score closer to average, mastery of the concepts in the FUNDAMENTAL questions is absolutely essential.

➢ As you might expect, the INTERMEDIATE questions are more difficult but are essential for test-takers who need an above-average score or higher.

• Finally, the RARE or ADVANCED questions involve a confusing wrinkle or subtle deception. Mastery of such questions is required only if you need a math score above the 90th percentile.

• As always, if you find yourself confused, bogged down with busy work, or stuck, don't be afraid to fall back on your "Plan B" strategies!

| Fundamental |

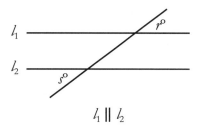

$l_1 \parallel l_2$

Quantity A	Quantity B

1. r s

2. In the diagram above, what is the value of y?

(A) 17.5 (B) 22.5 (C) 32.5 (D) 37.5 (E) 42.5

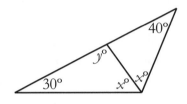

	Quantity A	Quantity B

3. h $180° - h$

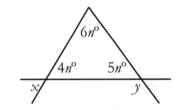

4.   In the figure above, what is the value of y?

(A) 80   (B) 85   (C) 90   (D) 95   (E) 100

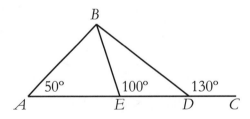

	Quantity A	Quantity B

5. x y

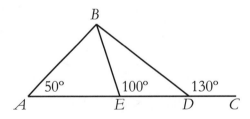

6.   In the figure above, what is the measure of $\angle ABD$?

(A) 60   (B) 65   (C) 70   (D) 75   (E) 80

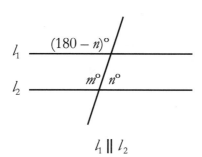

Quantity A	Quantity B

7. m 120°

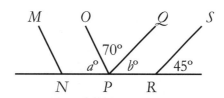

$MN \parallel OP$ and $PQ \parallel RS$.

8.   In the figure above, the value of $a - b =$

         (A) 15   (B) 20   (C) 25   (D) 30   (E) 40

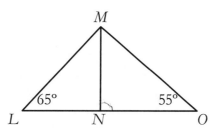

9.   If line segment MN bisects angle LMO, what is the measure of angle MNO?

         (A) 80   (B) 85   (C) 90   (D) 95   (E) 100

    X is the midpoint of line segment WZ and Y is the midpoint of line segment XZ.

Quantity A	Quantity B

10.   The value of $\dfrac{WX}{WY}$ $\dfrac{7}{11}$

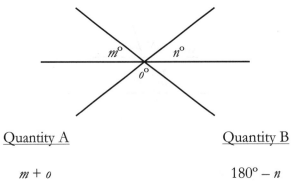

Quantity A	Quantity B
Quantity A	Quantity B

11. $m + o$ $180° - n$

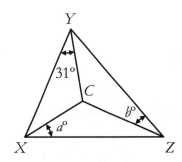

Segments CX, CY, and CZ are the angle bisectors of triangle XYZ.

Quantity A	Quantity B

12. $a + b$ $59°$

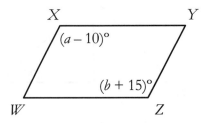

$WX \parallel YZ$ and $XY \parallel WZ$

13.   What is the value of $a - b$?

(A) –5   (B) 5   (C) 10   (D) 15   (E) 25

Intermediate

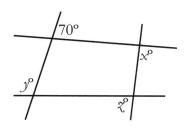

14. In the figure above, $x + y + z =$

   (A) 270° (B) 275° (C) 280° (D) 285° (E) 290°

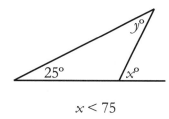

$x < 75$

15. Which of the following are possible values of y?

   Select all possible values.

   A 55   B 50   C 45   D 40   E 35

16. In the diagram above, $\dfrac{a}{a+b} = \dfrac{5}{12}$.

   $a = $ ☐

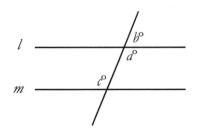

Lines *l* and *m* are parallel and $a - b = 80°$.

Quantity A	Quantity B
17. *c*	120°

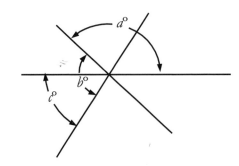

18.   In the figure above, if $a = 140$ and $b = 110$, then $c =$

         (A) 30   (B) 40   (C) 45   (D) 60   (E) 70

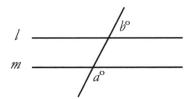

19.   In the diagram above, $l \parallel m$ and $\dfrac{4b - a}{b} = 2$. What is the value of *b*?

         (A) 45°   (B) 50°   (C) 60°   (D) 75°   (E) 90°

Quantity A	Quantity B

20. The total number of triangles shown above   11

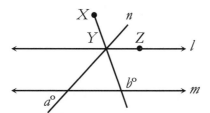

21. In the figure above, what is the value of $a - b$?

(A) 50   (B) 55   (C) 60   (D) 65   (E) 70

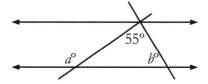

22. In the figure above, lines l and m are parallel and line n bisects angle XYZ. If $b = 110°$, what is the value of a?

(A) 35°   (B) 50°   (C) 55°   (D) 65°   (E) 70°

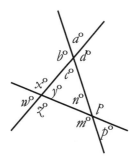

23. In the diagram above, if $b = 120°$, what is the value of $w + p$?

(A) 40   (B) 60   (C) 80   (D) 100   (E) 120

Rare or Advanced

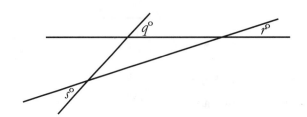

Quantity A	Quantity B

24. $q - r$ s

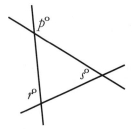

25. In the diagram above, if the measure of angle s is 30°, what is the value of $p + r$?

(A) 180° (B) 210° (C) 240° (D) 250° (E) 270°

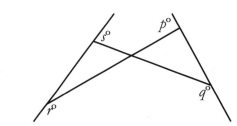

Quantity A	Quantity B

26. $r + s$ $p + q$

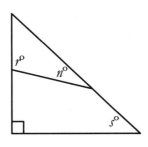

Quantity A	Quantity B
27. $r - s + n$	90°

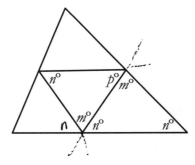

28.   In the diagram above, what is the value of p in terms of m and n?

Select <u>all</u> possible values.

A $180° - m - n$ B $180° - 2m - 3n$ C $360° - 2m - 3n$ D $360° - 3m + 2n$

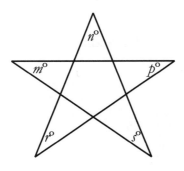

29.   In the diagram above, what is the value of $m + n + p + r + s$?

(A) 180°   (B) 360°   (C) 540°   (D) 720°   (E) 900°

(15) Solutions – Video solutions for each of the previous questions can be found on our website at **www.sherpaprep.com/masterkey**.

• BOOKMARK this address for future visits!

  ➢ To view the videos, you'll need to register your copy of <u>Master Key to the GRE: Geometry</u>.

• If you have yet to do so, please go to **www.sherpaprep.com/videos** and enter your email address.

• Be sure to provide the SAME email address that you used to purchase your copy of <u>Master Key to the GRE</u> or to enroll in your GRE course with Sherpa Prep!

  ➢ When checking your answers, we encourage you to watch the solution for any problem that you answered INCORRECTLY

• The same goes for any problem that took you MORE than TWO MINUTES to solve.

• After digesting the explanation, REVISIT your mistake a couple of days later to ensure that the problem no longer poses issues to you.

  ➢ If you struggle to solve the problem a SECOND time, add it to your "LOG of ERRORS" and redo it every few weeks.

• Solving tricky questions MORE THAN ONCE is the best way to learn from your mistakes and to avoid similar difficulties on your actual exam.

Fundamental		Intermediate	Rare or Advanced
1. C	11. C	14. E	24. C
2. E	12. C	15. C, D, E	25. B
3. D	13. E	16. 75	26. C
4. D		17. A	27. C
5. B		18. E	28. A, C
6. E		19. C	29. A
7. D		20. A	
8. B		21. B	
9. D		22. C	
10. A		23. E	

Chapter 3

Triangles

Triangles

To be discussed:

Fundamental Concepts

Whether you're aiming for a perfect score or a score closer to average, mastery of the following concepts is essential.

1 Introduction
2 Angles & Sides
3 Equilaterals & Isosceles
4 Right Triangles
5 45°–45°–90° Triangles
6 30°–60°–90° Triangles
7 Area & Altitudes
8 Perimeter & the Triangle Inequality Theorem
9 Spatial Reasoning Problems

Rare or Advanced Concepts

The following concepts are either advanced or are tested only on rare occasions. If you don't need an elite math score, don't waste your time!

10 Similar Triangles
11 Acute & Obtuse Triangles
12 Crazy Pythagorean Triangles
13 Hexagons & Octagons

Practice Questions

There's no substitute for elbow grease. Practice your new skills to ensure that you internalize what you've studied.

14 Problem Sets
15 Solutions

Fundamental Concepts

(1) Introduction – No shape is tested more frequently on the GRE than triangles.

• Not only do a third of all Geometry questions test triangles exclusively, but roughly half the other Geometry questions contain them as well.

> ➤ As you will see in the sections to come, problems involving circles, quadrilaterals, and coordinate geometry all have a funny way of becoming triangle problems in the end.

• The reason that triangles are tested so frequently is twofold. On the one hand, there's a LOT to know about them.

• On the other, triangles have a large number of SHORTCUTS. Exam-makers love to test concepts with shortcuts, since shortcuts distinguish test-takers who can find simple solutions to problems that seem complicated from those who can't.

> ➤ Before exploring triangles in full, let's take a moment to review what we have already covered.

• So far, we've learned that the 3 interior angles of a triangle add to 180°, regardless of the triangle's shape or size, and that the 3 exterior angles add to 360°:

$$x + y + z = 180° \qquad\qquad a + b + c = 360°$$

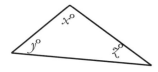 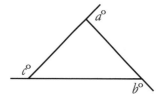

> ➤ We've also learned that any exterior angle equals the sum of the interior angles to which it is not adjacent.

• Thus, in the diagram to below, $a = c + d$, since a is the exterior angle, while c and d are the non-adjacent interior angles:

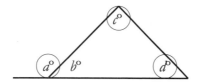

➢ Let's also introduce some basic background information. On the GRE, you will encounter 3 types of triangles.

• Any triangle that has a 90° angle is known as a **right triangle**. In a right triangle, the side opposite the right angle is known as the **hypotenuse**. The remaining sides are known as legs.

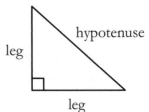

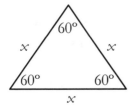

• A triangle that has THREE sides of EQUAL length is known as an **equilateral**. Each angle of an equilateral triangle has a measure of 60°.

• A triangle that has at least TWO sides of EQUAL length is known as an **isosceles**. The angles OPPOSITE the equal legs of an isosceles triangles are also equal.

➢ You will also encounter a fourth type of triangle, commonly known as a **scalene**, whose legs all have different lengths and whose angles all have different measures.

• Here's an example:

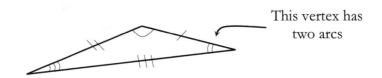

This vertex has two arcs

• In the figure above, the **slash marks** indicate that no two sides have the same length, and the **arcs** within the vertices indicate that no two angles have the same measure.

➢ Finally, when solving triangle problems, remember that you CANNOT trust the diagrams.

• Although in many cases angles and lines are roughly drawn to scale, they are sometimes drawn in MISLEADING manners, often without the warning "not drawn to scale".

• Triangle problems also feature the **"looks like" trap** quite a bit, so be careful not to assume that you have a right triangle, isosceles, or equilateral, unless you have PROOF that you do. Remember, just because a triangle LOOKS like a right triangle does not mean that it is.

(2) Angles & Sides – For EVERY triangle, there is a correlation between the size of an angle and the length of the side ACROSS from it.

• In the diagram below, note that the smallest angle is directly across from the smallest side, while the largest angle is across from the largest side:

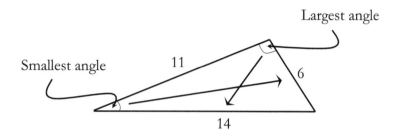

➤ To understand the basis for this correspondence, take a look at your thumb and forefinger.

• As the angle between them grows, notice how the distance between their two tips also grows. Conversely, as that angles shrinks, notice how the distance between them shrinks:

As the angle grows   As the angle shrinks

The opposing distance grows   The opposing distance shrinks

➤ Because the size of an angle and the length of the line across from it directly correspond, you can always use one to draw a conclusion about the other.

• For example, in the triangle below, we know that 62° is the largest angle, so we can deduce that side *C* is the largest of the three sides:

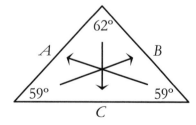

• Likewise, we know that the angles at the bottom of the triangle are equal, so we can deduce that sides *A* and *B* have the same length.

➢ It's important to note, however, that as the measure of an angle increases, its opposing side does NOT increase PROPORTIONALLY.

• For example, in the triangle below, angle *CAB* is half the size of angle *ACB*. This does not imply, however, that side *BC* is half the size of side *AB*.

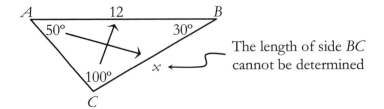

• Although we know that side *BC* is shorter than side *AB*, we cannot use the angle measurements to determine the exact value of *x* — at least without using Trigonometry, which you are NOT required to know for the GRE.

➢ When solving questions about Angles & Sides, we encourage you to DRAW ARROWS from the angles in question to their opposing sides.

• Doing so will help you avoid careless mistakes and simple traps:

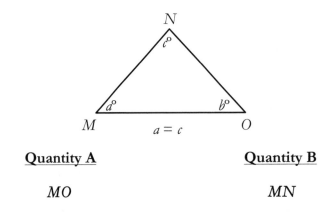

Quantity A	**Quantity B**
MO	*MN*

Answer: D. According to the problem, angle *a* has the same measure as angle *c*. As shown below, side *NO* is across from angle *a* and side *MO* is across from angle *c*. Thus, *NO* = *MO*.

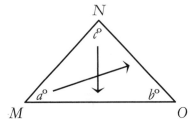

We have no information about angle *b* or side *MN*. The correct answer is therefore (D), since side *MN* could be smaller than, larger than, or equal to side *MO*.

(3) Equilaterals & Isosceles – As we saw earlier, an EQUILATERAL triangle has three sides of equal length and three angles whose measures are 60°.

• An ISOSCELES triangle has at least two sides of equal length, and two angles of equal measure. Those angles are OPPOSITE the two equal legs:

Equilateral   Isosceles

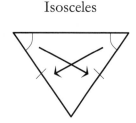

➢ It is commonly believed that the THIRD side of an isosceles triangle has a DIFFERENT length than the other two.

• This is MISTAKEN. The third side CAN have a different length, but it can also have the same length. In other words, an equilateral is just a special type of isosceles: it's the type in which the third side is equal.

• The GRE is unlikely to test this fact directly, but you should be careful not to ASSUME that the third leg of an isosceles triangle MUST be different.

➢ In the previous section, we also saw that there is a direct correlation between the angles within a triangle and the sides ACROSS from them.

• The greater the angle, the greater the opposing side. The smaller the angle, the smaller the opposing side. When working with isosceles triangles, be sure to remember that this correlation works RECIPROCALLY.

• For example, if two sides have the same length, then the angles across from them have the same measure. Likewise, if two angles have the same measure, then the opposing legs are equal. Thus:

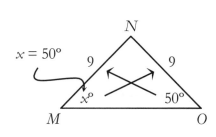

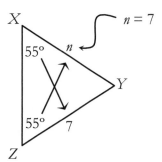

➤ Problems involving isosceles triangles often provide two side lengths and one angle, as in the figure below.

• Given such information, you can always determine the value of the remaining angles, since the interior angles of a triangle add to 180°.

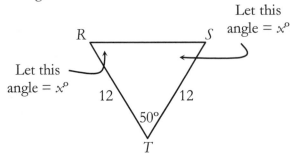

• To do so, simply label the unmarked angles x, and set all three angles equal to 180°. Here, for example, $x = 65°$, since:

$$x + x + 50° = 180°$$
$$2x = 130°$$
$$x = 65°$$

➤ Finally, isosceles triangles also lend themselves to tricky questions about PERIMETER. Questions like the one below are common for the GRE:

The sum of two sides of isosceles triangle ABC is 9. If the perimeter of the triangle is 14, which of the following could be a side length of triangle ABC?

Select <u>all</u> possible lengths.

A 4   **B** 4.5   **C** 5   **D** 5.5   **E** 6

• To answer questions of this sort, first take stock of what you know. Here, the sum of two sides is 9 and the perimeter is 14, so the remaining side MUST have a length of 5.

➤ Then consider whether there is ONLY one combination of side lengths that satisfies the constraints of the problem. In most cases, you will find TWO possibilities.

• Since at least two sides in an isosceles triangle have the same length, there are two possible combinations of side lengths in which the sum of two sides is 9 and the perimeter is 14.

• The first is obvious: 4, 5, 5. The second is not: 4.5, 4.5, 5. Both combinations add to 14, and have two sides that add to 9. In the first case, the two sides are 4 and 5. In the second, they're 4.5 and 4.5. Thus, the correct answer is A, B, and C.

(4) Right Triangles – As we saw earlier, any triangle that has a 90° angle is known as a RIGHT triangle.

• The side opposite the right angle is called the HYPOTENUSE, and the remaining sides are called LEGS.

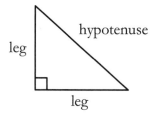

➢ The GRE LOVES to test right triangles, since all right triangles have a special property. You might remember it from your high school days.

• It's called the PYTHAGOREAN Theorem.

• In short, the theorem states that $a^2 + b^2 = c^2$, where a and b are the legs and c is the hypotenuse. In the triangle below, one leg = 3 and the hypotenuse = 5, so we can solve for the length of the other leg as follows:

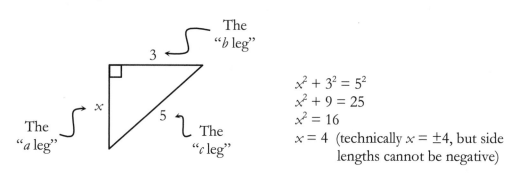

$$x^2 + 3^2 = 5^2$$
$$x^2 + 9 = 25$$
$$x^2 = 16$$
$$x = 4 \text{ (technically } x = \pm 4, \text{ but side}$$
$$\text{lengths cannot be negative)}$$

➢ Be sure to remember that the Pythagorean theorem ONLY applies to RIGHT triangles.

• We CANNOT solve for x in the triangle below, since we have no proof that triangle *ABC* is a right triangle:

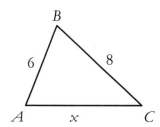

➤ Although the Pythagorean theorem is the central principle of any right triangle, it turns out that you rarely need to use it on the GRE.

• Because the exam prefers triangles whose side lengths are integers, you can often avoid the tedious computations of the theorem if you memorize a small group of triangles.

• These triangles are commonly known as PYTHAGOREAN TRIPLES.

➤ A Pythagorean triple is a triangle in which each side length is an integer such that $a^2 + b^2 = c^2$.

• The most well-known example of a Pythagorean triple is the 3–4–5. This combination of integers is a triple because $3^2 + 4^2 = 5^2$. In other words, $9 + 16 = 25$.

• While there are an infinite number of Pythagorean triples, only 4 are worth memorizing:

3–4–5	8–15–17
5–12–13	7–24–25

➤ When learning these combinations, remember that the first two numbers represent the LEGS of the triangle, and the largest number the HYPOTENUSE.

• You should also be aware that these combinations are RATIOS. Not only do their values satisfy the Pythagorean theorem, but their MULTIPLES do too.

• For example, if we double 3–4–5, we get 6–8–10. Likewise, if we triple 3–4–5, we get 9–12–15. In each case, notice how $a^2 + b^2 = c^2$:

$$6^2 + 8^2 = 10^2$$
$$36 + 64 = 100$$

$$9^2 + 12^2 = 15^2$$
$$81 + 144 = 225$$

➤ As you might guess, the GRE is more likely to test Pythagorean triples with small numbers than triples with large numbers.

• After all, the exam is interested in your ability to find solutions to thought-provoking problems, not your ability to be a human calculator.

• Thus, you're far more likely to encounter triples such as 6–8–10 and 9–12–15 than triples such as 10–24–26 (twice the ratio 5–12–13) or 15–20–25 (five times the ratio 3–4–5), since the numbers are less cumbersome.

➤ The table below will give you a sense of which triples are critical for the GRE, and which are not.

• We STRONGLY encourage you to memorize anything identified as "common" or "key". If you're shooting for a perfect score, we encourage you to memorize everything:

Triple	Frequency	Important Multiples
3–4–5	*Common*	6–8–10, 9–12–15, 12–16–20, 15–20–25
5–12–13	*Common*	10-24-26
8–15–17	*Rare*	None
7–24–25	*Rare*	None

➤ To understand why Pythagorean triples are so important for the GRE, consider the triangles below.

• For each, use the table above to identify the unknown length. Then use $a^2 + b^2 = c^2$ to confirm the solution. We think that you'll find the first strategy dramatically faster:

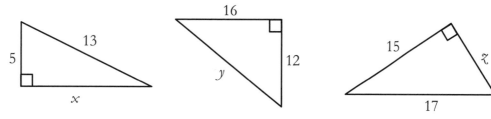

• Solutions: $x = 12$, $y = 20$, $z = 8$.

➤ Although not every right triangle on the GRE is a Pythagorean triple, many are. LOOK for them ACTIVELY.

• The sooner you can find them, the more time you'll save. Consider the following:

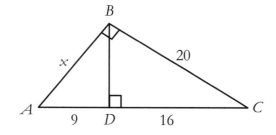

• Triangle *BCD* is a 12–16–20 triangle, so its missing leg is 12. Triangle *ABD*, therefore, has the legs 9–12–*x*. Since this is a 9–12–15 triangle, $x = 15$. Alternatively, triangle *ABC* has the legs *x*–20–25, so $x = 15$.

➤ On a final note, be sure to remember that ONLY right triangles can be Pythagorean triples.

• In the triangle below, we CANNOT determine the value of x, since triangle ABC is not a right triangle:

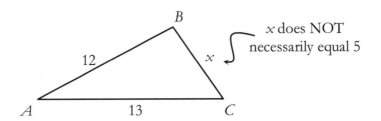

➤ Likewise, the LARGEST number in a Pythagorean triple always corresponds to the HYPOTENUSE of the triangle.

• In the triangle below, y does NOT equal 10, as many test-takers presume, since the leg of a right triangle cannot be longer than the hypotenuse:

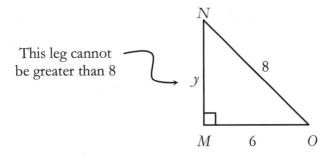

➤ Because triangle MNO is not a Pythagorean triple, we have to use the Pythagorean theorem to determine the value of y.

• We can do so as follows:

$$y^2 + 6^2 = 8^2$$
$$y^2 + 36 = 64$$
$$y^2 = 28$$

• Thus, $y = 2\sqrt{7}$, since $y = \sqrt{28} = \sqrt{2 \times 2 \times 7} = 2\sqrt{7}$.

(5) 45°–45°–90° Triangles – In addition to the Pythagorean triples, there are two more special right triangles that you ought to learn.

• The first of these is commonly known as the "45°–45°–90°". As you might guess, this name refers to the measures of the interior angles.

> ➢ Because the 45°–45°–90° has two angles of 45°, it is an ISOSCELES triangle. Therefore, its legs have EQUAL lengths.

• If you let x equal the lengths of these legs, the Pythagorean theorem proves that the hypotenuse has a length of $x\sqrt{2}$, since:

$$x^2 + x^2 = c^2$$
$$2x^2 = c^2$$
$$c = \sqrt{2x^2} = \sqrt{2 \cdot x \cdot x} = x\sqrt{2}$$

> ➢ Therefore, the sides of EVERY 45°–45°–90° triangle have the RATIO $x : x : x\sqrt{2}$, as is in the diagram below:

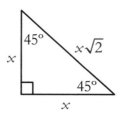

• This ratio is IMPORTANT because it allows you to determine the length of ALL three sides from a single leg length.

> ➢ For example, in the diagram below, **triangle ABC has side lengths of 5, 5, and $5\sqrt{2}$,** since leg AB has a length of 5.

• Likewise, **triangle XYZ has side lengths of 7, 7, and $7\sqrt{2}$,** since hypotenuse XY has a length of $7\sqrt{2}$:

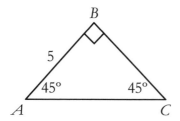
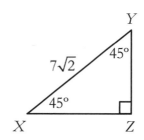

➤ In more advanced problems involving 45°–45°–90° triangles, you often come across triangles like the one below:

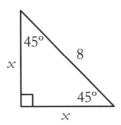

• Given that the sides of EVERY 45°–45°–90° triangle have the RATIO $x : x : x\sqrt{2}$, this triangle should look ODD to you since its hypotenuse LACKS a $\sqrt{2}$.

➤ In such situations, there are several ways to determine the length of the LEGS. One way is to set the HYPOTENUSE equal to $x\sqrt{2}$.

• For example, in the triangle above, the hypotenuse equals 8, so we could let $x\sqrt{2} = 8$ and solve for x as follows:

$$x\sqrt{2} = 8 \qquad \text{Let the hypotenuse} = x\sqrt{2}.$$
$$x = \frac{8}{\sqrt{2}} \qquad \text{Divide both sides by } \sqrt{2}.$$

• As discussed in the Roots chapter of our book on <u>Number Properties and Algebra</u>, however, if a fraction contains a radical in its denominator, it is not considered simplified.

➤ To simplify such fractions, we have to multiply their tops <u>and</u> their bottoms by the radical we want to remove.

• Thus, to remove the $\sqrt{2}$ from the bottom our fraction, we need to multiply its top and its bottom by $\sqrt{2}$.

• Doing so proves our fraction has **LEG lengths of $4\sqrt{2}$** , since:

$$x = \frac{8}{\sqrt{2}} \cdot \frac{\sqrt{2}}{\sqrt{2}} = \frac{8\sqrt{2}}{2} = 4\sqrt{2}$$

➤ Alternatively, we can use the Pythagorean theorem. For example, since the legs of the triangle are x and x, and the hypotenuse is 8, we can solve for x as follows:

$$x^2 + x^2 = 8^2 \quad \rightarrow \quad 2x^2 = 64 \quad \rightarrow \quad x^2 = 32$$

• Thus, $x = 4\sqrt{2}$, since $x = \sqrt{32} = \sqrt{4 \times 4 \times 2} = 4\sqrt{2}$.

➤ There is also a fast, simple way to determine the leg lengths in a 45°–45°–90° triangle when the hypotenuse LACKS a $\sqrt{2}$.

• Naturally, we call it the 45°–45°–90° Shortcut .

• To determine the leg lengths of a 45°–45°–90° triangle whose hypotenuse lacks a $\sqrt{2}$, simply CUT the hypotenuse in HALF and MULTIPLY the result by $\sqrt{2}$.

➤ For example, in the triangle below and to the left, the hypotenuse is 8. Therefore, $x = 4\sqrt{2}$, since 8 cut in half is 4, and $4 \times \sqrt{2} = 4\sqrt{2}$.

• Likewise, in the triangle to the right, $n = 6\sqrt{2}$, since 12 cut in half is 6, and $6 \times \sqrt{2} = 6\sqrt{2}$.

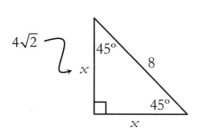
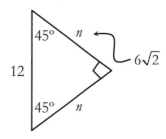

➤ To ensure that you've the hang of it, let's work through a sample problem together. Consider the following:

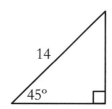

Quantity A	**Quantity B**
The perimeter of the triangle	$14 + 14\sqrt{2}$

Answer. C. The triangle above has angles of 45° and 90°. The remaining angle must also equal 45°, since the angles of any triangle add to 180°.

In a 45°–45°–90° triangle whose hypotenuse lacks a $\sqrt{2}$, the lengths of the legs can be determined by cutting the hypotenuse in half and multiplying the result by $\sqrt{2}$. The legs above, therefore, have lengths of $7\sqrt{2}$, because half of 14 is 7, and $7 \times \sqrt{2} = 7\sqrt{2}$.

Thus, the correct answer is (C), since the perimeter equals $14 + 7\sqrt{2} + 7\sqrt{2}$, or $14 + 14\sqrt{2}$.

(6) 30°–60°–90° Triangles – In addition to the Pythagorean triples and the 45°–45°–90°, there's one more special right triangle that you ought to learn.

• It's commonly known as the "30°–60°–90°". As with the 45°–45°–90°, the name refers to the measures of the interior angles.

➤ The sides of EVERY 30°–60°–90° triangle have the RATIO $x : x\sqrt{3} : 2x$, as in the diagram below:

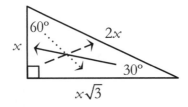

• The SMALLEST leg, x, is always across from the SMALLEST angle, 30°, and the LARGEST leg, $2x$, is always across from the LARGEST angle, 90°.

• Naturally, this means that the $x\sqrt{3}$ leg is always across from the 60° angle.

➤ This ratio is IMPORTANT because it allows you to determine the length of ALL three sides from a SINGLE leg length.

• For example, in triangle ABC, the $x\sqrt{3}$ leg (across from the 60° angle) has a length of $6\sqrt{3}$, so the x leg must have a length of 6 and the $2x$ leg must have a length of 12:

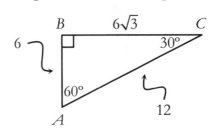

• Likewise, in triangle XYZ, the $2x$ leg (across from the 90° angle) has a length of 14, so the x leg must have a length of 7 and the $x\sqrt{3}$ leg must have a length of $7\sqrt{3}$:

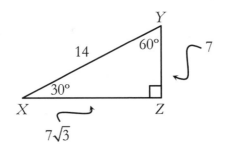

➢ As triangle problems become more difficult, exam-makers often DISGUISE 30°–60°–90° triangles by excluding their angles.

• Here's an example:

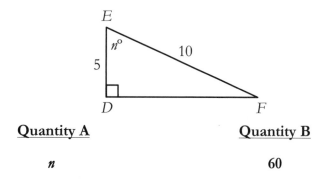

Quantity A

n

Quantity B

60

• To solve "hidden 30°–60°–90° problems" like this, it can be helpful to remember the following:

➢ For any RIGHT triangle, if the length of the hypotenuse is TWICE as large as the length of a leg, the triangle MUST be a 30°–60°–90°.

• To understand why, simply think back to the dimensions of the 30°–60°–90°. The smaller leg has a length of x and the hypotenuse a length of $2x$.

• In the problem above, **hypotenuse EF is twice as long as leg ED**, so triangle DEF must be a 30°–60°–90° triangle, where the "x leg" = 5, and the "$2x$ leg" = 10:

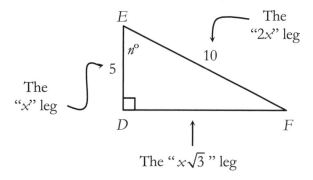

➢ Because angle n is across from the "$x\sqrt{3}$ leg", angle n must therefore have a measure of 60°.

• Thus, the correct answer is (C), since the two quantities are equal.

> ➢ Finally, it's worth noting that an EQUILATERAL triangle is composed of TWO 30°–60°–90° triangles.

• This is important because solving problems about equilateral triangles often requires cutting them into 30°–60°–90° triangles. Here's an example:

The length of each side of equilateral triangle T is 4

<u>Quantity A</u>	<u>Quantity B</u>
The height of triangle T	$2\sqrt{3}$

• The distance from the topmost point of a triangle to its base can be referred to as its HEIGHT. In every triangle, the height and the base meet at a 90° angle.

> ➢ Below, we've drawn an equilateral triangle with side lengths of 4. We've also drawn its height with a dotted line.

• Notice that the height SPLITS the equilateral into 30°–60°–90° triangles. Also, notice that the height of the equilateral EQUALS the height of either 30°–60°–90°:

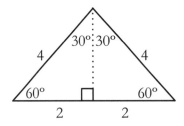

> ➢ Because the two heights are the same, we can use the height of the 30°–60°–90° to determine the height of the equilateral.

• The sides of EVERY 30°–60°–90° triangle have the RATIO $x : x\sqrt{3} : 2x$. Since the leg opposite the 30° has a length of 2 and the hypotenuse has a length of 4, the height of both triangles must therefore be $2\sqrt{3}$, as in the figure below:

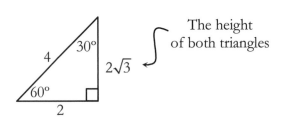

• Thus, the correct answer is (C), since the two quantities are equal.

(7) Area & Altitudes – The area of any triangle can be determined with the following formula:

$$\text{Area of a Triangle} = \tfrac{1}{2}(\text{Base} \times \text{Height})$$

- In most GRE problems, the base and the height are easy to identify.

  ➤ The base is the SIDE of the triangle that lies HORIZONTALLY, while the height is the VERTICAL distance line from the top of the triangle to the base.

- In every triangle, the height and the base are PERPENDICULAR to one another, as they are in the triangle below:

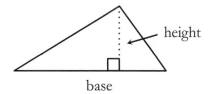

base

  ➤ For RIGHT triangles, you can simply think of the LEGS as the base and the height, since they too are perpendicular.

- Thus, the triangle on the left has an area of 24, as $\tfrac{1}{2}(6 \times 8) = 24$, and the triangle on the right has an area of 30, as $\tfrac{1}{2}(5 \times 12) = 30$:

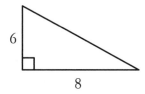

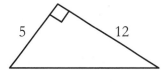

  ➤ In more advanced problems, however, the base and the height can be a bit trickier to identify.

- Technically, the base can be ANY side of the triangle, not just the horizontal side. In fact, some triangles don't even have horizontal sides. Here's an example:

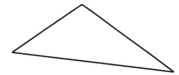

➢ Likewise, the height can be any PERPENDICULAR distance from a vertex to an OPPOSING base.

• Thus, there are SEVERAL ways we can conceive of the base and height for triangle *ABC*:

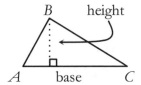 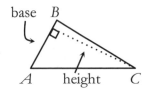 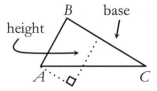

• The key thing, in each case, is that the base is a SIDE, and that the base and the height are PERPENDICULAR to one another.

➢ Fortunately, the GRE rarely designs area problems with strange bases and heights. You should, however, be prepared to tackle problems like the one below:

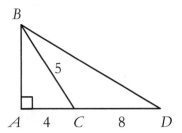

What is the area of triangle *BCD*?

(A) 6 (B) 12 (C) 18 (D) 20 (E) 30

Answer. B. The diagram above is composed of 3 triangles: *ABC*, *ABD*, and *BCD*. Because triangle *ABC* is a right triangle with a leg of 4 and a hypotenuse of 5, it's remaining leg has a length of 3, since it's a 3–4–5:

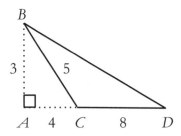

As you can see from the diagram above, triangle *BCD* has a horizontal side *CD*, so its base is 8. The perpendicular distance from the top of the triangle to the base is line segment *AB*. Thus, its height is 3. The area of triangle *BCD* is therefore 12, since $\frac{1}{2}(8 \times 3) = 12$.

➢ Finally, you should be aware that exam-makers sometimes use the term ALTITUDE to describe the HEIGHT of a triangle.

• Technically, an altitude extends from any VERTEX and intersects the OPPOSING SIDE at a 90°. Thus, as in triangle *XYZ* below, all triangles have THREE altitudes:

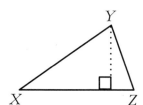 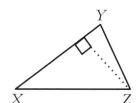 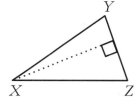

➢ The KEY thing to remember when working with altitudes is that the altitude and its opposing side are always PERPENDICULAR.

• It can also be helpful to remember that the altitude of an ISOSCELES triangle BISECTS the adjacent angle and the opposing side — so long as the two equal sides are on either side of the altitude:

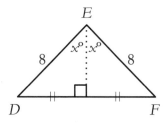

➢ Thus, in the triangle below, the altitude from vertex *C* bisects side *AB* and is perpendicular to it.

• Note that the altitude also carves triangle *ABC* into two 6–8–10 triangles, since each bisection of side *AB* has a length of 6 and the hypotenuse of both triangles has a length of 10:

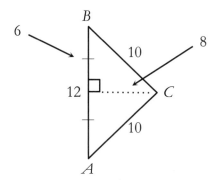

(8) Perimeter & the Triangle Inequality Theorem – As you likely know, the perimeter of a triangle can be determined by adding the lengths of its sides.

• What you may not know is there is a very specific RESTRICTION that governs the side lengths within any perimeter.

➤ This restriction, commonly known as the TRIANGLE INEQUALITY THEOREM, states:

• "The sum of any two sides of ANY triangle must be greater than the third. Conversely, the difference of any two sides must be less than the third."

• This theorem can be reduced to the following statement, which we encourage you to memorize:

$$\boxed{\textbf{LESS than the SUM, but GREATER than the DIFFERENCE}}.$$

➤ Thus, if a triangle has side lengths of 9 and 5, the third side would have a length BETWEEN 4 and 14, since $9 - 5 = 4$ and $9 + 5 = 14$.

• Likewise, if a triangle has side lengths of 7 and 4, the third side would have a length BETWEEN 3 and 11, since $7 - 4 = 3$ and $7 + 4 = 11$:

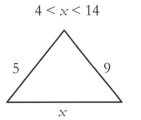
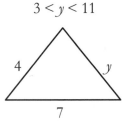

➤ To understand the basis for this rule, think of a triangle as a drawbridge. If the legs are too long or too short, the ENDS of the bridge can't meet.

• For example, in the triangles below, the legs on the left are too small for the ends to meet, while those on the right are too long:

The legs are too SMALL   The legs are too LONG

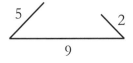
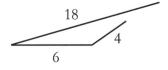

Sherpa
Prep

➤ When solving perimeter questions, you've got to keep the Triangle Inequality theorem in mind.

• A LOT of perimeter questions involve the theorem, especially those that seem to lack enough information. Examples like the following are commonplace on the GRE:

Triangle T has a perimeter composed of side lengths x, y, and z.

Quantity A	Quantity B
y	$x - z$

Answer. A. According to the Triangle Inequality theorem, the side length of a triangle must be **less than the sum** of the other two sides, **but greater than the difference**. Since y is a side length of triangle T, and $x - z$ is the difference of the other two, y must be greater than $x - z$.

➤ On a final note, it's worth pointing out that perimeter questions are occasionally like the one below:

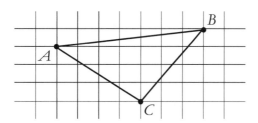

If the grid above consists of unit squares, what is the perimeter of triangle ABC?

(A) $5 + 5\sqrt{2}$ **(B)** 15 **(C)** 17 **(D)** 20 **(E)** $10 + 5\sqrt{2}$

• To solve such questions, simply BOX the triangle and determine the HYPOTENUSES of the resulting RIGHT triangles:

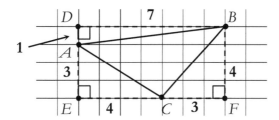

• Here, for example, triangles ACE and CBF have hypotenuses of length 5, since both are 3–4–5 triangles. Likewise, triangle ADB has a hypotenuse of length $5\sqrt{2}$, since (via the Pythagorean theorem) the lengths of its legs are 1 and 7. Thus, the correct answer is (E), as ABC has side lengths of 5, 5, and $5\sqrt{2}$.

(9) Spatial Reasoning Problems – You've now studied the fundamental properties of triangles.

• Almost every triangle question that you see on the GRE will test your understanding of one (or more) of these concepts.

➤ From time to time, however, triangle problems will also test your SPATIAL reasoning. Here's an example:

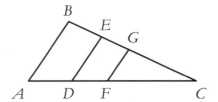

Line segments *AB*, *DE*, and *FG* are parallel.

Quantity A	**Quantity B**
The sum of the areas of triangles *FGC* and *DEC*	The area of triangle *ABC*

• Spatial reasoning problems require very little technical knowledge. In fact, to solve them you simply need to imagine two scenarios that are as DIFFERENT as possible.

➤ Remember, GRE diagrams are not necessarily accurate. By considering EXTREME possibilities, you can sometimes expose easy solutions that technical approaches miss.

• Take the problem above. For all we know, triangles *DEC* and *FGC* are both either extremely large or extremely small:

DEC and *FGC* are both LARGE   *DEC* and *FGC* are both SMALL

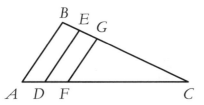
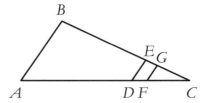

• As the figures above show, if triangles *DEC* and *FGC* are extremely large, the sum of their areas clearly exceeds that of *ABC*. Likewise, if *DEC* and *FGC* are extremely small, the sum of their areas is clearly smaller than that of *ABC*. The correct answer, therefore, must be (D), since we cannot determine the exact relationship between the two quantities.

➤ To give you a little more experience solving problems that involve spatial reasoning, let's work through one more example together.

• Consider the following:

Town _T_ has a rectangular park whose boundaries are 5 kilometers on each side. Three rest stations are located within the park.

<u>**Quantity A**</u>   <u>**Quantity B**</u>

The distance between any two stations   **6 kilometers**

• According to the problem, the boundaries of the park are 5 kilometers on each side, and all three stations are located within the park.

➤ Since the question does not specify the whereabouts of the rest stations, we can envision SEVERAL possible configurations.

• If two of the stations are closely bunched together, the distance between them would clearly be less than 6 kilometers. If, however, two of the stations are as far apart as possible, the distance between them would be quite large:

Closely bunched together   As far apart as possible

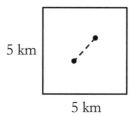   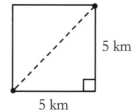

➤ In the diagram to the right, because the interior angles of a square equal 90°, the distance is equivalent to the hypotenuse of a right triangle with legs of 5 kilometers.

• That distance would equal $5\sqrt{2}$ kilometers, since a right triangle with equal legs is a 45°–45°–90° triangle, and the sides of every 45°–45°–90° triangle have the ratio $x : x : x\sqrt{2}$.

• Because $\sqrt{2} \approx 1.4$, a distance of $5\sqrt{2}$ kilometers is roughly equal to $5 \times 1.4 = 7$ kilometers. The correct answer, therefore, must be (D), since the distance between any two stations could be less than or greater than 6 kilometers.

Rare or Advanced Concepts

(10) Similar Triangles – Some of the most difficult Geometry problems on the GRE involve SIMILAR triangles.

• Similar triangles are triangles with the SAME angles. For example, the triangles below are similar, since their angles are IDENTICAL:

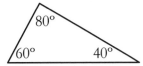 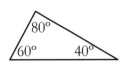 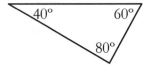

• As you can see, similar triangles don't need to have the same size or face the same direction. They only need equal angles.

➢ When triangles have identical angles, their side lengths are PROPORTIONAL. This means that the RATIO of ALL corresponding side lengths is the same.

• To understand what this means, consider the following triangles:

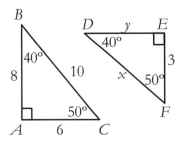

• According to the diagram, triangles *ABC* and *DEF* both have angles of 40°, 50°, and 90°. Thus, they are similar.

➢ Leg *EF* corresponds to leg *AC*, because both legs are opposite 40° angles. Therefore, the two legs are proportional.

• Leg *EF* has a length of 3 and Leg *AC* has a length of 6. Since 3 is HALF as large as 6, **EACH side of triangle *DEF* must be HALF as large as its counterpart in triangle *ABC*.**

• Thus, *x* = 5, since sides *DF* and *BC* are both hypotenuses, and 5 is half of 10. Likewise, *y* = 4, since legs *DE* and *AB* are both opposite 50° angles, and 4 is half of 8.

➤ There are THREE ways to prove that triangles are similar. The FIRST way is to prove that TWO angles are the same.

• If two angles are the same, the third must be as well, since the interior angles of any triangle add to 180°.

• For instance, if triangle *A* has angles of 40° and 90°, and triangle *B* also has angles of 40° and 90°, *A* and *B* must be similar, because the third angle of each triangle must be 50°.

➤ The SECOND way to prove that triangles are similar is to demonstrate that ALL three pairs of corresponding sides have the same RATIO.

• For example, in the diagram below, angle *x* must equal 50°, since each side in triangle *ABC* is TWICE as large as its counterpart in triangle *DEF*, proving that the two triangles have identical angles:

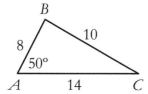 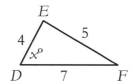

➤ The THIRD way to prove that triangles are similar is the LEAST obvious. It is also the way most commonly tested by the GRE.

• If TWO pairs of corresponding sides have the same RATIO and the angle BETWEEN them is equal, the triangles must be similar.

• This proof is commonly known as "Side Angle Side", since the equal angles are flanked by the proportional sides, just like the word "angle" is flanked by the words "side" in the name of the postulate.

➤ For example, the triangles *MNO* and *RST* are similar, since two pairs of sides have the same ratio and the angle between those side is equal:

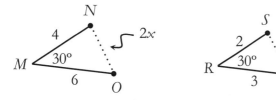 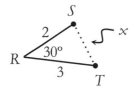

➢ The primary reason that questions involving similar triangles are often difficult is that similar triangles can be hard to recognize.

• Consider the following:

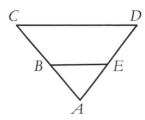

B is the midpoint of *AC* and *E* is the midpoint of *AD*.
$AC = 10$ and $CD = 8$.

<u>Quantity A</u>	<u>Quantity B</u>
BE	4

• While there is no "failsafe" way to recognize similar triangle problems, it's worth noting that any triangle containing MIDPOINTS or PARALLEL LINES masks similar triangles.

➢ In the problem above, triangles *ABE* and *ACD* are similar. To prove it, let's first insert the information we've been given:

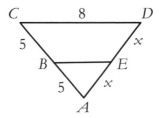

• Next, let's line up the triangles, side by side:

 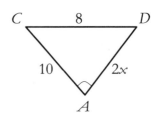

➢ As you can see, triangle *ABE* has side lengths of 5 and *x*, and triangle *ACD* has side lengths of 10 and 2*x*. In both triangles, angle *A* is between the proportional sides.

• Since 5 is half of 10 and *x* is half of 2*x*, side *BE* must therefore have a length of 4, since 4 is half of 8. Thus, the correct answer is (C).

• Here's a second example for you:

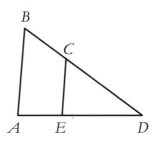

$AB \parallel CE$. $AB = 12$, $BC = 5$, and $CE = 9$.

Quantity A	**Quantity B**
CD	10

➤ In the problem above, triangles ABD and CDE are similar. To prove it, let's insert the information we've been given:

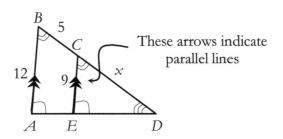

These arrows indicate parallel lines

• Note that the angles at points A and E are equal, since the corresponding angles of parallel lines are equal. For the same reason, the angles at points B and C are also equal. Thus, all three angles of triangles ABD and ECD must be equal, since both triangles also contain the angle at point D.

➤ Because the ratio of side AB to side CE is 12 to 9, the ratio of side BD to side CD must be the same.

• Thus, we can determine the length of side CD through the following proportion:

$$\frac{12}{9} = \frac{5+x}{x}$$

• Because x equals the length of side CD, the correct answer must be (A), since cross-multiplication proves that $x = 15$:

$$12x = 9(5+x) \quad \rightarrow \quad 12x = 45 + 9x \quad \rightarrow \quad 3x = 45$$

➢ On a final note, it's worth pointing out that if a RIGHT TRIANGLE is composed of two SMALLER right triangles, ALL THREE triangles are similar.

• To understand why, consider the figure below:

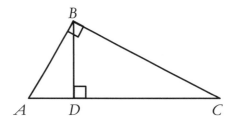

• Notice that triangles *ABC* and *ABD* both have an angle at vertex *A* and a right angle. Thus, they are similar, since they have TWO angles in common.

➢ Likewise, triangles *ABC* and *BCD* both have an angle at vertex *C* and a right angle. Thus, they too are similar, since they have TWO angles in common.

• Since triangle *ABC* is similar to triangle *ABD* <u>and</u> triangle *BCD*, all three triangles must be similar.

• In the figure below, right triangle *MNP* is composed of right triangles *MNO* and *MOP*. Since, all 3 triangles are similar, x must have a length of 1:

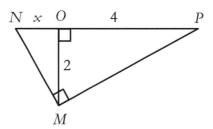

➢ To prove it, first rotate triangle *MNO* so that it has a base of x and a height of 2. Then rotate triangle *MOP* so that it has a base of 2 and a height of 4:

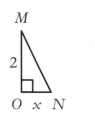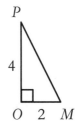

• As you can see, the height of triangle *MNO* is half as large as that of triangle *MOP*. Thus, the base of *MNO* must also be half as large. Since *MOP* has a base of 2, the base of *MNO* is therefore 1.

(11) Acute & Obtuse Triangles – By now, you know that the Pythagorean theorem can be used to measure the third side of a right triangle — if you know the remaining side lengths.

• What you may not know is that the Pythagorean theorem can also be used to determine WHETHER a triangle has a 90° angle.

➢ To make this determination, simply plug the side lengths of a triangle into the theorem. If $a^2 + b^2 = c^2$, the triangle HAS a right angle.

• If $a^2 + b^2 \neq c^2$, the triangle does NOT have right angle.

• For example, a triangle with side lengths of 8, 15, and 17 has a right angle, because $8^2 + 15^2 = 17^2$. However, a triangle with side lengths of 7, 14, and 16 does not have a right angle, because $7^2 + 14^2 \neq 16^2$. Thus:

$$8^2 + 15^2 = 17^2 \qquad\qquad 7^2 + 14^2 \neq 16^2$$
$$64 + 225 = 289 \qquad\qquad 49 + 196 \neq 256$$

➢ To get a sense of how this might help you on the GRE, consider the following question:

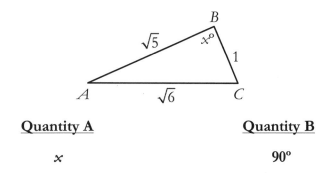

Quantity A	**Quantity B**
x	90°

• According to the problem, triangle ABC has side lengths of 1, $\sqrt{5}$, and $\sqrt{6}$. Since these values satisfy the Pythagorean theorem, it must have a 90° angle:

$$1^2 + \left(\sqrt{5}\right)^2 = \left(\sqrt{6}\right)^2$$
$$1 + 5 = 6$$

➢ Hence, if triangle ABC has one interior angle of 90°, the other two angles must be **less than 90°**, as the sum of the interior angles of a triangle cannot exceed 180°.

• The largest angle in any triangle is always across from the largest leg (and vice versa). Since side AC is the largest side in the triangle above, and 90° is the largest angle, x must therefore equal 90°, because angle x is across from side AC. Thus, the correct answer is (C).

> ➤ On occasion, the GRE will use this application of the Pythagorean theorem to test your knowledge of acute and obtuse triangles.

• In an acute triangle, all the angles are less than 90°. In an obtuse triangle, one angle is greater than 90°.

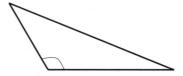

ACUTE triangle: OBTUSE triangle
all angles LESS than 90°   one angle GREATER than 90°

> ➤ If you plug the side lengths of a triangle into the theorem, and c^2 is GREATER than $a^2 + b^2$, the triangle is OBTUSE.

• Conversely, if c^2 is LESS than $a^2 + b^2$, the triangle is ACUTE.

• To understand why, think back to our discussion of Angles & Sides. As the angle between two sides grows, the distance between their two tips also grows. Conversely, as that angle shrinks, the distance between them shrinks:

As the angle grows   As the angle shrinks

The opposing distance grows   The opposing distance shrinks

> ➤ Thus, a triangle with an angle LARGER than 90° must have a side LARGER than a hypotenuse across from it, so $c^2 > a^2 + b^2$.

• Likewise, a triangle whose angles are SMALLER than 90° has no side as large as a hypotenuse, so $c^2 < a^2 + b^2$.

➢ To get a sense of how the GRE might test this knowledge, consider the following questions:

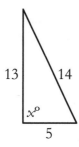

Quantity A	**Quantity B**
x	90°

Answer. A. Although angle x visually appears to equal 90°, we know that $x \neq 90°$, since 5, 13, and 14 don't satisfy the Pythagorean theorem. On the contrary, because angle x is across from the largest leg, we know that x is greater than 90°, as $c^2 > a^2 + b^2$:

$$14^2 > 5^2 + 13^2$$
$$196 > 25 + 169$$

The correct answer is therefore (A).

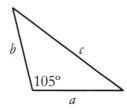

Quantity A	**Quantity B**
$a^2 + b^2$	c^2

Answer. B. According to the rules of the Pythagorean theorem, a triangle has:

A right angle when $a^2 + b^2 = c^2$.
Three acute angles when $a^2 + b^2 > c^2$.
An obtuse angle when $a^2 + b^2 < c^2$.

Because the triangle above has an angle greater than 90°, the correct answer must be (B), since $a^2 + b^2 < c^2$ for all obtuse triangles.

(12) Crazy Pythagorean Triangles – You now know that the Pythagorean theorem has a relationship with acute and obtuse triangles.

• If you're like most people preparing for the GRE, however, you're probably unaware the Pythagorean theorem has another important relationship.

➢ This one concerns the "FOIL" IDENTITIES that we discussed with you in our treatment of Algebra.

• Notice that if we rearrange the terms within the Pythagorean theorem, we get the most important of the identities: the DIFFERENCE between SQUARES.

$$a^2 + b^2 = c^2 \quad \rightarrow \quad b^2 = c^2 - a^2$$

➢ As you may recall, the difference between two squares, such as $x^2 - y^2$, can be rewritten as $(x + y)(x - y)$, since the product of $(x + y)(x - y) = x^2 - y^2$.

• Because this equation REMOVES the need to calculate the square of any term, it can be tremendously helpful in handling right triangles whose LEGS are LARGE, and therefore difficult to work with.

• To get a sense of exactly how helpful, consider the following:

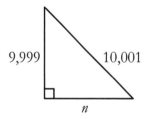

In the triangle above, what is the length of leg *n*?

(A) 100   (B) 200   (C) 400   (D) 800   (E) 1,000

Answer: B. According to the Pythagorean theorem, $9,999^2 + n^2 = 10,001^2$. If we isolate n^2, we get $n^2 = 10,001^2 - 9,999^2$. Because $x^2 - y^2 = (x + y)(x - y)$, this equation can be rewritten as follows:

$$n^2 = (10,001 + 9,999)(10,001 - 9,999)$$
$$n^2 = (20,000)(2) = 40,000$$
$$n = \pm 200$$

Since all distances must be positive, the correct answer is therefore (B).

> ➤ There are additional relationships between the Pythagorean and the "FOIL" identities.

• Fortunately, you don't need to know them, since they're not useful for solving GRE problems.

• The relationship with $x^2 - y^2 = (x + y)(x - y)$, however, can come in handy. So let's work through one more problem to ensure that you've got the hang of it:

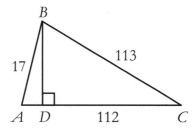

Note: figure not drawn to scale.

What is the perimeter of triangle ABC?

(A) 250 (B) 251 (C) 252 (D) 254 (E) 255

Answer. A. According to the problem, triangle BCD has side lengths of 112 and 113. We can therefore solve for the third leg of this triangle as follows:

$$BD^2 + 112^2 = 113^2$$
$$BD^2 = 113^2 - 112^2$$
$$BD^2 = (113 + 112)(113 - 112) = (225)(1)$$

Thus, side BD has a length of 15, since $\sqrt{225} = 15$.

If $BD = 15$, then triangle ABD has side lengths of 15 and 17. Side AD, therefore, must have a length of 8, since it is an 8–15–17 triangle. Alternatively, we can solve for AD as follows:

$$15^2 + AD^2 = 17^2$$
$$AD^2 = 17^2 - 15^2$$
$$AD^2 = (17 + 15)(17 - 15) = (32)(2) = 64$$

Because the square root of 64 is 8, the length of side AD is 8. Thus, the perimeter of triangle ABC must be 250, since the sum of its side lengths equals $17 + 113 + 112 + 8$:

$$17 + 113 + 112 + 8 = 130 + 120 = 250$$

(13) Hexagons and Octagons – Every now and then, the GRE asks test-takers to determine the areas of polygons such as hexagons and octagons.

• Despite their appearance, such questions are really triangle questions.

> ➤ In most cases, the key to solving them is to split the polygon into IDENTICAL triangles by drawing lines from the center of the shape to each VERTEX.

• You'll also need to determine the INTERIOR angles of the polygon. Doing so will tell you what sort of triangles you're working with.

• For example, imagine a REGULAR hexagon with a side length of 4. (Remember, all the sides of a regular polygon have the SAME length and all the angles have the SAME measure.)

> ➤ As shown below, we can split this shape into six equal triangles. Further, its six interior angles add to 720°, so EACH individual angle equals 120°.

• Because the lines to the vertices have the SAME length AND cut the interior angles in HALF, each of the triangles is therefore an equilateral:

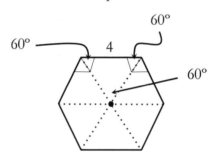

> ➤ Thus, to determine the area of the hexagon, we simply need to determine the area of one equilateral triangle and to multiply the result by 6 to account for all six triangles.

• Since all equilateral triangles are composed of two 30°–60°–90° triangles, each of the triangles above can be conceived of as follows:

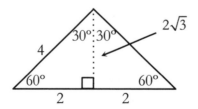

• The base of this triangle is 4 and its height is $2\sqrt{3}$, so its area equals $\frac{1}{2}(4 \times 2\sqrt{3}) = 4\sqrt{3}$. Thus, the area of the hexagon equals $24\sqrt{3}$, since $6 \times 4\sqrt{3} = 24\sqrt{3}$.

➤ In some cases, however, you might instead find it helpful to cut a polygon into a series of triangles and rectangles.

• This is especially true of octagons, because the eight interior angles add to $(8 - 2)180°$, making each individual angle 135°.

• A measure of 135° can be split into angles of 45° and 90°, so the area of any octagon is easily determined be carving it into four 45°–45°–90° triangles and five rectangles.

➤ Imagine, for example, an octagon with equal angles, whose horizontal and vertical sides have a length of 1 and whose diagonal sides have a length of $\sqrt{2}$.

• How would one calculate the area of the octagon? As shown below, such an octagon would be composed of five squares, each with a side length of 1, and four 45°–45°–90° triangles, each with a hypotenuse of $\sqrt{2}$.

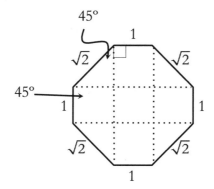

➤ Because the area of a square equals its length × its width, each of these squares would have an area of 1, as $1 \times 1 = 1$.

• Likewise, each triangle would have an area of $\frac{1}{2}$, since a 45°–45°–90° triangle with a hypotenuse of $\sqrt{2}$ has a base of 1 and a height of 1, so $\frac{1}{2}(\text{base} \times \text{height}) = \frac{1}{2}(1 \times 1) = \frac{1}{2}$:

• The octagon, therefore, would have an area of 7, since the 5 squares each have an area of 1, and the 4 triangles each have an area of $\frac{1}{2}$:

$$5(1) + 4\left(\frac{1}{2}\right) = 7$$

(14) Problem Sets – The following questions have been arranged into three groups: fundamental, intermediate, and rare or advanced.

• Whether you're aiming for a perfect score or a score closer to average, mastery of the concepts in the FUNDAMENTAL questions is absolutely essential.

➢ As you might expect, the INTERMEDIATE questions are more difficult but are essential for test-takers who need an above-average score or higher.

• Finally, the RARE or ADVANCED questions test concepts that are very sophisticated or seldom encountered on the GRE. Mastery of such questions is required only if you need a math score above the 90th percentile.

• As always, if you find yourself confused, bogged down with busy work, or stuck, don't be afraid to fall back on your "Plan B" strategies!

| Fundamental |

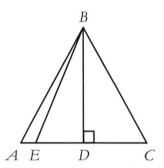

D is the midpoint of segment *AC*.

	Quantity A	Quantity B
1.	The length of segment *BE*	The length of segment *BC*

2. If triangle *Z* has sides of lengths 5, 12, and *x*, which of the following are a possible value for the length of side *x*?

Select <u>all</u> possible values.

A 7   B 8   C 13   D 16   E 18

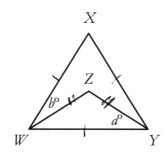

Note: Figure not drawn to scale.

3. In the figure above, *WXY* is an equilateral triangle and *WYZ* is an isosceles triangle. If *a* = 47, then *b* equals

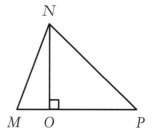

The product of *MP* and *NO* is 34.

Quantity A	Quantity B
4. The area of triangle *MNP*	18

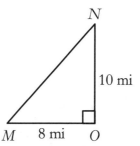

5. According to the figure above, traveling directly from point *M* to point *N*, rather than from point *M* to point *O* and then from point *O* to point *N*, would save approximately how many miles?

(A) 5 (B) 7 (C) 8 (D) 9 (E) 12

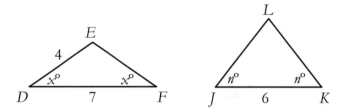

In triangle JLK, angle n has a measure of $60°$.

Quantity A	Quantity B
The perimeter of triangle DEF	The perimeter of triangle JLK

6.

Isosceles triangle M has a side of length 5. The sum of the lengths of two sides of triangle M is 9.

Quantity A	Quantity B
The length of its perimeter	14

7.

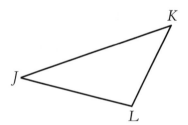

Quantity A	Quantity B
$JK + JL$	KL

8.

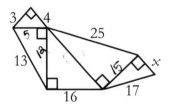

9. According to the figure above, $x =$

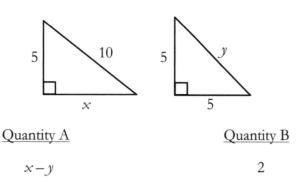

Quantity A	Quantity B
$x - y$	2

10.

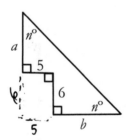

The map above shows the only roads that connect the four towns
and shows the distance along each road.

Quantity A	Quantity B

11. The straight-line distance between   The straight-line distance between
     Hillton and Seaside   Gasland and Riverville

Quantity A	Quantity B
a	b

12.

Isosceles right triangle T has an area of 18.

Quantity A	Quantity B

13. The hypotenuse of T 9

Intermediate

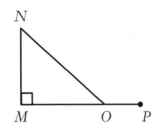

The length of line segment MN is 6, and the
lengths of line segments NO and MP are twice that of MN.

	Quantity A	Quantity B
14.	The length of line segment OP	$12 - 6\sqrt{3}$

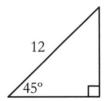

	Quantity A	Quantity B
15.	The area of the triangular region	36

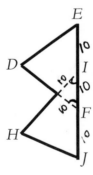

16. In the diagram above, triangles DEF and HIJ are equilateral. If EI, IF, and FJ each
have a length of 10, what is the length of the perimeter in bold?

17. If right triangle *ABC* has legs of equal length and a hypotenuse of length 20, what is the approximate length of the perimeter of the triangle?

(A) 40   (B) 50   (C) 60   (D) 70   (E) 80

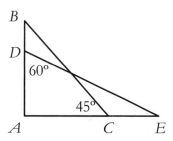

18. If *BC* = *DE* = 20 and line segment *AB* is perpendicular to line segment *AE*, what is the approximate difference between the lengths of line segments *BD* and *CE*?

(A) $\frac{1}{2}$ (B) $\frac{2}{3}$ (C) 1   (D) $\frac{3}{2}$ (E) 2

19. What is the area of an equilateral triangle with sides of length 10?

(A) 25   (B) $25\sqrt{3}$ (C) 50   (D) $50\sqrt{2}$ (E) 100

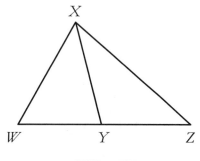

WY = YZ

Quantity A	Quantity B
20. The area of triangle *WXY*	The area of triangle *XYZ*

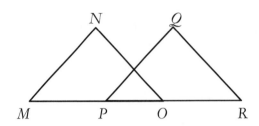

Triangles MNO and PQR have the same area.

$NO < QR.$

Quantity A	Quantity B
21.	
The altitude of triangle MNO from M to NO	The altitude of triangle PQR from P to QR

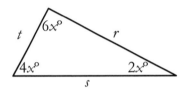

Quantity A	Quantity B
22.	
s^2	$r^2 + t^2$

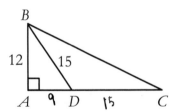

23.   In the figure above, line segment AC has a length of 24. The area of triangle $BCD =$

(A) 90   (B) 120   (C) 135   (D) 288   (E) 360

Rare or Advanced

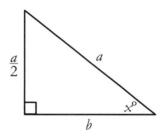

	Quantity A	Quantity B

24. x 45°

25.   Right triangle *ABC* has a leg of length 9,996 and a hypotenuse of length 10,004. What
       is the length of its unknown leg?

                   (A) 100   (B) 200   (C) 400   (D) 500   (E) 1,000

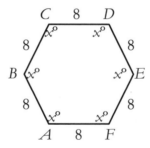

26.   In the figure above, what is the area of the hexagonal region?

                   (A) $54\sqrt{3}$ (B) 108   (C) $96\sqrt{3}$ (D) 216   (E) $144\sqrt{3}$

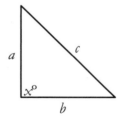

            In the triangle above, $a^2 + b^2 < 24$ and $c > 5$.

	Quantity A	Quantity B

27. x 90

28. Triangle T has a perimeter of 14. If the length of each of its legs is an integer, and no two legs are equal, which of the following CANNOT be the length of one side?

Select all such lengths.

A 1   B 3   C 5   D 7   E 9

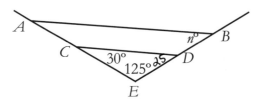

$AC = CE; BD = DE$

Quantity A	Quantity B
29. $n + 30$ $2n$

30. If the perimeter of isosceles right triangle XYZ is $16\sqrt{2} + 16$, its area equals

(A) 16   (B) 32   (C) 48   (D) 64   (E) 96

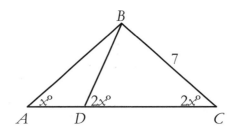

Figure not drawn to scale.

Quantity A	Quantity B
31. The length of line segment AD 7

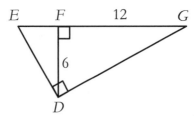

Quantity A	Quantity B
32. The area of triangle DEG 45

(15) Solutions – Video solutions for each of the previous questions can be found on our website at **www.sherpaprep.com/masterkey**.

• BOOKMARK this address for future visits!

  ➢ To view the videos, you'll need to register your copy of Master Key to the GRE: Geometry.

• If you have yet to do so, please go to **www.sherpaprep.com/videos** and enter your email address.

• Be sure to provide the SAME email address that you used to purchase your copy of Master Key to the GRE or to enroll in your GRE course with Sherpa Prep!

  ➢ When checking your answers, we encourage you to watch the solution for any problem that you answered INCORRECTLY

• The same goes for any problem that took you MORE than TWO MINUTES to solve.

• After digesting the explanation, REVISIT your mistake a couple of days later to ensure that the problem no longer poses issues to you.

  ➢ If you struggle to solve the problem a SECOND time, add it to your "LOG of ERRORS" and redo it every few weeks.

• Solving tricky questions MORE THAN ONCE is the best way to learn from your mistakes and to avoid similar difficulties on your actual exam.

Fundamental		Intermediate	Rare or Advanced
1. B	11. D	14. C	24. B
2. B, C, D	12. B	15. C	25. C
3. 13	13. B	16. 90	26. C
4. B		17. B	27. A
5. A		18. C	28. A, D, E
6. B		19. B	29. A
7. D		20. C	30. D
8. A		21. A	31. C
9. 8		22. C	32. C
10. B		23. A	

Chapter 4

Quadrilaterals & Rectangular Solids

Quadrilaterals & Rectangular Solids

To be discussed:

Fundamental Concepts

Whether you're aiming for a perfect score or a score closer to average, mastery of the following concepts is essential.

1. Quadrilaterals
2. Parallelograms
3. Rectangles & Squares
4. Trapezoids
5. Unusual Shapes
6. Shaded Areas
7. Rectangular Solids & Cubes
8. Questions Without Values

Rare or Advanced Concepts

The following concepts are either advanced or are tested only on rare occasions. If you don't need an elite math score, don't waste your time!

9. The Volume Trap
10. Rhombuses
11. Maximizing Volume
12. The Area & Perimeter "Guess Trick"

Practice Questions

There's no substitute for elbow grease. Practice your new skills to ensure that you internalize what you've studied.

13. Problem Sets
14. Solutions

> [!Fundamental Concepts]

(1) Quadrilaterals – Mercifully, Quadrilaterals are a lot simpler than Triangles.

• In fact, if you know how to determine the perimeter and area of a Rectangle, you already know much of what you need to know to solve many basic quadrilateral problems.

    ➤ The GRE also designs questions with special Quadrilaterals such as Trapezoids and Parallelograms, but such problems tend to boil down to a few basic facts.

• More advanced quadrilateral problems often test the properties of Triangles. This is particularly true of questions involving Squares and Rectangles.

• If you've worked through the preceding chapter, and felt comfortable with its core concepts, you'll find such questions to be similar to ones you've already solved.

    ➤ Challenging quadrilateral problems also tend to involve unusual figures, questions without values, and shaded areas.

• To solve such problems, you'll need to know a few key but simple strategies. Before we get to those strategies, however, let's quickly review a few things we've already discussed.

• First, every Quadrilateral has 4 sides and 4 interior angles. The sum of the interior angles is always 360°. Likewise, every Quadrilateral has 4 exterior angles. These angles also add to 360°, as they do for any polygon:

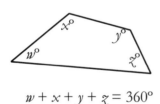
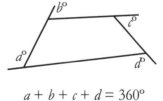

$$w + x + y + z = 360° \qquad\qquad a + b + c + d = 360°$$

    ➤ Further, remember that you CANNOT trust the diagrams. Although many shapes are drawn to scale, some are intentionally drawn in MISLEADING manners.

• Finally, be sure to watch out for the "LOOKS LIKE" trap. Because something LOOKS like a square, rectangle, or parallelogram does not mean that it is.

• You cannot assume a shape has equal side lengths or 90° angles unless you have PROOF that it does.

(2) Parallelograms – Any quadrilateral in which both pairs of opposite sides are PARALLEL is known as a PARALLELOGRAM.

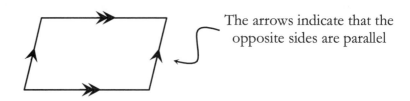

The arrows indicate that the opposite sides are parallel

• In every parallelogram, the opposite SIDES have the SAME length and the opposite ANGLES are EQUAL:

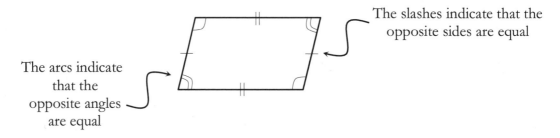

The arcs indicate that the opposite angles are equal

The slashes indicate that the opposite sides are equal

➤ While opposite angles are equal, ADJACENT angles (angles that are next to one another) always ADD to 180°.

• Thus, in the diagram below, EVERY combination of x and y adds to 180°, since every angle x is next to an angle y:

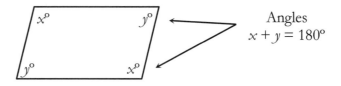

Angles
$x + y = 180°$

➤ The DIAGONALS of a parallelogram are also important, since they BISECT one another and split the parallelogram into two EQUAL triangles.

• In the figures below, $AC = 8$ and $BD = 6$, and triangle WXY has an area of 12:

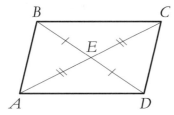

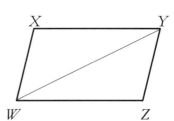

Sherpa
Prep

- Therefore, $AE = CE = 4$ and $BE = DE = 3$, and triangle WYZ also has an area of 12, since diagonals AC and BD bisect one another, and diagonal WY splits parallelogram $WXYZ$ into equal triangles.

  ➢ Finally, the PERIMETER of any parallelogram is equal to the SUM of its side lengths, and the AREA is equal to the BASE × the HEIGHT.

- As with triangles, you can think of the base of a parallelogram as any SIDE that lies HORIZONTALLY and the height as the VERTICAL distance from the top of the parallelogram to the base.

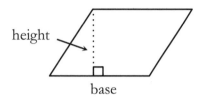

- Note that the height and the base MUST be PERPENDICULAR to one another, as indicated in the figure above.

  ➢ Parallelogram $ABCD$, shown below, has two sides of length 8 and two sides of length 12, so its perimeter is $2(8) + 2(12) = 40$.

- Since its base has a length of 12 and its height a length of 6, its area is $12 \times 6 = 72$. The HEIGHT is not 8, because sides AB and AD are not PERPENDICULAR to one another.

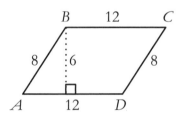 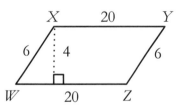

  ➢ Likewise, parallelogram $WXYZ$, shown above, has two sides of length 6 and two sides of length 20, since the opposite sides of parallelograms are always EQUAL.

- Thus, its perimeter equals $2(6) + 2(20) = 52$. Its base has a length of 20 and its height a length of 4, so its area equals $20 \times 4 = 80$.

- As with parallelogram $ABCD$, the height of parallelogram $WXYZ$ cannot equal the length of its slanted legs, since the height of any parallelogram MUST be PERPENDICULAR to the base.

➤ To get a sense of how the GRE might test your knowledge of parallelograms, consider the following:

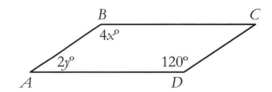

ABCD is a parallelogram.

Quantity A	Quantity B
x	y

Answer. C. In every parallelogram, opposite angles are equal. Since angles B and D are opposite one another, we therefore know that $4x° = 120°$. Thus, $x = 30$.

Conversely, the adjacent angles of every parallelogram add to 180°. Since angles A and D are next to one another, we also know that $2y + 120° = 180°$. Thus, $2y = 60°$, so $y = 30$. The correct answer is therefore (C), since x and y both equal 30.

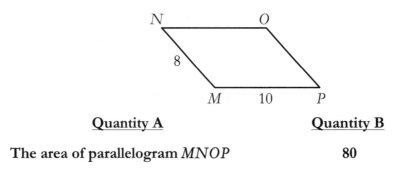

Quantity A	Quantity B
The area of parallelogram $MNOP$	80

Answer. B. According to the figure above, parallelogram $MNOP$ has a base of 10. Its height can be depicted as follows:

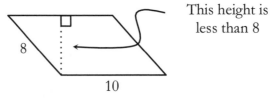

This height is less than 8

As you can see, the height of the parallelogram forms a right triangle in which the hypotenuse has a length of 8 and one leg is the height of the parallelogram. Because **the legs of a right triangle must be shorter than the hypotenuse**, the height of the triangle must be less than 8. Thus, the area of this parallelogram must be less than 80, since a base of 10 × a height less than 8 = a product less than 80.

<u>**(3) Rectangles & Squares**</u> – A RECTANGLE is a special type of parallelogram.

• Like all parallelograms, a rectangle has opposite sides that are parallel and of equal length, as well as opposite angles that are equal and adjacent angles that add to 180°.

> ➤ A rectangle is special in that all four interior angles of a rectangle have a measure of 90° and the sides are referred to by the terms LENGTH and WIDTH:

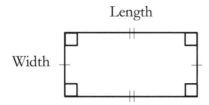

• As with any parallelogram, the PERIMETER of a rectangle is equal to the SUM of its side lengths. However, since the length and the width of a rectangle are perpendicular to one another, the AREA is defined as LENGTH × WIDTH.

> ➤ The rectangle below has a length of 8 and a width of 4. Since the opposite sides of a rectangle are always EQUAL, its perimeter equals 2(8) + 2(4) = 24.

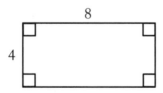

• When calculating the area of a rectangle, it doesn't matter which side you consider the length and which the width. Just be sure to multiply two side lengths that are perpendicular to one another. Thus, in the rectangle above, the area is 4 × 8 = 32.

> ➤ Finally, as with other parallelograms, the DIAGONALS of a rectangle BISECT one another.

• Unlike generic parallelograms, however, all four bisections of a rectangle have the SAME length, since the diagonals of a rectangle are also equal:

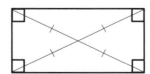

➢ A SQUARE is a special type of rectangle. Everything that is true of rectangles is true of squares.

• The main difference between a square and a rectangle is that a square has four sides of equal length. The perimeter still equals the SUM of the side lengths, and the area still equals the PRODUCT of the side lengths.

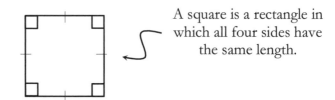

A square is a rectangle in which all four sides have the same length.

• For example, if the square above had a side length of 8, its perimeter would equal 32, since 4(8) = 32. Likewise, that square would have an area of 64, since 8 × 8 = 64.

➢ The other key difference between a rectangle and a square is that the diagonals of a square BISECT the corner ANGLES.

• As shown below, this means that each diagonal SPLITS a square into TWO 45°–45°–90° triangles:

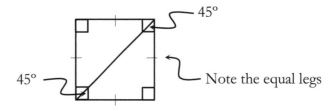

➢ Further, since all four bisections of a rectangle are equal, it also means that both diagonals, when drawn together, split a square into FOUR 45°–45°–90° triangles.

• In the diagram below, notice how all 8 corner angles equal 45°. Since the interior angles of a triangle equal 180°, each of the 4 angles at the center of the square must therefore equal 90°:

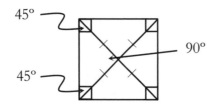

➢ To get a basic feel for how the GRE might test your knowledge of rectangles and squares, consider the following:

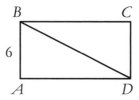

If rectangle *ABCD* has a perimeter of 28, what is the length of diagonal *BD*?

(A) 8   (B) 9   (C) 10   (D) 12   (E) 14

Answer. C. Rectangle *ABCD* has a width of 6, a perimeter of 28, and its length is unstated. Since the opposite sides of a rectangle have equal lengths, **twice the rectangle's length plus twice its width must equal the perimeter**. Thus, the length of the rectangle is 8, as:

$$2(l) + 2(6) = 28 \;\rightarrow\; 2l = 16 \;\rightarrow\; l = 8$$

The interior angles of a rectangle are 90°, and triangles *ABD* and *BCD* both have legs of length 6 and 8, so each is a 6–8–10 triangle. Because diagonal *BD* is also the hypotenuse of both triangles, *BD* must therefore have a length of 10.

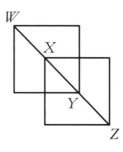

X and Y are the centers of two squares with side lengths of 2.

Quantity A	Quantity B
The length of *WZ*	$3\sqrt{2}$

Answer. C. A diagonal splits a square into two 45°–45°–90° triangles. The legs of such triangles have the ratio $x : x : x\sqrt{2}$, so diagonals *WY* and *XZ* must each have a length of $2\sqrt{2}$, since the side length of each square is 2.

Because *X* is the center of *WY*, and *Y* is the center of *XZ*, line segments *WX*, *XY*, and *YZ* each have a length of $\sqrt{2}$, which is half of $2\sqrt{2}$. The correct answer is therefore (C), since $\sqrt{2} + \sqrt{2} + \sqrt{2} = 3\sqrt{2}$.

(4) Trapezoids – In American English, a quadrilateral in which ONE pair of sides is parallel is referred to as a TRAPEZOID.

• In British English, such a shape is called a TRAPEZIUM.

➤ The parallel sides of a trapezoid are known as BASES, and the other sides as LEGS. The quadrilaterals below are all trapezoids, since each has one pair of parallel sides:

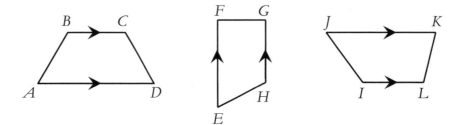

• A trapezoid in which the legs have the same length and the base angles have the same measure is commonly known as an ISOSCELES trapezoid:

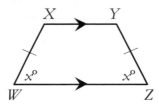

➤ Most GRE questions involving trapezoids will test your ability to determine their AREAS. There are two ways you can do so.

• The easiest way is with the following formula:

Area of a TRAPEZOID = the Average of the BASES × the HEIGHT

• You can think of the height of a trapezoid as a PERPENDICULAR line from one base to the other. The trapezoid below has bases of lengths 8 and 16, and the perpendicular distance between them is 4.

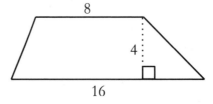

• Thus, its area is 48, since the average of 8 and 16 is 12, and $12 \times 4 = 48$.

> In some cases, however, you may need to SPLIT a trapezoid into a rectangle and one or more right triangles to determine its area.

- Here's an example:

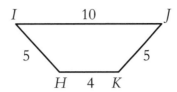

In the figure above, _IJ_ is parallel to _HK_.

Quantity A   **Quantity B**

The area of _HIJK_   **30**

- To determine the area of trapezoid _HIJK_, we need to know its height. We can get this information by splitting up the trapezoid as follows:

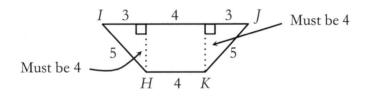

> As you can see, the height of the trapezoid forms two right triangles, each of which has a leg of length 3 and a hypotenuse of length 5.

- Thus, the height of the trapezoid is 4, since each of these triangles is a 3–4–5.

- Because _IJ_ and _HK_ are parallel, the bases of _HIJK_ have lengths of 4 and 10. The average of these bases is 7. The area of the trapezoid must therefore be 28, since the average of the bases × the height equals 7 × 4 = 28.

> Alternatively, we can determine the area of _HIJK_ by adding the areas of the rectangle and the right triangles from which it is composed.

- Each 3–4–5 triangle has an area of 6, since $\frac{1}{2}(3 \times 4) = 6$. The rectangle between them has a length of 4 and a width of 4, so its area is 16.

- Since 6 + 6 + 16 = 28, the area of trapezoid _HIJK_ is therefore less than 30, so the correct answer is (B).

(5) Unusual Shapes – On the GRE, quadrilateral problems sometimes feature figures with unusual shapes.

• Here's an example:

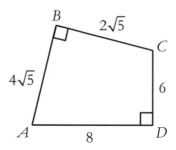

The area of quadrilateral _ABCD_ is equal to

(A) 42   (B) 44   (C) 45   (D) 46   (E) 48

• As with trapezoids, the key to working with such figures is to SPLIT them into familiar shapes such as right triangles and rectangles.

➢   When doing so, remember that exam-makers are NOT interested in your ability to do a lot of BUSY work.

• There should always be a simple breakdown that allows you to find what you need easily. For example, we can split up the shape above in a variety of ways. A simple diagonal down the middle, however, creates two basic right triangles:

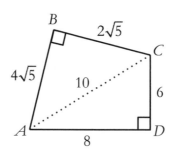

➢   Triangle _ACD_ has legs of 6 and 8, so its area is $\frac{1}{2}(6 \times 8) = 24$. Likewise, triangle _ABC_ has legs of $2\sqrt{5}$ and $4\sqrt{5}$, so its area is 20, as:

$$\frac{1}{2}(2\sqrt{5} \times 4\sqrt{5}) \quad \rightarrow \quad \frac{1}{\cancel{2}} \cdot \cancel{2} \cdot \sqrt{5} \cdot 4 \cdot \sqrt{5} \quad \rightarrow \quad 5 \cdot 4 = 20$$

• Thus, quadrilateral _ABCD_ has an area of 44, since the areas of the triangles within it are 24 and 20. The correct answer is therefore (B).

(6) Shaded Regions – Quadrilateral problems on the GRE also tend to involve shaded regions.

• Here's a typical example:

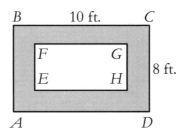

In the figure above, a rug is 10 feet long by 8 feet wide, and has a brown border that is 1 foot wide on all sides.

Quantity A

The area of the rug's border

Quantity B

40 square feet

• To solve problems with shaded regions, first get the area of the LARGER shape. Then get the area of the SMALLER shape.

  ➢ The DIFFERENCE between the two AREAS will represent the area of the shaded region.

• For example, in the problem above, the area of rectangle *ABCD* is 10 × 8 = 80 square feet. Likewise, the area of rectangle *EFGH* is 8 × 6 = 48 square feet, since the rug has a border that is 1 foot wide on all sides:

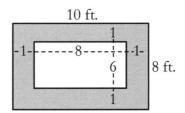

• Thus, the area of the shaded region must be 32 square feet, because 80 – 48 = 32. The correct answer is therefore (B), since the shaded region in the figures above represents the area of the rug's border.

➤ When solving shaded region questions, we encourage you to WRITE down the shaded region FORMULA before solving the problem:

BIG Area – SMALL Area = SHADED Region

• BENEATH the formula, insert any information that's been provided. Doing so will organize your thoughts, helping you solve trickier problems like the one below:

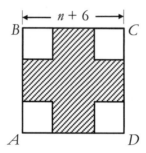

In the figure above, square *ABCD* has sides of length *n* + 6, and each of the smaller squares has sides of length 3. If the area of the shaded region is 45, what is the value of *n*?

(A) 3   (B) $3\sqrt{2}$ (C) 6   (D) $6\sqrt{2}$ (E) 9

Answer. A. According to the problem, the shaded region has an area of 45 and each of the smaller squares has a side length of 3. There are four smaller squares, so their collective areas must add to 36, since each has an area of $3 \times 3 = 9$.

If we insert this information into the shaded region formula, we can see that area of the big square must equal 81, since:

$$\text{BIG} - \text{SMALL} = \text{SHADED} \qquad b = 45 + 36 = 81$$
$$b - 36 = 45$$

Therefore, if the area of the big square equals 81, then each of its sides must have a length of 9, as $9 \times 9 = 81$. According to the problem, however, the sides of square *ABCD* have a length of *n* + 6. Thus, we know that *n* + 6 equals 9. We can use this equation to solve for *n*:

$$n + 6 = 9$$
$$n = 3$$

Since *n* = 3, the correct answer must be (A).

(7) Rectangular Solids – In Geometry, there are several basic three-dimensional figures.

• The most common of these figures are rectangular solids, cubes, cylinders, spheres, pyramids, and cones.

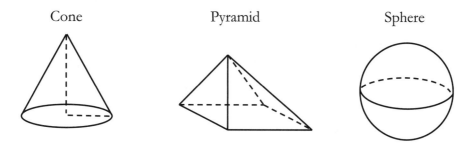

Cone   Pyramid   Sphere

• If you were back in high-school, you would study each of these figures and learn their respective formulas.

> ➤ Mercifully, the GRE will only test your knowledge of rectangular solids, cubes, and cylinders.

• On extremely rare occasions, a GRE question might refer to a cone or a sphere. Such questions, however, are simply tests of visual reasoning.

• You do not need to know a single thing about cones or spheres in order to solve them. You just need to know what they look like.

> ➤ In this section, we will discuss rectangular solids and cubes with you. You will find our discussion of cylinders in the chapter titled "Circles and Cylinders".

• As you may know, a RECTANGULAR SOLID is composed of six rectangles, known as FACES. Each side of a face is known as an EDGE, and each point at which two edges meet is known as a VERTEX.

• A CUBE is simply a rectangular solid in which each face is a SQUARE.

Rectangular Solid   Cube

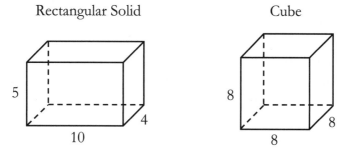

> ➤ To solve most problems involving rectangular solids or cubes, you'll need to determine one of two things: a surface area or a volume.

• The SURFACE AREA of a shape is the COLLECTIVE space on its surface. As an example, think of the wrapping paper on a box that's been gift-wrapped.

• To determine the surface area of a rectangular solid or cube, simply **ADD the AREAS of the SIX faces**. When doing so, remember that the top and bottom faces have the SAME areas, as do the left and right faces, and the front and back faces.

> ➤ For example, in the rectangular solid below, the BOTTOM face has an area of $4 \times 10 = 40$. Thus, the TOP face also has an area of 40.

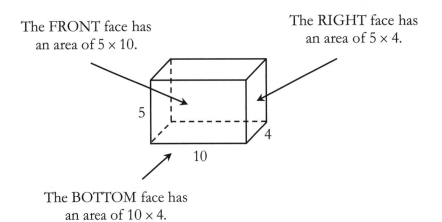

The FRONT face has an area of 5×10.

The RIGHT face has an area of 5×4.

The BOTTOM face has an area of 10×4.

• Likewise, the RIGHT face has an area of $5 \times 4 = 20$, so the LEFT face also has an area of 20. Finally, the FRONT face has an area of $5 \times 10 = 50$, so the BACK face also has an area of 50.

> ➤ Thus, the surface area of the rectangular solid is 220, since the sum of the six faces is $40(2) + 20(2) + 50(2) = 220$.

• When calculating surface area, the UNITS should be SQUARED. For example, if the lengths of the figure above had been given in inches, the surface area would have been 220 inches^2, since inches $\times$ inches $=$ inches^2.

• Similarly, a cube with side lengths of 5 feet would have a surface area of 150 feet^2, since each of the six faces would have an area of 5 feet $\times$ 5 feet $= 25$ feet^2, and 6×25 feet$^2 = 150$ feet^2.

➤ The VOLUME of a shape is the amount of three-dimensional space that it OCCUPIES or ENCLOSES.

• You can determine the volume of a rectangular solid by multiplying its length, width, and height, as follows:

Volume of a Rectangular Solid = Length × Width × Height

• For example, the rectangular solid below has a length of 10, and width of 4, and a height of 5, so its volume equals $10 \times 4 \times 5 = 200$.

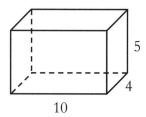

➤ In a CUBE, the length, width, and height are equal, so you can determine the volume by CUBING the length of a single side.

• Thus, a cube with a side length of 4 has a volume of 64, since $4 \times 4 \times 4 = 64$.

• When calculating volume, the UNITS should be CUBED. For example, a cube with a side length of 3 yards would have a volume of 3 yards × 3 yards × 3 yards = 27 yards^3.

➤ Every now and then, GRE problems involve the DIAGONAL of a rectangular solid.

• The diagonal of a rectangular solid extends from one vertex to another, spanning the entire length, width, and height of the shape.

• Here's an example:

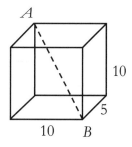

➢ The EASIEST way to determine the lengths of such three-dimensional diagonals is with the following formula, where l = length, w = width, and h = height:

The Diagonal of a Rectangular Solid = $\sqrt{l^2 + w^2 + h^2}$

• For example, in the diagram on the previous page, diagonal AB has a length of 15, since the rectangular solid has a length of 10, a width of 5, and a height of 10:

$$AB = \sqrt{10^2 + 5^2 + 10^2} = \sqrt{100 + 25 + 100} = \sqrt{225} = 15$$

➢ This formula can ALSO be used to determine the length of PARTIAL diagonals, such as the one below:

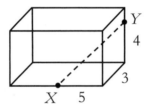

• The measurements in the diagram pertain to partial diagonal XY, not the rectangular solid. Thus, XY has a length of $5\sqrt{2}$, since:

$$XY = \sqrt{5^2 + 3^2 + 4^2} = \sqrt{25 + 9 + 16} = \sqrt{50} = \sqrt{5 \cdot 5 \cdot 2} = 5\sqrt{2}$$

➢ It's worth remembering that the length of a diagonal of a CUBE can be determined with its own formula, where s = side length:

The Diagonal of a Cube = $s\sqrt{3}$

• For example, a cube with a side length of 5 would have a diagonal of $5\sqrt{3}$. Likewise, in the cube below, the diagonal must be $8\sqrt{3}$, since the sides have a length of 8:

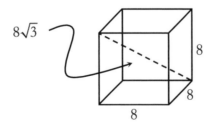

• The BASIS for this formula is simply the formula at the top of the page. Since the length, width, and height of a cube are equal, $\sqrt{l^2 + w^2 + h^2} = \sqrt{s^2 + s^2 + s^2} = \sqrt{3s^2} = \sqrt{3 \cdot s \cdot s} = s\sqrt{3}$.

(8) Questions Without Values – Problems involving quadrilaterals and rectangular solids frequently lack values.

• Here's a typical example:

Liam and Micah each have flat rectangular gardens. The length of Micah's garden is 10 percent longer than Liam's, but the width is 10 percent shorter.

Quantity A	**Quantity B**
The area of Liam's garden	The area of Micah's garden

• As detailed in section ▨8▨ of the "Plan B" chapter of our book on <u>Arithmetic & "Plan B" Strategies</u>, the KEY to problems without CONCRETE values is to PICK NUMBERS.

    ➤ When picking, choose numbers that are SMALL and EASY to work with and respect any constraints, should your problem have them.

• In the problem above, neither garden has a concrete value, so we can start the problem by assigning values.

• To keep the math simple, let's make the length and width of Liam's garden both equal 10. Remember, a square is a special type of rectangle, so it's okay to make his garden a square.

    ➤ Since 10% of 10 = 1, Micah's garden thus has a length of 10 + 1 = 11, but a width of 10 − 1 = 9.

• Given these measurements, the area of the two gardens can therefore be calculated as follows:

The area of Liam's garden	The area of Micah's garden
$10 \times 10 = 100$	$11 \times 9 = 99$

• Thus, the correct answer is (A), since Liam's garden is larger.

    ➤ Notice that it doesn't matter what numbers we pick. If a problem has no concrete values, ANY numbers that we pick will give us the SAME answer.

• Hence, if the length of Liam's garden were 30 and its width 20, its area would be 600. Since 10% of 30 = 3 and 10% of 20 = 2, Micah's garden would have a width of 30 + 3 = 33 and a length of 20 − 2 = 18.

• Liam would still have the larger garden, since $33 \times 18 = 594$.

➤ To ensure that you realize exactly how effective picking numbers can be, let's work through another sample problem together.

• Consider the following:

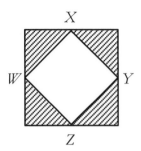

W, X, Y, and Z are midpoints of the sides of the square.

Quantity A   **Quantity B**

The total area of the shaded regions   **The area of the unshaded region**

Answer: C. According to the problem, W, X, Y, and Z are midpoints. Because the question supplies no concrete values, let's give the square a side length of 2.

➤ A midpoint splits a side length in half, so the legs of each triangle would have a length of 1:

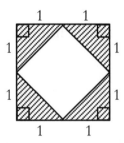

• The interior angles of a square have a measure of 90°, so we know that each shaded region is a right triangle.

• We also know that each of these triangles is a 45°–45°–90° triangle, since their legs have equal lengths.

➤ **The areas of the shaded regions, therefore, have a sum of 2**, because each of the 4 triangles has an area of $\frac{1}{2}(1 \times 1) = \frac{1}{2}$, and $4 \times \frac{1}{2} = 2$.

• Further, if the square has side lengths of 2, then its area is $2 \times 2 = 4$. Thus, **the area of the unshaded region must also be 2**, since the areas of the shaded triangles and unshaded quadrilateral combine to form the area of the square. Hence, the answer is (C).

Rare or Advanced Concepts

(9) The "Volume Trap" – Every now and then, volume problems on the GRE have a simple wrinkle that's easy to miss.

- Here's an example:

A rectangular chest has a volume of 1,000 cubic inches.

Quantity A	Quantity B
The number of boxes, each with a volume of 100 cubic inches, that can be packed inside the chest.	10

- If you're like most test-takers, you might believe that the correct answer should be (C), since 100 divides into 1,000 ten times:

$$\frac{1,000 \text{ in}^3}{100 \text{ in}^3} = 10$$

➢ Unfortunately, this sort of reasoning is mistaken. Because we don't know the EXACT DIMENSIONS of the chest or the boxes, the actual answer is (D).

- To understand why, first imagine that the chest has dimensions of 5 in × 10 in × 20 in and that each box has dimensions of 2 in × 5 in × 10 in. With such dimensions, the two quantities would in fact be equal, since all 10 boxes would fit neatly inside the chest:

$$\frac{\cancel{5} \text{ in} \times \cancel{10} \text{ in} \times 20 \text{ in}}{2 \text{ in} \times \cancel{5} \text{ in} \times \cancel{10} \text{ in}} = \frac{20}{2} = 10$$

➢ Now imagine that the chest has dimensions of 10 in × 10 in × 10 in, but that each box has dimensions of 1 in × 1 in × 100 in.

- NO boxes would fit inside the chest because the boxes would be TOO BIG. A box with a length, width, or height of 100 inches cannot fit inside a chest in that is only 10 inches wide, deep, and tall.

- Since the two quantities can be equal or dissimilar, we cannot determine the relationship between them. This is why the correct answer is (D).

> ➢ So, be careful when working with volume. If you don't know the SPECIFIC dimensions of a shape, be sure to consider DIFFERENT possibilities.

• Let's work through one more sample question:

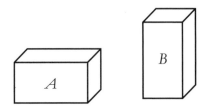

Rectangular solids _A_ and _B_ each have a volume of 15 cubic centimeters.

Quantity A	**Quantity B**
The surface area of _A_	**The surface area of _B_**

• According to the problem, rectangular solids _A_ and _B_ each have a volume of 15 cm^3.

> ➢ Because the two solids have the same volume, we might be tempted to believe that they also have the same surface area.

• Unfortunately we don't know the specific dimensions of each solid.

• If _A_ and _B_ have the same dimensions, their surface areas would be equal. However, if _A_ has dimensions of 1 cm × 3 cm × 5 cm, and _B_ has dimensions of 1 cm × 1 cm × 15 cm, their surface areas may be different.

> ➢ To prove it, let's quickly consider the surface areas of two such solids.

• A rectangular solid with a length, width, and height of 1 cm, 3 cm, and 5 cm would have two faces that measure 1 × 3 = 3 cm^2, two that measure 1 cm × 5 cm = 5 cm^2, and two that measure 3 × 5 = 15 cm^2. However, a rectangular solid with a length, width, and height of 1 cm, 1 cm, and 15 cm would have two faces that measure 1 × 1 = 1 cm^2 and four that measure 1 cm × 15 cm = 15 cm^2.

• Since these faces clearly have different sums, we have proved that the two surface areas can be different or (as we saw earlier) the same. The correct answer, therefore, must be (D).

(10) Rhombuses – On very rare occasions, the GRE may test your knowledge of rhombuses.

- A rhombus is a special type of parallelogram.

  ➤ Like all parallelograms, a rhombus has opposite sides that are parallel and of equal length, as well as opposite angles that are equal, and adjacent angles that add to 180°.

- What makes a rhombus special is that all four sides have the SAME length (as do squares):

All parallelograms   Rhombuses

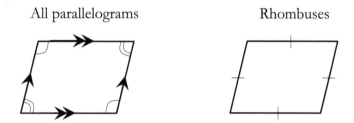

  ➤ Because all sides of a rhombus are equal, rhombuses have several SPECIAL PROPERTIES. Of these, two are worth memorizing.

- The first is that the area of a rhombus equals HALF the PRODUCT of its DIAGONALS. This property can be stated as:

$$\text{Area of a Rhombus} = \frac{1}{2}(\text{Diagonal}_1 \times \text{Diagonal}_2)$$

- Thus, a rhombus in which the diagonals have lengths of 9 and 6 would have an area of 27, since $\frac{1}{2}(9 \times 6) = 27$.

  ➤ The other special property is that the DIAGONALS of a rhombus are PERPENDICULAR to one another.

- This means that every rhombus is composed of four RIGHT triangles, as in the diagram below:

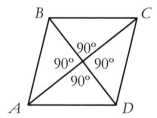

➢ To give you a sense of how the GRE might test your knowledge of rhombuses, consider the following:

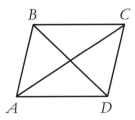

Parallelogram *ABCD* has four sides of equal length.
$AC = 8$ and $BD = 6$.

<u>**Quantity A**</u>   <u>**Quantity B**</u>

The area of *ABCD*   **The perimeter of *ABCD***

Answer. A. According to the problem, parallelogram *ABCD* has four sides of equal length. Thus, it is a rhombus. In any rhombus, the area equals half the product of its diagonals. Since *AC* and *BD* are the diagonals of the rhombus, the area equals 24:

$$\frac{1}{2}(8 \times 6) = 24$$

Determining the perimeter is a little trickier. In any parallelogram, the diagonals bisect one another. *AC* has a length of 8, so *BD* splits it into two lengths of 4. Likewise, *BD* has a length of 6, so *AC* splits it into two lengths of 3:

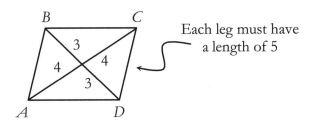

Since the diagonals of a rhombus are perpendicular, each of the triangles within parallelogram *ABCD* has a right angle at the point where the diagonals intersect. Thus, each triangle is a 3–4–5.

Because each side of the rhombus has a length of 5, the perimeter of parallelogram *ABCD* must be 4(5) = 20. The correct answer is therefore (A), since the area is greater than the perimeter.

(11) Maximizing Area – From time to time, the GRE will test your understanding of what maximizes the area of a quadrilateral.

- Here's an example:

> **If parallelogram $ABCD$ has a perimeter of 24 inches, what is its maximum possible area, in square inches?**
>
> **(A) 30   (B) 32   (C) 34   (D) 36   (E) 38**

- Although questions like this can seem daunting, they are actually quite simple. To solve them, you only need to know one thing:

  ➢ The more SQUARE-like a quadrilateral becomes, the GREATER its area will be.

- To understand why, first consider a RECTANGLE in which the length and width ADD to 8. Notice how the area INCREASES as the dimensions become more similar:

If the Length and Width are…	…the Area would be
1 and 7	$1 \times 7 = 7$
2 and 6	$2 \times 6 = 12$
3 and 5	$3 \times 5 = 15$
4 and 4	$4 \times 4 = 16$

  ➢ Now consider a PARALLELOGRAM in which some angles are extremely large and others extremely small.

- Notice how the area GROWS as ALL four angles draw CLOSER to 90°:

Extreme angles   Angles near 90°

  ➢ Thus, to answer the question above, we simply need to determine the largest square possible, given a perimeter of 24 inches.

- A square with a side length of 6 inches has a perimeter of 24 inches. Therefore, the answer to the question must be (D), since a square with such sides has an area of $6 \times 6 = 36$ in^2.

➤ As you may have noticed, the "square principle" also implies a corollary: the more SQUARE-like a quadrilateral becomes, the SMALLER its perimeter will be.

• Consider a RECTANGLE with an area of 16. Notice how the perimeter DECREASES as the dimensions become more similar:

If the Length and Width are…	…the Perimeter would be
1×16	$2(1 + 16) = 34$
2×8	$2(2 + 8) = 20$
4×4	$2(4 + 4) = 16$

➤ Likewise, notice how the perimeter of a parallelogram with an area of 16 DECREASES as the angles draw closer to 90°:

Extreme Angles	Angles near 90°
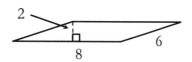	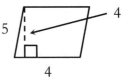
Area = $2 \times 8 = 16$, but Perimeter = $2(8 + 6) = 28$	Area = $4 \times 4 = 16$, but Perimeter = $2(5 + 4) = 18$

➤ On a final note, it's also worth pointing out that these principles apply to TRIANGLES.

• Because a 45°–45°–90° triangle is half a SQUARE, the area of a triangle increases as its legs become more similar or the angle between them grows closer to 90°.

Different Legs and Obtuse   Similar Legs and a 90° Angle

• Thus, in the diagrams above, the leg lengths of each triangle add to 10, but the area of the triangle with the 90° angle and the legs of equal length is clearly greater.

(12) The Area & Perimeter "Guess Trick" – Every now and then, the GRE will design quadrilateral problems that involve the interplay of area and perimeter.

• Here's a typical example:

A rectangle has an area of 40 square inches and a perimeter of 28 inches. The length of the shortest side is *a* and the length of the longest side is *b*.

Quantity A	Quantity B
$\dfrac{a}{b}$	$\dfrac{2}{5}$

• Such questions can either be solved with a series of involved and time-consuming algebra computations or by "guessing" the dimensions.

  ➤ To "guess" the dimensions, first consider the INTEGERS that MULTIPLY to the given area.

• Then, determine which PAIR can produce the given perimeter.

• For example, in the problem above, the integers that multiply to 40 are 1×40, 2×20, 4×10, and 5×8. Of these, the only combination that can produce a perimeter of 28 is 4 and 10, since $2(4) + 2(10) = 28$.

  ➤ Thus, the rectangle has side lengths of 4 and 10 integers. Because *a* is length of the shortest side and *b* is the length of the longest, we know that $a = 4$ and $b = 10$.

• The correct answer is therefore (C), since $\dfrac{a}{b} = \dfrac{4}{10} = \dfrac{2}{5}$.

• To get a sense of why the "guess trick" is important, let's solve this problem without the shortcut. To do so, we would first need to create two equations: $lw = 40$ and $2l + 2w = 28$.

  ➤ Next, we would need to reduce $2l + 2w = 28$ to $l + w = 14$ and to rewrite $lw = 40$ as $w = \dfrac{40}{l}$ in order to combine the equations:

$$l + w = 14 \quad \rightarrow \quad l + \frac{40}{l} = 14$$

• From here, we would need to multiply both sides of the equation by *l* and set the resulting quadratic equal to zero:

$$l + \frac{40}{l} = 14 \quad \rightarrow \quad l^2 + 40 = 14l \quad \rightarrow \quad l^2 - 14l + 40 = 0$$

➤ Finally, we would need to factor the equation as $(l-4)(l-10) = 0$ in order to solve for l.

• Doing so tells us that the length of the rectangle must be 4 or 10. If the length is 4, then the width would have to be 10, since:

$$lw = 40 \quad \rightarrow \quad 4w = 40 \quad \rightarrow \quad w = 10$$

• For the same reason, if the length is 10, the width would have to be 4. The dimensions of the rectangle therefore must be 4 and 10 — just as the "guess trick" showed us.

➤ As you can see, the "guess trick" is a dramatically superior strategy. Not only is it easier and faster, it's just as reliable.

• To ensure that you've got the hang of it, let's work through one more example together. This time, let's make it a little harder by involving a diagonal:

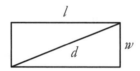

If $d^2 = 20$ and $l + w = 6$, what is the area of the rectangle above?

(A) 6   (B) 8   (C) 10   (D) 12   (E) 15

Answer. (B). According to the problem, the rectangle has a length l, a width w, and a diagonal d. Since all four interior angles of a rectangle have a measure of 90°, the triangles formed by l, d, and w must be right triangles.

• In any right triangle, $a^2 + b^2 = c^2$. Thus, we know that $l^2 + w^2 = d^2$. Since the problem states that $d^2 = 20$, we further know that $l^2 + w^2 = 20$.

➤ If $l + w = 6$, there are only three possible integer combinations for l and w: (1, 5), (2, 4), and (3, 3).

• Of these, only 2 and 4 add to 20, when squared:

$$2^2 + 4^2 = 4 + 16 = 20$$

• The correct answer must therefore be (B), since a rectangle with side lengths of 2 and 4 has an area of $2 \times 4 = 8$.

(13) Problem Sets – The following questions have been arranged into three groups: fundamental, intermediate, and rare or advanced.

• Whether you're aiming for a perfect score or a score closer to average, mastery of the concepts in the FUNDAMENTAL questions is absolutely essential.

➤ As you might expect, the INTERMEDIATE questions are more difficult but are essential for test-takers who need an above-average score or higher.

• Finally, the RARE or ADVANCED questions test concepts that are very sophisticated or seldom encountered on the GRE. Mastery of such questions is required only if you need a math score above the 90th percentile.

• As always, if you find yourself confused, bogged down with busy work, or stuck, don't be afraid to fall back on your "Plan B" strategies!

Fundamental

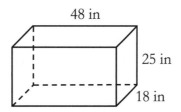

1.   What is the maximum number of rectangular blocks, each with dimensions of 8 inches by 5 inches by 3 inches, that can be packed into a rectangular box with inside dimensions as shown?

(A) 120 (B) 150 (C) 160 (D) 180 (E) 210

2.   What is the perimeter, in meters, of a rectangle 17 meters wide that has the same area as a rectangle 42 meters long and 34 meters wide?

meters

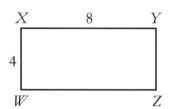

Quantity A	Quantity B

3.   The area of a square region with a   36
     perimeter equal to the perimeter
     of rectangular region WXYZ

4.   If the total surface area of a cube is 24, what is the volume of the cube?

(A) 8   (B) 24   (C) 48   (D) 64   (E) 216

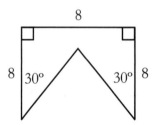

5.   What is the perimeter in the figure above?

(A) 24   (B) 28   (C) 32   (D) 36   (E) 40

6.   A rectangular region has a perimeter of 22. Which of the following could be the area
     of the region?

Select all possible values.

A 10   B 18   C 24   D 28   E 30

7.   A certain rectangle is twice as wide as it is long. If its perimeter is 18 feet, what is the
     difference, in feet, between its width and its length?

feet

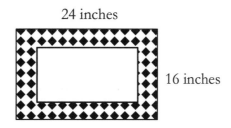

24 inches

16 inches

8. A rug, as shown above, has a checkered border 4 inches wide on all sides. What is the area, in square inches, of that portion of the rug that excludes the border?

(A) 128   (B) 240   (C) 316   (D) 320   (E) 336

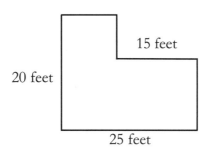

15 feet

20 feet

25 feet

The figure above shows the dimensions of an L-shaped room. All angles shown are right angles. The cost to carpet the room is $20 per square foot.

Quantity A	Quantity B
9. The cost to carpet the entire floor	$7,000

10. A rectangular box has a capacity of 15 cubic feet. If the box were three times as long, twice as wide, and equally tall, what would its capacity be, in cubic feet?

(A) 60   (B) 75   (C) 90   (D) 120   (E) 180

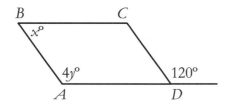

B C

$x°$

$4y°$ $120°$

A D

11. If quadrilateral $ABCD$ is a parallelogram, what is the difference between the value of x and the value of y?

(A) 20   (B) 30   (C) 40   (D) 50   (E) 60

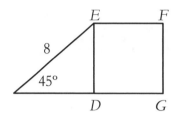

12. In the figure above, what is the area of square *DEFG*?

    (A) 16   (B) $24\sqrt{2}$ (C) 32   (D) $36\sqrt{2}$ (E) 54

13. The exterior of a rectangular chest needs to be painted. The chest has dimensions 8 feet × 2.5 feet × 2 feet. If each square foot of the chest costs 20 cents to paint, how much will it cost to paint the entire chest, in terms of dollars?

    (A) 8   (B) 12   (C) 16.40   (D) 21.20   (E) 24

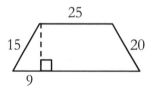

	Quantity A	Quantity B
14.	The area of the trapezoid region	400

15. A rectangular container has a square base. If each side of the base has a length of 3 feet and the volume of the container is 135 cubic feet, what is the surface area of the container, in square feet?

    (A) 112   (B) 128   (C) 144   (D) 198   (E) 256

The volume of a certain cube is 64 cubic inches.

	Quantity A	Quantity B
16.	Twice the shortest distance, in inches, from the center of the cube to one side	The greatest distance, in inches, between any two points on the cube

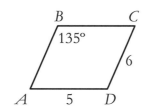

ABCD is a parallelogram

Quantity A	Quantity B

17. The area of region *ABCD*   30

18. A rectangular field 24 feet by 12 feet is completely covered with sod that costs *g* dollars per square yard. In terms of *g*, how many dollars will the carpeting cost? (1 yd = 3 ft)

      (A) 32*g* (B) 36*g* (C) 96*g* (D) 288*g* (E) 864*g*

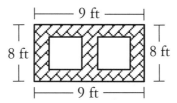

19. The top of an 8-foot by 9-foot rectangular table consists of two panes of glass surrounded by wooden trim, as indicated in the figure above. If the trim is uniformly 1 foot wide, what fraction of the table's top surface is covered by trim?

      (A) $\frac{1}{3}$ (B) $\frac{2}{5}$ (C) $\frac{1}{2}$ (D) $\frac{3}{5}$ (E) $\frac{2}{3}$

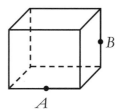

20. The cube shown above has edges of length 10, and points *A* and *B* are midpoints on their respective edges. What is the length of line segment *AB* (not shown)?

      (A) 10 (B) $5\sqrt{6}$ (C) 15 (D) $12\sqrt{2}$ (E) 20

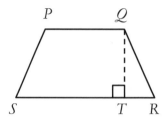

Figure <u>not</u> drawn to scale.

21. In the figure above, *PQ* ‖ *SR* and point *T* is the midpoint of *SR*. If *PQ* = 6, *QT* = 7, and triangle *QTR* has an area of 24.5, what is the area of *PQRS*?

22. If rectangular solid *X* is identical to cube *Y* in all ways except that its height has been tripled, what is the ratio of the surface area of solid *X* to the surface area of cube *Y*?

(A) 3 to 1   (B) 6 to 1   (C) 7 to 3   (D) 9 to 2   (E) 27 to 1

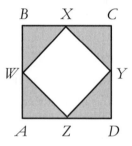

23. In the figure above, quadrilaterals *ABCD* and *WXYZ* are squares. If the vertices of square *WXYZ* bisect the sides of square *ABCD*, what is the ratio of the collective area of the shaded regions to the area of square *WXYZ*?

(A) 1 to 2   (B) 2 to 3   (C) 1 to 1   (D) 3 to 2   (E) 2 to 1

Rare or Advanced

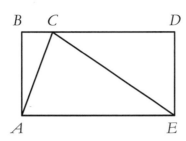

Figure *ABDE* is a rectangle.

Quantity A	Quantity B

24.   The sum of the areas of   The area of triangle *ACE*
        triangles *ABC* and *CDE*

25.   If parallelogram *ABCD* has an area of 36 square inches, which of the following could
        be the length of its perimeter?

Select <u>all</u> possible values.

A. 18   B. 20   C. 21   D. 24   E. 30

In rhombus *JKLM*, diagonal *JL* has a length of 12
and diagonal *KM* has a length of 16.

Quantity A	Quantity B

26.   Half the area of rhombus *JKLM*   The perimeter of rhombus *JKLM*

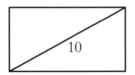

27.   If the rectangular region above has an area of 50, its perimeter is most nearly equal to

(A) 24   (B) 28   (C) 36   (D) 48   (E) 50

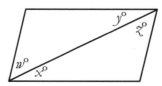

	Quantity A	Quantity B
28.	$w + z$	$x + y$

Two adjacent faces of a rectangular solid have areas of 15 and 24, respectively.

	Quantity A	Quantity B
29.	The volume of the solid	120

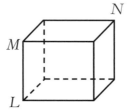

Figure *LMN* is a cube.

30. The positive difference between line segments *LN* and *MN* is approximately what percentage of the distance from point *L* to point *M*?

(A) 30%   (B) 50%   (C) 60%   (D) 70%   (E) 80%

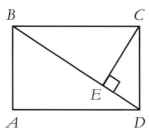

	Quantity A	Quantity B
31.	The area of rectangle *ABCD*	$BD \times CE$

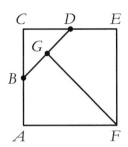

In the figure above, *ACEF* is a square, and *B*, *D*, and *G* are midpoints of sides *AC*, *CE*, and *BD*, respectively.

Quantity A	Quantity B
$\dfrac{\text{The area of } DEFG}{\text{The area of } ACEF}$	$\dfrac{\text{The area of } BCD}{\text{The area of } DEFG}$

32.

(14) Solutions – Video solutions for each of the previous questions can be found on our website at **www.sherpaprep.com/masterkey**.

• BOOKMARK this address for future visits!

> ➤ To view the videos, you'll need to register your copy of <u>Master Key to the GRE: Geometry</u>.

• If you have yet to do so, please go to **www.sherpaprep.com/videos** and enter your email address.

• Be sure to provide the SAME email address that you used to purchase your copy of <u>Master Key to the GRE</u> or to enroll in your GRE course with Sherpa Prep!

> ➤ When checking your answers, we encourage you to watch the solution for any problem that you answered INCORRECTLY

• The same goes for any problem that took you MORE than TWO MINUTES to solve.

• After digesting the explanation, REVISIT your mistake a couple of days later to ensure that the problem no longer poses issues to you.

> ➤ If you struggle to solve the problem a SECOND time, add it to your "LOG of ERRORS" and redo it every few weeks.

• Solving tricky questions MORE THAN ONCE is the best way to learn from your mistakes and to avoid similar difficulties on your actual exam.

Fundamental		Intermediate		Rare or Advanced
1. D	11. B	12. C	22. C	24. C
2. 202		13. C	23. C	25. D, E
3. C		14. A		26. A
4. A		15. D		27. B
5. E		16. B		28. D
6. A, B, C, D, E		17. B		29. D
7. 3		18. A		30. A
8. A		19. C		31. C
9. D		20. B		32. A
10. C		21. 70		

Circles & Cylinders

Circles & Cylinders

To be discussed:

Fundamental Concepts

Whether you're aiming for a perfect score or a score closer to average, mastery of the following concepts is essential.

1 Introduction
2 Circumference & Area
3 Arcs & Sectors
4 Inscribed Angles
5 Inscribed & Circumscribed Polygons
6 Chords & Tangents
7 Cylinders

Strategy Concepts

Geometry is more than a collection of facts and formulas. To solve the most difficult questions, you need to complement the essential concepts with the following tactics.

8 Don't Forget the Center
9 Label Every Radius
10 Problems Without Values
11 Asswholes
12 Unusual Shapes
13 Spatial Reasoning

Practice Questions

There's no substitute for elbow grease. Practice your new skills to ensure that you internalize what you've studied.

14 Problem Sets
15 Solutions

Fundamental Concepts

(1) Introduction – As you likely know, a circle is a set of points that are equidistant from a central point.

- That central point is known as the **CENTER**.

  ➢ Technically, the center of a circle is NOT part of the circle. It is only a point WITHIN the circle.

- Thus, in the diagram below, points A and B would be said to "lie on the circle", but center O would not:

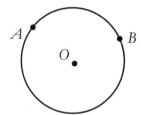

Point O lies inside the circle, but is not part of it

  ➢ The distance from ANY point on a circle to the CENTER is known as the **RADIUS**. In any circle, EVERY radius has the same length.

- In the diagram below, point O is the center of the circle. Therefore line segments AO, BO, and CO have the same length, since all three are RADII:

Line segments AO, BO, and CO are all radii

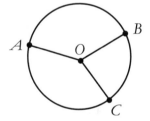

  ➢ The **DIAMETER** of a circle runs through the CENTER, connecting two points directly ACROSS from one another.

- The diameter of a circle is always TWICE the radius, since every diameter is composed of two radii:

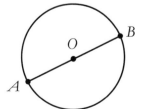

Radii AO and BO form diameter AB

Chapter 5: Circles & Cylinders

(2) Circumference & Area – The majority of circle questions on the GRE involve a circle's circumference or area.

- The term CIRCUMFERENCE refers to the distance around a circle. You can also think of it as the length of a circle's PERIMETER.

  ➢ To determine the circumference of a circle, you simply need to know the following formula, where C = circumference and r = radius:

$$C = 2\pi r$$

- Thus, a circle with a radius of 6 has a circumference of $2\pi r = 2\pi(6) = 12\pi$. Conversely, a circle with a circumference of 8π has a radius of 4, since:

$$C = 8\pi \quad \rightarrow \quad 2\pi r = 8\pi \quad \rightarrow \quad r = \frac{8\cancel{\pi}}{2\cancel{\pi}} = 4$$

- This formula can ALSO be stated as $C = \pi d$, where d = diameter, since the diameter of a circle equals twice the radius ($d = 2r$).

  ➢ When working with circles, it is customary to LEAVE the Greek letter π (pronounced "pie") as part of the answer.

- From time to time, however, you will come across questions in which you need to replace π with its numerical equivalent.

- As you likely know, π is a never-ending number that approximately equals 3.14. For most GRE problems, you can safely think of π as 3.1 to save time (though there are sporadic problems in which you need to recognize numbers such as 6.28 and 9.42 as multiples of π).

  ➢ What you may not know is that π can ALSO be approximated by the FRACTION $\frac{22}{7}$, since $\frac{22}{7} \approx 3.14$.

- If you come across a problem in which you need to resolve π, but find 3.1 or 3.14 difficult to work with, we encourage you to use $\frac{22}{7}$ instead.

- Exam-makers know that most test-takers are unaware that π equals anything other than 3.14 and therefore design problems that hinge on the knowledge that π can also equal $\frac{22}{7}$.

➤ While the term CIRCUMFERENCE refers to the distance around a circle, the term AREA refers to the space INSIDE.

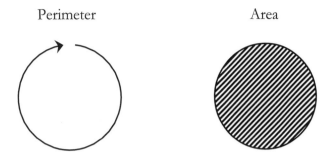

Perimeter   Area

• As with circumference, you can determine the area of any circle with a simple formula. In this formula, A = area:

$$A = \pi r^2$$

• Thus, a circle with a radius of 6 has an area of $\pi r^2 = \pi(6)^2 = 36\pi$. Conversely, a circle with an area of 16π has a radius of 4, since the positive square root of 16 is 4:

$$A = 16\pi \;\; \rightarrow \;\; \pi r^2 = 16\pi \;\; \rightarrow \;\; r^2 = \frac{16\cancel{\pi}}{\cancel{\pi}} = 16$$

➤ For any circle, you've now seen that the CIRCUMFERENCE = $2\pi r$, the AREA = πr^2, and the DIAMETER = $2r$.

• Notice that ALL of these formulas have something in common: the RADIUS. This is important, because it proves that if we know ANY of these values, we have enough information to determine the OTHERS. For example, if a circle has a circumference of 14π, its radius is 7, since:

$$C = 14\pi \;\; \rightarrow \;\; 2\pi r = 14\pi \;\; \rightarrow \;\; r = \frac{14\cancel{\pi}}{2\cancel{\pi}} = 7$$

• Therefore, that circle must have a diameter of 14, since $d = 2r = 2(7) = 14$, and a circumference of 14π, since $2\pi r = 2\pi(7) = 14\pi$.

➤ Likewise, if a circle has a diameter of 8, we know it has a radius of 4, since for any circle the diameter is always twice the radius.

• Thus, its circumference must equal 8π, since $2\pi r = 2\pi(4) = 8\pi$, and its area must equal 16π, since $\pi r^2 = \pi(4)^2 = 16\pi$.

➢ In general, using one measurement of a circle to determine another is KEY to solving problems that involve circles.

• To give you a little more experience doing so, let's work through a practice problem together:

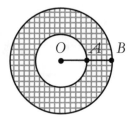

Circles A and B have circumferences of 10π and 20π, respectively.

Quantity A	Quantity B
The area the shaded region	**75π**

Answer. C. According to the problem, circle A has a circumference of 10π, and circle B has a circumference of 20π. The circumference of any circle equals $2\pi r$, so circle A must have a radius of 5 and circle B a radius of 10, since:

Circle A	Circle B
$2\pi r = 10\pi \rightarrow r = \dfrac{10\pi}{2\pi} = 5$	$2\pi r = 20\pi \rightarrow r = \dfrac{20\pi}{2\pi} = 10$

The area of any circle equals πr^2. If circle A has a radius of 5, its area must equal 25π, since $\pi r^2 = \pi(5)^2 = 25\pi$. Likewise, if circle B has a radius of 10, its area must equal 100π, since $\pi r^2 = \pi(10)^2 = 100\pi$.

As discussed in our chapter on Quadrilaterals & Rectangular Solids, the area of a shaded region equals the difference between the area of the large region and the area of the small region.

Here, the large region belongs to circle B and the small region to circle A. The two quantities are therefore equal, since the difference between the two regions equals $100\pi - 25\pi = 75\pi$. Thus, the correct answer is (C).

(3) Arcs & Sectors – As circle questions become more complicated, they often involve arcs or sections.

- The term ARC simply refers to a PORTION of a circle's circumference.

    ➤ When referencing arcs, it is customary for the GRE to use THREE points to do so, in order to avoid ambiguity.

- Thus, in the diagrams below, arc *ABC* refers to the SHORTER arc between points *A* and *C*, while arc *ADC* refers to the LONGER arc between points *A* and *C*:

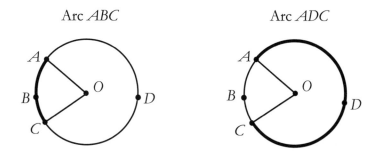

Arc *ABC*   Arc *ADC*

    ➤ Similarly, a SECTOR is a portion of a circle's area. The GRE typically uses shaded regions to differentiate sectors.

- Thus, in the diagram below, SMALL sector *AOB* would likely be referred to as shaded region *AOB* or shaded sector *AOB* to distinguish it from LARGE sector *AOB*:

Shaded sector *AOB*

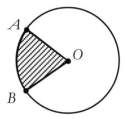

- When working with sectors, be sure that one vertex lies at the CENTER of the circle. The area of a region WITHOUT a vertex at the center of the circle CANNOT be determined by using basic geometry properties.

➢ To find the length of an arc or the area of a sector, simply think of the arc or sector as a FRACTION of the circle.

• In the figure below, arc *ABC* has a measure of 60°. This measure is commonly known as the CENTRAL ANGLE, since its vertex lies at the center of the circle.

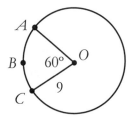

Arc *ABC* has
a central
angle of 60°

Point *O* is the center of the circle.

• Because every circle has a measure of 360°, arc *ABC* represents $\frac{60°}{360°}$, or $\frac{1}{6}$, of the circle. Thus, to find its length, we simply need to determine $\frac{1}{6}$ of the circle's circumference.

➢ Since the circle has a radius of 9, its circumference equals $2\pi r = 2\pi(9) = 18\pi$. Therefore, arc *ABC* has a length of 3π, since $\frac{1}{6}$ of $18\pi = 3\pi$.

• Likewise, in the figure below, sector *COD* has a measure of 120°, so it represents $\frac{120°}{360°}$, or $\frac{1}{3}$, of the circle. Thus, to find its area, we simply need to determine $\frac{1}{3}$ of the circle's area:

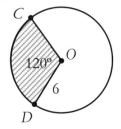

Sector *COD* has
a central
angle of 120°

Point *O* is the center of the circle.

• Since the circle has a radius of 6, its area equals $\pi r^2 = \pi(6)^2 = 36\pi$. Therefore, sector *COD* has an area of 12π, since $\frac{1}{3}$ of $36\pi = 12\pi$.

➤ Alternatively, you can express the length of an arc or the area of a sector with the following formulas.

• In each case, x = the CENTRAL ANGLE, so $\frac{x}{360°}$ = the FRACTION of the circle that you're solving for:

$$\text{Arc} = \text{Circumference} \cdot \frac{x}{360°} \qquad\qquad \text{Sector} = \text{Area} \cdot \frac{x}{360°}$$

• When looking at these formulas, notice that each contains THREE UNKNOWNS: (1) the central angle, (2) the circumference or area, and (3) the arc length or sector.

➤ One of the tricks to working with arcs and sectors is to realize that if you know any TWO of these unknowns, you can use them to get the THIRD.

• Consider the following:

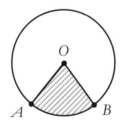

Circle C, pictured above, has a center O and an area of 64π. If the shaded region has an area of 8π, what is the measure of angle AOB?

(A) 30° (B) 45° (C) 50° (D) 60° (E) 72°

• According to the problem, circle C has an area of 64π and the shaded region has an area of 8π. Since $\frac{8\pi}{64\pi} = \frac{1}{8}$, the shaded region therefore represents $\frac{1}{8}$ of the circle.

➤ Every circle has a measure of 360°, so the measure of angle AOB must be 45°, since $\frac{1}{8}$ of that measure equals 45°.

• Here's the arithmetic:

$$\frac{1}{8} \cdot 360° = \frac{360°}{8} = \frac{\cancel{4}(90°)}{\cancel{4}(2)} = 45°$$

• The correct answer, therefore, is (B).

> ➢ To give you a little more experience working with arcs and sectors, let's do one more practice problem together.

• Consider the following:

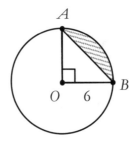

The circle above has a center O and a radius of 6. What is the area of the shaded region?

(A) $4(\pi - 1)$ (B) $6(\pi - 3)$ (C) $9(\pi - 2)$ (D) $12(\pi - 3)$ (E) $18(\pi - 2)$

• The area of a shaded region equals the difference between the areas of the large and small regions that define it.

> ➢ In the figure above, the large region is sector AOB and the small region is right triangle AOB.

• According to the problem, sector AOB has a central angle of 90°, so it represents $\frac{90°}{360°}$, or $\frac{1}{4}$, of the circle.

• Since the circle has a radius of 6, its area equals $\pi r^2 = \pi(6)^2 = 36\pi$. Therefore, sector AOB has an area of 9π, since $\frac{1}{4}$ of $36\pi = 9\pi$.

> ➢ The height and base of right triangle AOB each have a length of 6, since both are radii. Thus, the area of the triangle must equal 18, since $\frac{1}{2}(6 \times 6) = 18$.

• Because 9π and 18 have a common factor of 9, their difference equals $9(\pi - 2)$, so the correct answer is (C):

$$9\pi - 18 = 9(\pi - 2)$$

(4) Inscribed Angles: Half the Central Angle – As you've seen, the CENTRAL angle of an arc or sector has its vertex at a circle's center.

• Arcs and sectors also have another sort of angle, commonly known as an INSCRIBED angle.

> ➤ An inscribed angle differs from a central angle in that an inscribed angle has a vertex that LIES ON the circle itself.

• To illustrate the difference, compare the diagrams below:

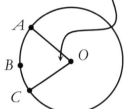
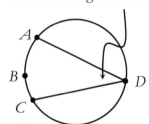

Central Angle *AOC*   Inscribed Angle *ADC*

• Notice how BOTH angles intercept arc *ABC*, but that central angle *AOC* has its vertex at center *O* while inscribed angle *ADC* has its vertex on the circle at point *D*.

> ➤ For the GRE, there are two things you need to know about inscribed angles. The first is the most important:

• For any arc, the measure of an inscribed angle is always HALF the measure of its central angle.

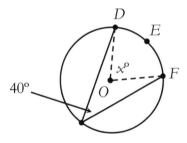

Point *O* is the center of the circle.

• Thus, in the diagram above, the measure of central angle *x* is 80°, since arc *DEF* has an inscribed angle whose measure is 40°.

➤ The other thing you need to know about inscribed angles is that inscribed angles with EQUAL measures have arcs of EQUAL length.

• For example, in the diagram below, arcs *ABC* and *DEF* have the SAME length, since their inscribed angles have the SAME measure:

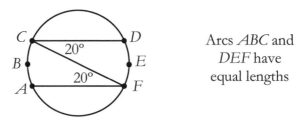

Arcs *ABC* and
DEF have
equal lengths

Points *C* and *F* lie on the circle above.

➤ The converse of this property is also true. If two arcs have the EQUAL lengths, their inscribed angles have EQUAL measures.

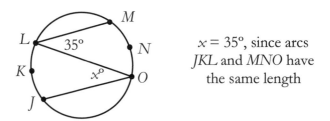

$x = 35°$, since arcs
JKL and *MNO* have
the same length

Arcs *JKL* and *MNO* both have a length of 4π.

• Hence, arcs *JKL* and *MNO*, drawn above, both have lengths of 4π, so inscribed angles *JOL* and *MLO* both equal 35°:

➤ Questions involving the inscribed angle of an arc or sector are relatively uncommon for the GRE.

• However, they do show up from time to time, sometimes in very simple ways, so let's work through a practice problem together to get a little experience.

• Consider the following:

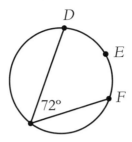

The circle above has a radius of 5.

Quantity A	Quantity B
The length of arc DEF	4π

Answer: C. According to the problem, arc DEF has an inscribed angle of 72°. Since the measure of an arc's inscribed angle is half the measure of its central angle, arc DEF has a central angle of 144°, as shown below:

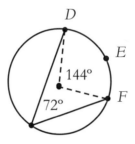

Therefore, arc DEF represents $\frac{144°}{360°}$, or $\frac{2}{5}$, of the circle, since:

$$\frac{144°}{360°} = \frac{\cancel{12}(12)}{\cancel{12}(30)} = \frac{\cancel{6}(2)}{\cancel{6}(5)} = \frac{2}{5}$$

Because the circle has a radius of 5, it's circumference equals $2\pi r = 2\pi(5) = 10\pi$. Thus, arc DEF has a length of 4π, since $\frac{2}{5}$ of $10\pi = 4\pi$. The correct answer is therefore (C), since the two quantities are equal.

(5) Inscribed & Circumscribed Polygons – From time to time, circle problems on the GRE feature inscribed or circumscribed polygons.

- A polygon is INSCRIBED in a circle if all of its vertices lie on the circle.

  ➢ Similarly, a polygon is CIRCUMSCRIBED about a circle if each of its sides touches the circle at exactly one point.

- Thus, triangle *ABC* is inscribed in the circle with center *O*, and rectangle *WXYZ* is circumscribed about the circle with center *V*:

<table>
<tr><td>Inscribed triangle ABC</td><td>Circumscribed rectangle WXYZ</td></tr>
</table>

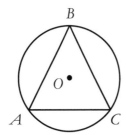 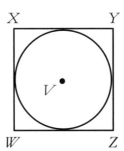

  ➢ When working with circles featuring inscribed or circumscribed polygons, there are a few things you should bear in mind.

- First, the DIAGONAL of an inscribed RECTANGLE will always intersect the CENTER of the circle. This is also true of squares, since a square is a special type of rectangle.

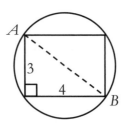

Rectangle *R* is inscribed in circle *C*.

- Thus, in the diagram above, line segment *AB* is the DIAMETER of circle *C*, since it is the diagonal of rectangle *R*. *AB* also has a length of 5, since a right triangle with legs of 3 and 4 is a 3–4–5 triangle.

➢ Second, for any SQUARE circumscribed about a circle, the side length of the SQUARE is equal to the DIAMETER of the circle.

• Thus, in the diagram below, diameters *AC* and *BD* have a length of 5, since square *S* has side lengths of 5:

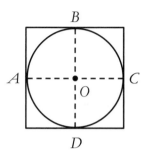

Square *S* has center *O* and a side length of 5.

➢ Finally, if ONE side of an inscribed triangle is a DIAMETER of the circle, the triangle is a RIGHT triangle.

• For example, in the figure below, triangle *XYZ* is a right triangle, since leg *XZ* runs through point *w*, the center of the circle:

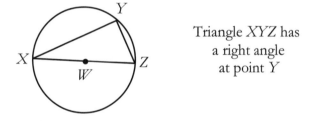

Triangle *XYZ* has a right angle at point *Y*

• The converse of this property is also true. If a right triangle is inscribed in a circle, one of its sides must be the diameter of the circle.

➢ To understand the basis for this last property, recall that the measure of an inscribed angle is always HALF the measure of a central angle.

• Since the inscribed angle at point *Y* lies <u>opposite</u> semicircle *XZ*, which is an arc with a central angle of 180°, the measure of its angle must therefore be half of 180°:

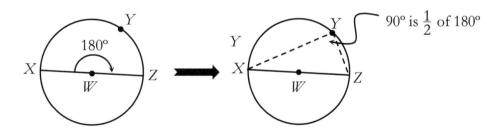

$90°$ is $\frac{1}{2}$ of 180°

➢ To get a sense of how the GRE might test your knowledge of inscribed shapes, let's work through a practice problem together.

• Consider the following:

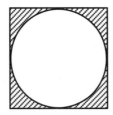

The circle above is inscribed in square S.

If square S has a side length of 10, then the area of the shaded region approximately equals

(A) 18   (B) 22   (C) 25   (D) 27   (E) 30

Answer. B. The area of a shaded region equals the difference between the areas of the large and small regions that define it. Here, the large region is square S and the small region is the circle inscribed within square S.

According to the problem, square S has a side length of 10, so we know two things: one, the area of the square equals $10 \times 10 = 100$; two, the diameter of the inscribed circle has a length of 10, as shown in the diagram below:

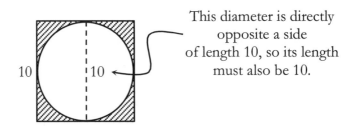

Because the diameter of any circle is twice the length of its radius, the inscribed circle has a radius of 5. A circle with a radius of 5 has an area of $\pi r^2 = \pi(5)^2 = 25\pi$. Thus, the approximate area of the circle is $25\pi \approx 25(3.14) \approx 78.5$.

Since the area of the shaded region equals the difference between the areas of the square and the circle, the correct answer must be (B), as $100 - 78.5 \approx 22$.

(6) Chords & Tangents – Every now and then, circle problems on the GRE involve chords or tangents.

• A CHORD is a STRAIGHT line drawn from one point on a circle to another.

> ➤ In the diagram below, line segment *EF* is a chord, since it runs in a straight line from point *E* to point *F*:

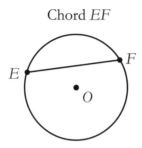

Chord *EF*

Point *O* is the center of the circle.

• The LONGEST possible chord that can be drawn in any circle is a DIAMETER, since it runs through the center of the circle.

> ➤ When working with chords, there are TWO things that you should bear in mind. Both are fairly intuitive.

• First, a chord gets LARGER as it gets closer to the center of the circle:

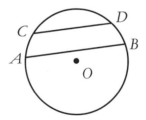

Point *O* is the center of the circle.

• Thus, in the diagram above, chord *AB* is longer than chord *CD*, since chord *AB* is closer to center *O*.

> ➤ Second, a RADIUS that is PERPENDICULAR to a chord BISECTS the chord.

• Hence, in the diagram below, radius OC is perpendicular to chord AB, so $x = 6$, since the radius bisects the chord:

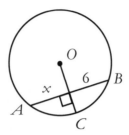

Point O is the center of the circle.

• The converse of this property is also true: a chord that is bisected by a radius is perpendicular to that radius.

> ➤ A TANGENT is a straight line that intersects a circle at a SINGLE point. The point of intersection is known as the POINT of TANGENCY.

• When working with tangents, there is only ONE thing that you need to know: a radius drawn to the point of tangency is PERPENDICULAR to the tangent.

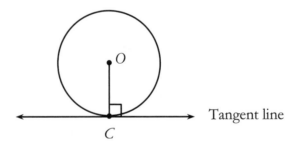

Point O is the center of the circle.

• In the diagram above, the line at the bottom of the circle is a tangent, since it intersects the circle at a single point. Radius OC is perpendicular to the tangent, since it intersects the tangent at the point of tangency.

➤ Problems involving tangents are relatively uncommon on the GRE. Problems involving chords are even rarer.

• However, they do show up from time to time — sometimes in very simple ways — so let's work through a practice problem together to get a little experience.

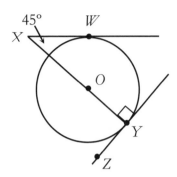

O is the center of the circle.

Line XW intersects the circle at point W, and line ZY intersects the circle at point Y. If the circle has a radius of 6, then $XY =$

(A) $6\sqrt{2}$ (B) 12   (C) $12+\sqrt{2}$ (D) $12+\sqrt{3}$ (E) $6+6\sqrt{2}$

• When solving problems with tangents, first DRAW a radius to the point of tangency and MARK the 90° angle at which they meet.

➤ That 90° angle is usually the KEY to solving the problem. Doing so here, for example, proves that triangle XWO is a right triangle.

• As shown below, triangle XWO has one angle of 90° and a second of 45°. Thus, it must be a 45°–45°–90° triangle with legs of length 6, since the circle has a radius of 6:

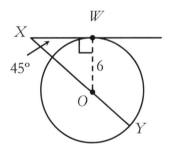

• Because the sides of a 45°–45°–90° triangle have the ratio $x : x : x\sqrt{2}$, the length of hypotenuse XO must therefore equal $6\sqrt{2}$. XY is composed of radius OY and hypotenuse XO, so the correct answer must be (E), since those segments add to $6+6\sqrt{2}$.

(7) Cylinders – On occasion, the GRE designs questions involving cylinders.

• A CYLINDER is a three-dimensional shape consisting of two circular bases and a lateral surface that connects them.

> ➤ In any cylinder, the circular bases have the SAME radius and are joined at their centers by a height that is perpendicular to both.

• In the diagram below, the circular bases have centers *A* and *B*, and the line that runs between them is height *AB*.

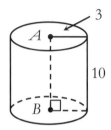

This cylinder has a radius of 3 and a height of 10.

> ➤ On the GRE, all cylinders are referred to as RIGHT CIRCULAR cylinders. Don't let the notation scare you.

• In advanced mathematics, there are other sorts of cylinders.

• By using the term "right circular", the GRE is just letting you know that you're working with regular, "soup-can shaped" cylinders, like the one above.

> ➤ To solve most problems involving cylinders, you'll need to determine one of two things: a surface area or a volume.

• As you may recall from our discussion of rectangular solids, the volume of a shape measures the amount of space that it occupies or encloses.

• The surface area, however, measures the "skin", or collective space on the surface, of a shape.

➤ You can determine the VOLUME of a cylinder with the following formula, in which r = radius and h = height:

The Volume of a Cylinder = $\pi r^2 h$

• For example, the cylinder below has a radius of 4 and a height of 10. Thus, its volume equals 160π, since $\pi r^2 h = \pi(4)^2(10) = \pi(16)(10) = 160\pi$.

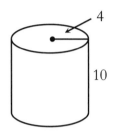

This cylinder has a volume of 160π.

➤ When working with cylinders, it's important to remember that cylinders with DIFFERENT dimensions can have the SAME volume.

• For example, the "thin" cylinder below has a radius of 2 and a height of 16, while the "fat" cylinder has a radius of 4 and a height of 4:

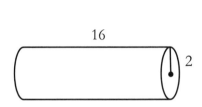   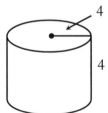

• Both, however, have a volume of 64π, since:

"Thin" cylinder	"Fat" cylinder
$\pi r^2 h = \pi(2)^2(16) = \pi(4)(16) = 64\pi$	$\pi r^2 h = \pi(4)^2(4) = \pi(16)(4) = 64\pi$

➤ Finally, as with any three-dimensional shape, the UNITS for the volume of a cylinder are CUBED.

• Thus, if a cylinder has a radius of 3 inches and a height of 5 inches, its volume would be $\pi r^2 h = \pi(3)^2(5) = \pi(9)(5) = 45\pi$ cubic inches (or inches^3).

> ➤ The SURFACE AREA of a cylinder can be determined with the following formula, where r = radius and h = height:

Surface Area of a Cylinder = $2(\pi r^2) + 2\pi rh$

• For example, the cylinder below has a radius of 3 and a height of 5. Thus, its surface area equals 48π, since:

$$2\pi rh + 2(\pi r^2) = 2\pi(3)(5) + 2(\pi \cdot 3^2) = 30\pi + 18\pi = 48\pi$$

> ➤ To solve certain problems involving cylinders, you need to understand which PARTS of the surface area formula correspond to which PARTS of the cylinder.

• Notice that the top and bottom of a cylinder are circles and that these circles are connected by a curled-up rectangle (think of the label on a can of soup):

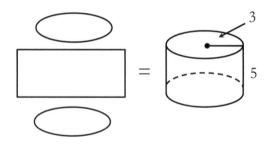

• The area of the TWO CIRCLES equals $2(\pi r^2)$, since area of a single circle is πr^2.

> ➤ The area of the RECTANGLE equals its length × its width. As you can see from the figure above, the length of the rectangle equals the **circumference** of the circle ($2\pi r$).

• Likewise, the width of the rectangle equals the height of the cylinder (h). Thus, the area of curled-up rectangle equals $2\pi r$ (circumference) × h (height).

• The formula for the surface area of a cylinder, therefore, can be analyzed as follows:

$$2(\pi r^2) + 2\pi rh = 2 \text{ circles} + \text{rectangle}$$

➤ From time to time, cylinder problems will ask you to find the surface area of a BAND, LABEL, or RIBBON.

• Here's an example:

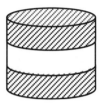

The radius of the cylinder is 2 inches.

The right circular cylinder, shown above, has a white band painted around its circumference. The width of the band is 4 inches.

Quantity A	**Quantity B**
The surface area, in square inches, of the painted band	**16π**

• The key to solving such problems is to use ONLY the portions of the surface area formula that you need.

➤ In the problem above, for example, we don't want the surface area of the cylinder's top or bottom, so there's no need to use the $2(\pi r^2)$ portion of the formula.

• Likewise, we don't want the surface area of the ENTIRE region between the cylinder's top and bottom. We just want the surface area of the painted band.

• To get that area, therefore, we simply need to use the $2\pi rh$ portion of the formula, substituting the width of the painted band (w) for the height of the cylinder (h).

➤ According to the problem, the cylinder has a radius of 2 inches and the painted band has a width of 4 inches.

• The correct answer must therefore be (C), since the surface area of the painted band equals 16π square inches:

$$2\pi rw = 2\pi(2)(4) = 16\pi \text{ inches}^2$$

Strategy Concepts

(8) Don't Forget the Center – Every now and then, the GRE designs circle problems without clearly defined centers.

• Here's an example:

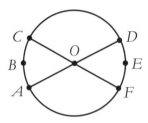

Points A, B, C, D, E, and F lie on the circle as shown.

Quantity A	**Quantity B**
The area of sector AOC	**The area of sector DOF**

• When solving such problems, you CANNOT trust the appearance of the diagram. Just because something seems to intersect the center of the circle does not mean that it does.

➢ In the problem above, for example, the two quantities may APPEAR equal, since line segments AD and CF intersect at point O.

• However, we have NO PROOF that point O is the center of the circle.

• The problem tells us nothing about point O, and the information we've been given does not allow us to infer that point O lies at the center of the circle, either.

➢ As the diagrams below illustrate, the answer to this problem has to be (D), since point O might lie to either side of the circle's center.

• Thus, if point O lies to the left, then sector DOF is larger than sector AOC; conversely, if point O lies to the right, then sector AOC is larger than sector DOF:

Sector DOF is larger

Sector AOC is larger

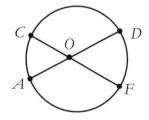 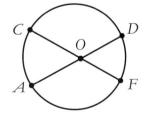

Sherpa
Prep

(9) Label Every Radius – Solving circle problems sometimes requires more than facts and formulas.

- From time to time, you need a bit of strategy, too.

    ➤ When working with circles, it's important that you LABEL EVERY RADIUS that's been drawn.

- Exam-makers like to design diagrams with multiple shapes or lines as a way of HIDING critical relationships. Labeling every radius is a simple way of exposing those relationships.

- Consider the following:

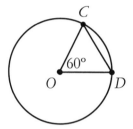

If point O is the center of the circle and CD has a length of 5, the perimeter of $\triangle COD =$

(A) 5   (B) $5+5\sqrt{2}$ (C) 15   (D) $5+10\sqrt{3}$ (E) 25

Answer: C. According to the problem, point O is the center of the circle and points C and D lie on the circle. Therefore, line segments OC and OD are both radii, as shown below:

Marks like this indicate that sides OC and OD are equal.

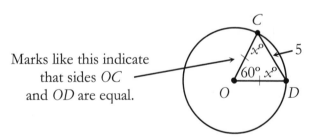

All radii have the same length, so triangle COD is an isosceles. In any isosceles triangle, the angles facing the equal legs are equal and all 3 interior angles add to 180°. Thus, the angles at points C and D equal 60°, as:

$$60° + x + x = 180° \rightarrow 2x = 120° \rightarrow x = 60°$$

Because every angle in triangle COD equals 60°, it is <u>also</u> an equilateral. Side CD has a length of 5, so the correct answer is (C), as a triangle with 3 side lengths of 5 has a perimeter of 15.

➤ To reinforce the importance of this strategy, let's work through a second problem together. This one is more difficult than the first:

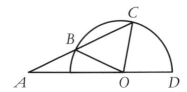

Point O is the center of semicircle S.

In the figure above, points A, B, and C lie on semicircle S, and the length of line segment AB is equal to the length of line segment OD. If the measure of angle BCO is 40°, what is the measure of angle BAO?

(A) 20° (B) 25° (C) 30° (D) 35° (E) 40°

Answer: A. According to the problem, points B, C, and D all lie on the semicircle and point O is the center. Thus, OB, OC, and OD are all radii. The problem also states that the lengths of lines segments AB and OD are equal and that angle BCO has a measure of 40°.

We can depict this information as follows:

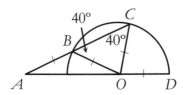

As can be seen from the figure above, triangles BCO is an isosceles. In any isosceles triangle, the angles facing the equal legs are equal, so angle OCB must equal 40°.

Further, angles ABO and OBC form a straight line, so the measure of angle ABO must equal 140°, since the measure of a straight line is 180°:

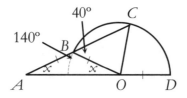

Finally, as shown above, triangle ABO is an isosceles, so the angles facing the equal legs are equal. Because the interior angles of any triangle add to 180°, angle BAO (labeled x) must therefore equal 20°, making (A) the correct answer:

$$140° + x + x = 180° \rightarrow 2x = 40° \rightarrow x = 20°$$

<u>(10) Problems Without Values</u> – Like problems involving quadrilaterals or rectangular solids, problems involving circles or cylinders frequently lack values.

- Here's a typical example:

If the radius of a circle is increased by 20 percent, by what percent will the area of the circular region be increased?

(A) 10%   (B) 40%   (C) 44%   (D) 56%   (E) 60%

- As discussed in our treatment of "Plan B" strategies, the KEY to solving problems without CONCRETE values is to PICK NUMBERS.

  ➤ When picking, choose numbers that are SMALL and EASY to work with, and respect any constraints, should your problem have them.

- In the problem above, the radius of the circle has no concrete value, so we can start the problem by assigning values.

- To keep the math simple, let's make the length of the radius 10. Since 20% of 10 = 2, the length of the increased radius would be 12.

  ➤ Before the increase, the area of the circle would equal $\pi r^2 = \pi(10)^2 = 100\pi$. After the increase, the area of the circle would equal $\pi r^2 = \pi(12)^2 = 144\pi$.

- To calculate the percent by which the area of the circle increased, we simply need to divide the difference between new and original quantities by the original quantity:

$$\frac{\text{difference}}{\text{original}} = \frac{144\pi - 100\pi}{100\pi} = \frac{44}{100}$$

- The correct answer is therefore (C), since $\frac{44}{100} \cdot 100 = 44\%$.

  ➤ Notice that it doesn't matter what numbers we pick. If a problem has no concrete values, ANY numbers that we pick will give us the SAME answer.

- Thus, if the length of the radius were 1, the circle's area would be $\pi r^2 = \pi(1)^2 = \pi$. As 20% of 1 = 0.2, the enlarged circle would have a radius of 1.2 and an area of $\pi r^2 = \pi(1.2)^2 = 1.44\pi$.

- The percent by which the area of the circle increased would still be 44%, since:

$$\frac{\text{difference}}{\text{original}} = \frac{1.44\pi - \pi}{\pi} = \frac{0.44}{1} = \frac{44}{100}$$

> ➤ To ensure that you realize exactly how effective picking numbers can be, let's work through a second example together.

• Consider the following:

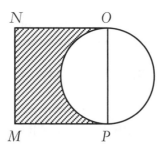

MNOP is a square and OP is the diameter of the circle.

Quantity A	Quantity B
The area of the shaded region	$\frac{2}{3}$ **the area of the square**

Answer: B. According to the problem, *MNOP* is a square and *OP* is the diameter of the circle. Because this problem supplies no concrete values, let's give the square a side length of 2. A side length of 2 would give the circle a diameter of 2 and a radius of 1:

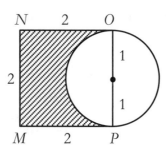

The area of square *MNOP* would be 4, since 2 × 2 = 4. Likewise, the area of the circle would be π, since $\pi r^2 = \pi(1)^2 = \pi$.

The area of a shaded region equals the difference between the areas of the big shape and the small shape. Here, the big shape is the square and the small shape is half the circle. Thus, the area of the shaded region equals:

$$4 - \frac{1}{2}\pi \quad \rightarrow \quad 4 - \frac{1}{2}(3.14) \quad \rightarrow \quad 4 - 1.57 = 2.43$$

Similarly, $\frac{2}{3}$ the area of the square equals $\frac{2}{3} \cdot 4 = \frac{8}{3} = 2\frac{2}{3} \approx 2.67$. Thus, the correct answer is (B), since 2.67 is greater than 2.43.

(11) Asswholes – In our book on <u>Arithmetic & "Plan B" Strategies</u>, we also introduced a type of problem that we like to call "Asswholes".

• As you may recall, Asswholes contain VARIABLES in the ANSWER choices.

    ➢ In most cases, the easiest way to solve such problems is to ASSIGN WHOLE numbers to variables WITHIN the question.

• To do so, first REPLACE any variables in the problem by picking numbers. Then solve the problem using those numbers.

• Once you've solved the problem, PLUG the values you've picked into the answer choices to see which answer MATCHES your solution.

    ➢ When choosing numbers, it's important that you choose numbers that are EASY to work with and work well together.

• It's also important that you OBEY a small set of rules.

• Exam-makers are aware that some test-takers pick numbers, and occasionally design answer choices to foil commonly chosen numbers.

    ➢ Obeying the following rules will help you avoid traps that exam-makers can build into certain problems:

       ☑ Do not pick the same number more than once.
       ☑ Avoid numbers you see in the question or in the answer choices.
       ☑ Stay away from 0, 1, and 100.

• In other words, if you have to choose values for two variables, do NOT pick the same number for both. And if you see the number 5 in the question or the number 10 in the answer choices, don't pick 5 or 10.

    ➢ Finally, when plugging numbers into the answer choices, try answer choice (A) first. If (A) doesn't work, try (E) next.

• As with "Which of the Following Questions", the correct answer to Asswhole problems is often (A) or (E).

• Trying (A) and then (E) may save you time.

> ➢ Although any type of Geometry problem can be an Asswhole, many Asswholes involve circles.

• In fact, many of the more difficult circle problems happen to be Asswholes. Fortunately, such problems are easily solved with this strategy.

• Consider the following:

If a circular region has area k and circumference C, then area k, in terms of C, equals

$$\text{(A) } \frac{4\pi}{C} \quad \text{(B) } \pi C^2 \quad \text{(C) } \frac{2C^2}{\pi} \quad \text{(D) } 2\pi C \quad \text{(E) } \frac{C^2}{4\pi}$$

• Because this problem has **variables in its answer choices**, we can solve it by picking numbers.

> ➢ To start, let's make $k = 25\pi$. Any value will do, but it's always best to choose values that are easy to work with.

• 25π is easy to work with, since a circle with an area of 25π has a radius of 5:

$$A = 25\pi \quad \rightarrow \quad \pi r^2 = 25\pi \quad \rightarrow \quad r^2 = \frac{25\pi}{\pi} = 25$$

• Further, a circle with a radius of 5 has a circumference of 10π, since $2\pi r = 2\pi(5) = 10\pi$. Thus, if the circle has an area k that equals 25π, it has a circumference C that equals 10π.

> ➢ To finish the problem, therefore, we only have to **plug $C = 10\pi$ into the answer choices** to see which of them produces a k that equals 25π.

• Let's start with (A). (A) is not the correct answer since it does not equal 25π:

$$\text{(A)} \longrightarrow \frac{4\pi}{C} = \frac{4\pi}{10\pi} = \frac{2}{5} = \boxed{0.4}$$

• Next, let's test (E). Since (E) equals 25π, it is the correct answer:

$$\text{(E)} \longrightarrow \frac{C^2}{4\pi} = \frac{(10\pi)^2}{4\pi} = \frac{100\pi^2}{4\pi} = \boxed{25\pi}$$

• We could plug $C = 10\pi$ into the remaining answer choices, but there's no need: we've already found the answer that equals 25π.

➢ If you were able to solve the previous problem algebraically: great! We still encourage you to incorporate the Asswhole strategy into your "bag of tricks".

• Although picking numbers may feel "wrong", doing so is almost always a fast, simple way to solve problems — especially difficult ones.

• To prove it, let's work through one more example together:

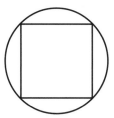

As shown above, square S is inscribed in a circle with a radius r.
The area of the square region equals

(A) $\frac{r^2}{2\pi}$ (B) $\frac{\pi r^2}{2}$ (C) πr^2 (D) r^2 (E) $2r^2$

• Like the previous problem, this problem has variables in its answer choices. Thus, we can solve it by picking numbers.

➢ Before doing so, however, first recall that when a rectangle (or square) is inscribed within a circle, the diagonal of the rectangle equals the diameter of the circle.

• Also recall that the diagonal of a square splits a square into two 45°–45°–90° triangles. Thus, if we were to give the square a side length of 2, the circle would have a diameter of $2\sqrt{2}$, since the sides of a 45°–45°–90° triangle have the ratio $x : x : x\sqrt{2}$:

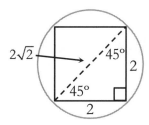

• Further, the radius of the circle would be $\sqrt{2}$, since $\sqrt{2}$ is half of $2\sqrt{2}$. Finally, the area of the square would be $2 \times 2 = 4$. Thus, if we let $r = \sqrt{2}$, we know that the correct answer is (E), since (E) is the only choice that gives the square an area of 4 when we plug in $\sqrt{2}$ for r.

$$(E) \longrightarrow 2r^2 = 2(\sqrt{2})^2 = 2(2) = \boxed{4}$$

(12) Unusual Shapes – Like quadrilateral problems, circle problems sometimes involve unusual shapes or regions.

• Here's an example:

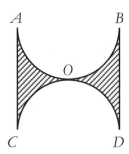

Semicircles *AOB* and *COD* each have a diameter of 8 and are tangent at point *O*.

<u>Quantity A</u>	<u>Quantity B</u>
The area of the shaded region	**16(4 − π)**

• When working with such figures, it's important to remember that there is ALWAYS a SIMPLE way to deconstruct them.

➢ The GRE does NOT design questions involving complicated geometric figures. No matter how weird a figure may look, it will always be a combination of basic shapes.

• For example, the diagram above consists of two semicircles within a square. We know this because the radii of semicircles *AOB* and *COD* can be depicted as follows:

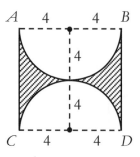

• Thus, to get the area of the shaded region, we need to get the area of square *ABCD* and subtract the areas of semicircles *AOB* and *COD*.

• The area of the square is $8 \times 8 = 64$, since its base and height each have a length of 8. Likewise, the two semicircles form a full circle with a radius of length 4, so their areas add to 16π, since $\pi r^2 = \pi(4)^2 = 16\pi$. The correct answer is therefore (C), since $64 - 16\pi = 16(4 - \pi)$.

(13) Spatial Reasoning – Like other sorts of Geometry problems, circle problems will occasionally test your spatial reasoning.

• Here's an example:

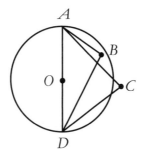

Point *O* is the center of the circle.

Quantity A

The measure of angle *ABD*

Quantity B

The measure of angle *ACD*

• As you may recall, spatial reasoning problems require little technical knowledge. In fact, to solve them you simply need to imagine two scenarios that are as DIFFERENT as possible.

➤ Remember, GRE diagrams are not necessarily accurate. By considering EXTREME possibilities, you can sometimes expose easy solutions that technical approaches miss.

• Take the problem above. We know that point *B* is inside the circle and that point *C* is outside it. We just don't know how CLOSE either is to the circle itself. Notice, however, what happens if we exaggerate their positions:

Point *C* moving further OUTSIDE   Point *B* moving further INSIDE

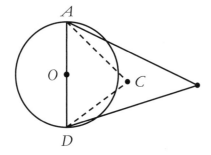
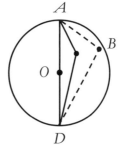

➤ As you can see, both angles DECREASE in measure as they move further from the center and both angles INCREASE in measure as they move closer to the center.

• The correct answer, therefore, must be (A), since angle *ABD* is inside the circle and thus closer to center *O* than angle *ACD*.

(14) Problem Sets – The following questions have been arranged into three groups: fundamental, intermediate, and rare or advanced.

• Whether you're aiming for a perfect score or a score closer to average, mastery of the concepts in the FUNDAMENTAL questions is absolutely essential.

➢ As you might expect, the INTERMEDIATE questions are more difficult but are essential for test-takers who need an above-average score or higher.

• Finally, the RARE or ADVANCED questions test concepts that are very sophisticated or seldom encountered on the GRE. Mastery of such questions is required only if you need a math score above the 90th percentile.

• As always, if you find yourself confused, bogged down with busy work, or stuck, don't be afraid to fall back on your "Plan B" strategies!

Fundamental

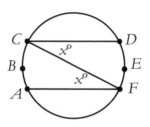

1. If arc *ABC* has a length of 5π, what is the length of arc *DEF*?

    (A) 2π (B) 4π (C) 5π (D) 8π (E) 10π

2. In the figure above, the checkered area represents the border of a rug with center *O*. If the border is 3 feet wide, what is the area of the border?

    (A) 9π (B) 25π (C) 39π (D) 49π (E) 64π

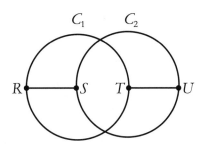

In the figure above, $RS = TU$ and C_1 has a diameter of 10.

	Quantity A	Quantity B

3.   The area of circle C_2 25π

4.   What is the area of a circular region that has a circumference of 8π?

(A) 4π (B) 8π (C) 16π (D) 32π (E) 64π

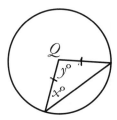

5.   Point Q is the center of the circle above. If $x = 30$, what is the value of y?

6.   If the radius of circle K has a length of $\frac{14}{11}$, its circumference is approximately equal to which of the following?

(A) 7.8   (B) 7.9   (C) 8.0   (D) 8.1   (E) 8.2

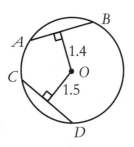

Circle with center O

Quantity A	Quantity B

7.　　　　The length of chord AB　　　　The length of chord CD

8.　If the diameter of a circle decreases by 20 percent, by what percent does the area of the circle decrease?

(A) 20%　(B) 36%　(C) 40%　(D) 60%　(E) 64%

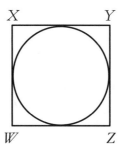

The radius of the inscribed circle is 5

Quantity A	Quantity B

9.　　　　The perimeter of square $WXYZ$　　　　10π

10.　If a rectangular solid that is 4 feet by 5 feet by 8 feet is placed inside a right circular cylinder with a radius of 5 feet and a height of 8 feet, what is the volume of the unoccupied portion of the cylinder in cubic feet?

(A) $80\pi - 16$　(B) $120\pi - 16$　(C) $160 - 80\pi$　(D) $200\pi - 160$　(E) $320\pi - 160$

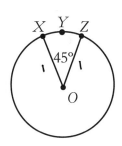

The circle has center O and radius 1.

Quantity A	Quantity B

11.   The length of arc XYZ $\frac{\pi}{4}$

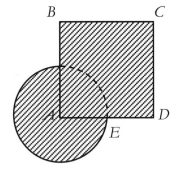

12.   In the figure above, vertex A of square $ABCD$ is the center of the circle. If $AE = ED = 5$, what is the area of the shaded region?

    (A) $25 + \frac{75}{4}\pi$ (B) $25 + 75\pi$ (C) $100 + \frac{75}{4}\pi$ (D) $100 + 25\pi$ (E) $100 + 75\pi$

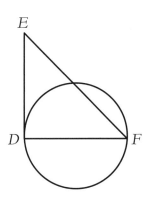

DF is the diameter of the circle, and ED is tangent to the circle.

Quantity A	Quantity B

13.   The angle at vertex E The angle at vertex F

Intermediate

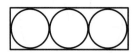

Viewed from above, three identical cylinders are situated within a fence so that they fit exactly inside, as shown.

Quantity A	Quantity B

14.   The combined length of the three cylinders   The circumference of one of the cylinders

Circle *C* has an area of 9 square meters.

Quantity A	Quantity B

15.   The radius, in meters, of circle *C* $\dfrac{4}{3}$

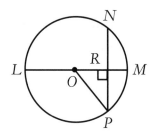

Point *O* is the center of the circle, and line segments *OP* and *NP* have lengths of 10 and 16, respectively.

Quantity A	Quantity B

16.   The length of line segment *RM*   4

17.   A right circular cylinder with height 4 and radius 5 has volume *K*. In terms of *K*, what is the volume of a right circular cylinder with height 2 and radius 10?

(A) *K*   (B) 2*K*   (C) 4*K*   (D) 6*K*   (E) 8*K*

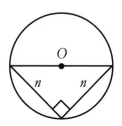

The area of the circular region with center O is 36π.

Quantity A	Quantity B

18. n 6

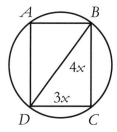

The circles are tangent at point I and $HJ = 6$.

19. If the circumference of the circle with center H is twice the circumference of the circle with center J, what is the diameter of the larger circle?

         (A) 2   (B) 4   (C) 5   (D) 6   (E) 8

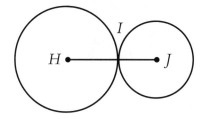

20. If the area of inscribed rectangle $ABCD$ is 108, the circumference of the circle equals

         (A) 10π (B) 12π (C) 15π (D) 18π (E) 25π

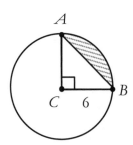

21. If point C is the center of the circle, what is the approximate area of the shaded region?

(A) 10   (B) 12   (C) 16   (D) 20   (E) 25

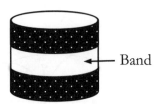

A rectangular band is painted on a right circular cylinder with radius r. The band, which encircles the cylinder, has width w and an area equal to the area of the base of the cylinder.

Quantity A	Quantity B

22. r $2w$

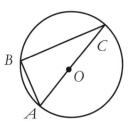

Triangle ABC is inscribed in a circle with center O.

Quantity A	Quantity B

23.   The measure of the angle at vertex B 90°

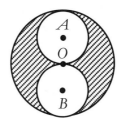

The inscribed circles with centers A and B are tangent at center O.

Quantity A	Quantity B

24.   The sum of the areas of the circles   The area of the shaded region
       with centers A and B

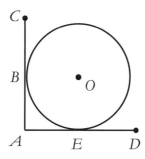

25.   In the figure above, the circle has center O and is tangent to perpendicular line
       segments AC and AD at points B and E, respectively. If the distance from point A to
       point O has a length of k, what is the diameter of the circle, expressed in terms of k?

       (A) $k\sqrt{2}$ (B) $2k\sqrt{2}$ (C) $3k$ (D) $3k\sqrt{2}$ (E) $4k\sqrt{3}$

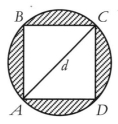

26.   In the figure above, square $ABCD$ is inscribed in a circle with a diameter d. In terms
       of d, what is the total area of the shaded regions?

       (A) $\dfrac{d^2(\pi-2)}{4}$ (B) $d(2-\pi)$ (C) $\dfrac{\pi(d^2-2)}{4}$ (D) $\dfrac{\pi d^2-4}{2}$ (E) $\dfrac{\pi d^2-1}{4}$

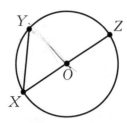

Point O is the center of the circle, and XY has a length of 8.

27. If the angle at point X has a measure of 45°, what is the approximate perimeter of the region XYZ?

(A) 22   (B) 24   (C) 26   (D) 28   (E) 30

28. The inside dimensions of a rectangular crate are 4 feet by 6 feet by 8 feet. A right circular cylinder is to be placed inside the crate so that it will stand upright on one of its circular bases when the closed crate rests on one of its six faces. Of all such cylinders that could be placed within the crate, what is the radius, in feet, of the one with the largest volume?

(A) 2   (B) 3   (C) 4   (D) 5   (E) 6

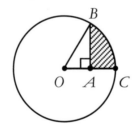

Point O is the center of the circle, and $OA = \frac{1}{2}OB$.

Quantity A	Quantity B
29. The area of triangle OBA	The area of the shaded region

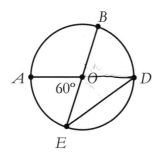

Point *O* is the center of the circle.

30.   If line segment *AO* has a length of 6, and points *A*, *O*, and *D* lie on the diameter of the circle, what is the approximate area of region *BED*?

(A) 8π   (B) 9π   (C) 11π   (D) 12π   (E) 15π

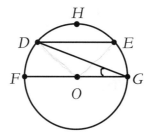

DE ∥ *FG* and point *O* is the center of the circle.

31.   The angle at point *G* is 30° and inscribed on the circle. If *FG* has a length of 18, what is the length of arc *DHE*?

(A) 2π   (B) 3π   (C) 4π   (D) 5π   (E) 6π

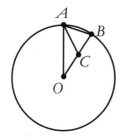

Point *O* is the center of the circle.

32.   In the figure above, if line segments *AB*, *AC*, and *OC* are congruent, what is the measure of angle *AOC*?

(A) 20°   (B) 24°   (C) 30°   (D) 32°   (E) 36°

(15) Solutions – Video solutions for each of the previous questions can be found on our website at **www.sherpaprep.com/masterkey**.

• BOOKMARK this address for future visits!

➢ To view the videos, you'll need to register your copy of <u>Master Key to the GRE</u>: <u>Geometry</u>.

• If you have yet to do so, please go to **www.sherpaprep.com/videos** and enter your email address.

• Be sure to provide the SAME email address that you used to purchase your copy of <u>Master Key to the GRE</u> or to enroll in your GRE course with Sherpa Prep!

➢ When checking your answers, we encourage you to watch the solution for any problem that you answered INCORRECTLY

• The same goes for any problem that took you MORE than TWO MINUTES to solve.

• After digesting the explanation, REVISIT your mistake a couple of days later to ensure that the problem no longer poses issues to you.

➢ If you struggle to solve the problem a SECOND time, add it to your "LOG of ERRORS" and redo it every few weeks.

• Solving tricky questions MORE THAN ONCE is the best way to learn from your mistakes and to avoid similar difficulties on your actual exam.

Fundamental		Intermediate	Rare or Advanced
1. C	11. C	14. B	24. C
2. C	12. C	15. A	25. A
3. D	13. D	16. C	26. A
4. C		17. B	27. D
5. 120		18. A	28. B
6. C		19. E	29. B
7. A		20. C	30. C
8. B		21. A	31. B
9. A		22. C	32. E
10. D		23. C	

Coordinate Geometry

Coordinate Geometry

To be discussed:

Fundamental Concepts

Whether you're aiming for a perfect score or a score closer to average, mastery of the following concepts is essential.

Rare or Advanced Concepts

The following concepts are either advanced or are tested only on rare occasions. If you don't need an elite math score, don't waste your time!

Practice Questions

There's no substitute for elbow grease. Practice your new skills to ensure that you internalize what you've studied.

Fundamental Concepts

(1) Introduction – Coordinate Geometry is the use of Algebra to study Geometry.

• At its heart lies the ***xy*–coordinate plane**, a two-dimensional grid composed of intersecting number lines.

> ➤ The HORIZONTAL number line is known as the ***x*–axis**, and the VERTICAL number line is known as the ***y*–axis**.

• The point at which the two number lines meet is known as the **origin**. The origin marks the ZERO POINT of each number line.

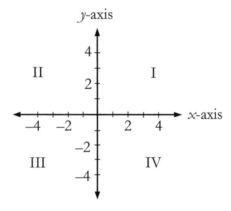

• As shown above, the axes divide the coordinate plane into four **quadrants**, I, II, III, and IV.

> ➤ Each point in the coordinate plane has an *x*-coordinate and a *y*-coordinate. A point is identified by two numbers (x, y) known as an **ordered pair**.

• The FIRST number represents a point's *x*-coordinate, and the SECOND number represents a point's *y*-coordinate.

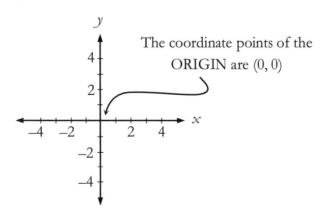

The coordinate points of the ORIGIN are $(0, 0)$

➤ Any point to the RIGHT of the origin has a POSITIVE *x*-coordinate, and any point to the LEFT of the origin has a NEGATIVE *x*-coordinate.

• Likewise, any point ABOVE the origin has a POSITIVE *y*-coordinate, and any point BELOW the origin has a NEGATIVE *y*-coordinate.

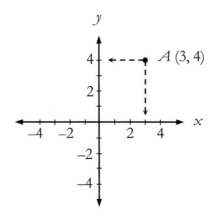

• Thus, in the figure above, point *A* has coordinates (3, 4), since it is 3 units to the RIGHT of the origin and 4 units ABOVE it.

➤ Similarly, in the figure below, point *B* has coordinates (–3, 3), since it is 3 units to the LEFT of the origin and 3 units ABOVE it.

• Point *C* is 2 units to the RIGHT of the origin and 4 units BELOW it, so its coordinates are (2, –4):

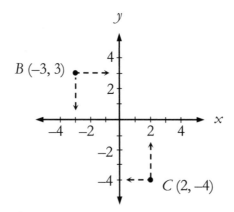

➢ Note that you can INFER significant information about a point if you know the QUADRANT in which it lies.

• In the figure below, we know that point A has a negative x-coordinate and a positive y-coordinate, since every point in quadrant II lies to the LEFT of the origin and ABOVE it:

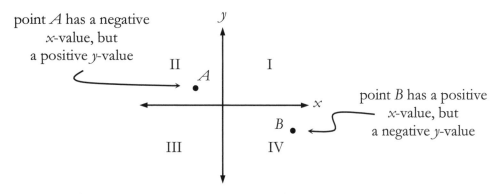

• Likewise, we know that point B has a positive x-coordinate and a negative y-coordinate, since every point in quadrant IV lies to the RIGHT of the origin and BELOW it.

➢ The GRE often designs questions that require such inferences. Here's a typical example:

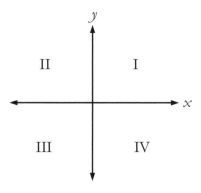

(a, b) is a point in region I, and (x, y) is a point in region III.

Quantity A	**Quantity B**
$a + b$	$x + y$

Answer. A. Every point in region I lies above the origin and to its right. Thus, the x- and y-coordinates of point (a, b) are both positive. Likewise, every point in region III lies below the origin and to its left. Thus, the x- and y-coordinates of point (x, y) are both negative. The correct answer is (A), since the sum of two positive values is greater than that of two negative values.

(2) Distance & Midpoints – From time to time, GRE questions require test-takers to identify the distance between two points.

- Here's an example:

Point A (–5, 4) and point B (3, –2) lie on the coordinate plane.

Quantity A	**Quantity B**
The length of line segment AB	**10**

- The simplest way to determine the distance between two points is to USE the PYTHAGOREAN theorem.

  ➤ To start, sketch out a RIGHT triangle in which the HYPOTENUSE represents the distance between the two points.

- For example, the distance between points AB can be depicted as follows:

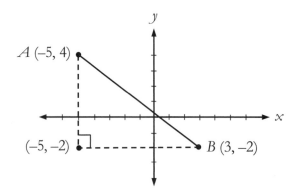

  ➤ Then determine the length of the two legs. In the diagram above, the VERTICAL leg has a length of 6, since the **y-coordinates** shift from –2 to 4.

- Likewise, the HORIZONTAL leg has a length of 8, since the **x-coordinates** shift from –5 to 3. Thus, the length of the hypotenuse is 10, since the Pythagorean theorem states:

$$6^2 + 8^2 = c^2 \rightarrow 36 + 64 = c^2 \rightarrow 100 = c^2 \rightarrow 10 = c$$

- Alternatively, you can recognize that a right triangle with leg lengths of 6 and 8 is a 6–8–10 triangle. The correct answer is therefore (C), since line segment AB is the hypotenuse of the right triangle.

➤ On rare occasions, a GRE question will require test-takers to determine the MIDPOINT between two points.

• To determine the location of a midpoint, first AVERAGE the x-coordinates of the given points. Then AVERAGE the y-coordinates.

• For example, the points $(1, 5)$ and $(–3, 7)$ have a midpoint of $(–1, 6)$, since the average of the x- and y-coordinates can be calculated as follows:

The average of the x-coordinates	The average of the y-coordinates
$\dfrac{1+(-3)}{2} = \dfrac{-2}{2} = -1$	$\dfrac{5+7}{2} = \dfrac{12}{2} = 6$

➤ To ensure that you're comfortable working with distances and midpoints, let's work through another practice problem.

• Consider the following:

In the xy-coordinate plane, point A lies at $(–1, 2)$ and point B lies at $(7, 6)$. What is the distance between the midpoint of the two points and the origin?

(A) $\sqrt{3}$ (B) 4   (C) $3\sqrt{2}$ (D) 5   (E) $4\sqrt{3}$

Answer: D. The location of a midpoint can be determined by averaging the x- and y-coordinates of any two points. Thus, the midpoint of points A and B lies at $(3, 4)$, since:

The average of the x-coordinates	The average of the y-coordinates
$\dfrac{(-1)+7}{2} = \dfrac{6}{2} = 3$	$\dfrac{2+6}{2} = \dfrac{8}{2} = 4$

The coordinates of the origin in the xy-coordinate plane are $(0, 0)$. Thus, we can determine the distance between the midpoint and the origin by drawing the following right triangle:

The horizontal leg has a length of 3, since it runs 3 spaces right of the origin

The vertical leg has a length of 4, since it rises 4 spaces above the origin

$(3, 4)$

The correct answer must therefore be (D), since a right triangle with leg lengths of 3 and 4 always has a hypotenuse of length 5.

(3) Slope & The Slope Formula – To solve certain Coordinate Geometry questions, it's important that you be able to identify the slope of a line.

• The term SLOPE refers to how "steep" a line is.

> ➤ A line with a SMALL positive slope will rise GENTLY, while a line with a STEEP positive slope will rise SHARPLY.

• Thus, the line on the left has a relatively small slope, since it rises gently, while the line on the right has a relatively large slope, since it rises sharply:

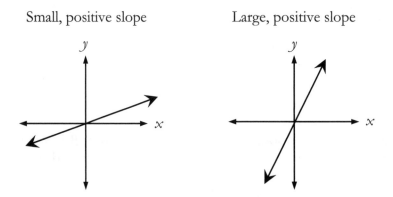

Small, positive slope   Large, positive slope

> ➤ Likewise, a line with a SMALL negative slope will fall GENTLY, while a line with a STEEP negative slope will fall SHARPLY.

• Thus, the line on the left has a small negative slope, since it falls gently, while the line on the right has a large negative slope, since it falls sharply:

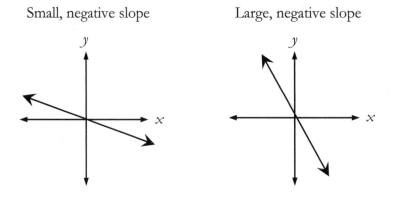

Small, negative slope   Large, negative slope

➤ Given two points (x_1, y_1) and (x_2, y_2), the slope of the line passing through them can be measured with a simple formula.

• It's commonly known as the SLOPE FORMULA:

$$\text{SLOPE of a Line} = \frac{y_2 - y_1}{x_2 - x_1}$$

• This formula is also known as "RISE over RUN", where "rise" refers to how much the line rises VERTICALLY between the two points, and "run" refers to how much the line runs HORIZONTALLY.

➤ In the xy-coordinate plane below, a line passes through points (–2, –3) and (4, 3). The difference between the y-coordinates is 3 – (–3) = 6.

• The difference between its x-coordinates is 4 – (–2) = 6. Its slope, therefore, is 1, since $\frac{\text{rise}}{\text{run}} = \frac{6}{6} = 1$.

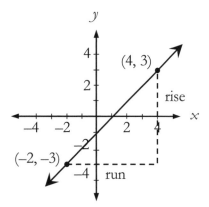

• Likewise, a line that passes through points (1, 5) and (4, 7) has a slope of $\frac{2}{3}$, since the difference between the y-coordinates is 7 – 5 = 2 and the difference between the x-coordinates is 4 – 1 = 3.

➤ When plugging points into the slope formula, it DOESN'T matter which point you label (x_1, y_1) and which point you label (x_2, y_2).

• Take the points (3, 1) and (5, 2). Notice that we get a slope of $\frac{1}{2}$, regardless of whether we let (5, 2) = (x_2, y_2) and (3, 1) = (x_1, y_1) or vice versa:

$$\frac{y_2 - y_1}{x_2 - x_1} = \frac{2 - 1}{5 - 3} = \frac{1}{2} \qquad\qquad \frac{y_2 - y_1}{x_2 - x_1} = \frac{1 - 2}{3 - 5} = \frac{-1}{-2} = \frac{1}{2}$$

Chapter 6: Coordinate Geometry

(4) Graphing Equations – In Coordinate Geometry, all lines can be expressed as equations.

- Although the order of such equations can be expressed in any form, it's generally preferable to arrange them in the order $y = mx + b$.

  ➤ In this order, m represents the SLOPE of the line and b represents the y-INTERCEPT.

- For example, the line $y = \frac{2}{3}x + 1$ has a slope of $\frac{2}{3}$ and intercepts the y-axis at 1, since:

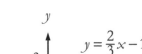

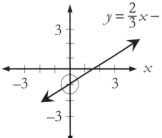

  ➤ As we saw in the preceding section, the slope of a line indicates how STEEP a line is and whether it rises or falls.

- An equation with a positive m, such as $y = \frac{2}{3}x - 1$, has a rising slope, while an equation with a negative m, such as $y = -\frac{1}{2}x + 2$, has a falling slope:

Positive slope   Negative Slope

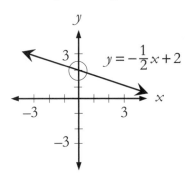

  ➤ The y-intercept indicates WHERE the line INTERSECTS the y-axis.

- In the diagrams above, the y-intercepts have been circled. Note that a negative y-intercept, like that found in the equation $y = \frac{2}{3}x - 1$, indicates a point of intersection below the x-axis.

- Likewise, a positive y-intercept, like that found in the equation $y = -\frac{1}{2}x + 2$, indicates a point of intersection above the x-axis.

➤ To solve Coordinate Geometry problems on the GRE, you sometimes have to GRAPH equations.

• To do so, first identify the equation's slope and *y*-intercept.

• For example, the equation $-3x + 2y = -2$ has a slope of $\frac{3}{2}$ and a *y*-intercept of -1, since it be can rewritten as $y = \frac{3}{2}x - 1$:

$$2y = 3x - 2 \qquad \text{Add } 3x \text{ to both sides.}$$
$$y = \frac{3}{2}x - 1 \qquad \text{Divide both sides by 2.}$$

➤ Then PLOT the *y*-intercept on the coordinate plane.

• Here, we know the equation $y = \frac{3}{2}x - 1$ intersects the *y*-axis at -1, so we can plot a point as follows:

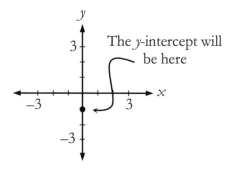

➤ Finally, use the SLOPE to plot a second point and CONNECT the two points with a straight line.

• The line above has a slope of $\frac{3}{2}$. Since slope $= \frac{\text{rise}}{\text{run}}$, this line "rises" 3 spaces for every 2 spaces that it "runs". If we rise 3 spaces and run 2 spaces from $(0, -1)$, we end up at $(2, 2)$:

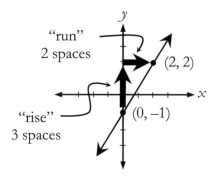

• Thus, the equation $-3x + 2y = -2$ can be graphed as shown, since the line above connects the points $(0, -1)$ and $(2, 2)$.

➢ To ensure that you've got it, let's graph $y = -\frac{1}{4}x + 3$.

• This equation has a slope of $-\frac{1}{4}$ and a y-intercept of 3. To start, let's plot a point at (0, 3), since that's where the line will intercept the y-axis:

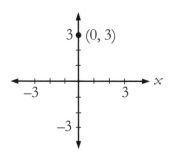

➢ Next, let's use the slope to plot a second point. Since $-\frac{1}{4}$ is a NEGATIVE slope, this line must go DOWN and to the RIGHT.

• Thus, instead of "rising" 1 space, it must "fall" 1 space for every 4 spaces that it "runs". If we fall 1 space and run 4 spaces from (0, 3), we end up at (4, 2):

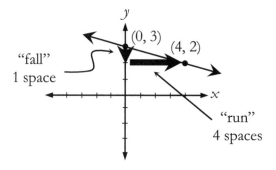

• The equation $y = -\frac{1}{4}x + 3$ can therefore be graphed as shown, since the line above connects points (0, 3) and (4, 2).

➢ When graphing equations, it's important to remember that equations **WITHOUT an m term**, such as $y = x + 2$ or $y = x - 3$, have a slope of 1.

• In Algebra, we use the notation x in place of $1x$, since the 1 can be inferred. The same is true of $-x$. The equation $y = -x + 4$ has a slope of -1, since $-x$ is shorthand for $-1x$.

• Likewise, equations **WITHOUT a b term**, such as $y = -\frac{2}{3}x$ or $y = x$, have a y-intercept of 0 (the <u>origin</u>), since the notation $y = -\frac{2}{3}x$ is shorthand for $y = -\frac{2}{3}x + 0$.

(5) Finding the *x*-Intercept – In the previous section, we saw that the point where a line intersects the *y*-axis is known as the *y*-intercept.

• We also saw that the *y*-intercept of a line can be determined by finding the "*b* term" in the equation $y = mx + b$.

➢ From time to time, however, the GRE will also ask questions about an equation's **x-intercept**.

• As you can infer, the *x*-intercept is the point where a line intersects the *x*-axis.

• In the diagram below, the *x*-intercept lies at (–1, 0), since the line intercepts the *x*-axis at $x = –1$:

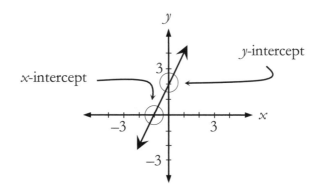

➢ Because ALL *x*-intercepts lie on the *x*-axis (as in the diagram above), EVERY *x*-intercept has a *y*-value of 0. (Remember, the *x*-axis is the line where $y = 0$.)

• To find the *x*-intercept of any equation, therefore, you simply need to **LET $y = 0$** and solve for *x*. For example, the equation $y = –2x + 6$ has an *x*-intercept of 3, since:

$0 = –2x + 6$	Let $y = 0$.
$2x = 6$	Add $2x$ to both sides.
$x = 3$	Divide both sides by 3.

• Likewise, the equation $–2x + 4y – 5 = 7$ has an *x*-intercept of –6, since:

$–2x – 4(0) – 5 = 7$	Let $y = 0$.
$–2x = 12$	Add 5 to both sides.
$x = –6$	Divide both sides by –2.

➤ To give you a sense of how the GRE might test your knowledge of *x*-intercepts, let's work through a practice problem together.

• Consider the following:

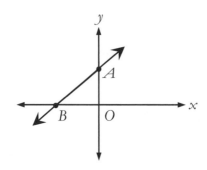

The equation of the line graphed above on the *xy*-coordinate plane is
6*y* − 5*x* = 12 and point *O* is the origin.

Quantity A	Quantity B
AO	*BO*

Answer. B. The line above intercepts the *y*-axis at point *A* and the *x*-axis at point *B*. Thus, point *A* is its *y*-intercept and point *B* is its *x*-intercept. To calculate the lengths of line segments *AO* and *BO*, therefore, we need to determine the values of the two intercepts.

To find the value of the *y*-intercept, we can arrange the equation in the order $y = mx + b$:

$$6y = 5x + 12 \qquad \text{Add } 5x \text{ to both sides.}$$
$$y = \frac{5}{6}x + 2 \qquad \text{Divide both sides by 6.}$$

Since the equation $y = \frac{5}{6}x + 2$ has a *b* term of 2, point *A* has the coordinates (0, 2).

To determine the value of the *x*-intercept, we need to let $y = 0$ and solve for *x*. Using the original equation, we can do so as follows:

$$6(0) - 5x = 12 \qquad \text{Set } y = 0.$$
$$x = -\frac{12}{5} \qquad \text{Divide both sides by } -5.$$

Point *B*, therefore, has the coordinates $(-\frac{12}{5}, 0)$.

Since point *A* is 2 spaces ABOVE the origin, line segment *AO* has a length of 2. Likewise, point *B* is $\frac{12}{5} = 2\frac{2}{5} = 2.4$ spaces to the LEFT of the origin, so line segment *BO* has a length of 2.4. Even though point *B* is to the left of the origin, the correct answer is (B), since the LENGTH of any line segment is positive.

(6) Horizontal & Vertical Lines – Unlike other lines, horizontal and vertical lines are not expressed in the form $y = mx + b$.

• To understand why, consider the statements $x = 1$ and $y = 2$.

➢ If you graph EVERY point at $x = 1$, the points form a VERTICAL line one space to the right of the origin.

• Likewise, if you graph EVERY point at $y = 2$, the points form a HORIZONTAL line two spaces above the origin:

All the points at $x = 1$ All the points at $y = 2$

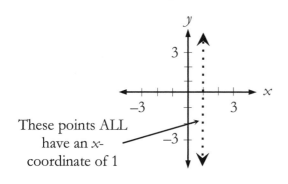 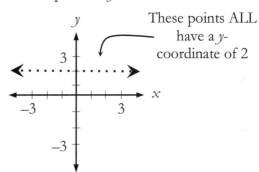

These points ALL have an x-coordinate of 1

These points ALL have a y-coordinate of 2

➢ Thus, horizontal and vertical lines are represented by equations such as $x = 1$ and $y = 2$, rather than equations in the form $y = mx + b$.

• What's UNEXPECTED about equations like $x = 1$ and $y = 2$ is that they form lines in the OPPOSITE direction of the axes.

• For example, the equation $x = 5$ represents a <u>vertical</u> line at $x = 5$, even though the x-axis is <u>horizontal</u>. Likewise, the equation $y = -2$ represents a horizontal line at $y = -2$, even though the y-axis is vertical.

➢ Every now and then, you may need to IDENTIFY the SLOPE of a horizontal or vertical line.

• To do so, simply remember that the slope of any line equals its "rise" over its "run". A horizontal line runs infinitely, but never rises, while a vertical line rises infinitely, but never runs, so:

A HORIZONTAL line A VERTICAL line

$$\text{slope} = \frac{\text{rise}}{\text{run}} = \frac{0}{\text{infinity}} = 0 \qquad \text{slope} = \frac{\text{rise}}{\text{run}} = \frac{\text{infinity}}{0} = \text{undefined}$$

(7) Parallel & Perpendicular Lines – From time to time, the GRE will design questions involving parallel or perpendicular lines.

• As you likely know, PARELLEL lines lie in the same plane but never meet, while PERPENDICULAR lines intersect one another at a 90° angle.

➤ In Coordinate Geometry, two lines are said to be parallel if their SLOPES are EQUAL.

Parallel Lines

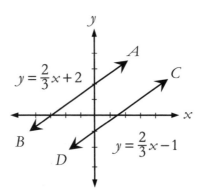

• In the figure above, lines AB and CD are parallel—even though they have different y-intercepts—since each line has a slope of $\frac{2}{3}$.

➤ Conversely, two lines are said to be perpendicular if the PRODUCT of their SLOPES equals –1 (or if one is horizontal and the other is vertical).

Perpendicular Lines

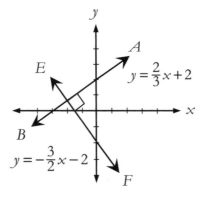

• In the figure above, lines AB and EF are perpendicular, since their slopes multiply to –1:

$$-\frac{3}{2} \times \frac{2}{3} = -1$$

➤ To give you a sense of how the GRE might test your knowledge of parallel and perpendicular lines, let's work through a practice problem together.

• Consider the following:

Which of the following lines are perpendicular to the line $-x = 2y$ in the xy-coordinate plane?

Indicate all such lines.

$\boxed{A}$ $-2x + y = 0$ $\boxed{B}$ $x = \frac{1}{2}$ $\boxed{C}$ $y + 2x = 0$ $\boxed{D}$ $y = -2$ $\boxed{E}$ $-2x + y = 3$

Answer. A, E. To determine whether two lines are perpendicular, we need to know their slopes. We can find the slope of $-x = 2y$ by arranging it in the form $y = mx + b$:

$$2y = -x \qquad \text{Reverse the order of the equation.}$$
$$y = -\frac{1}{2}x \qquad \text{Divide both sides by 2.}$$

Although the equation $y = -\frac{1}{2}x$ has no b term (thus, its y-intercept is the origin), its m term equals $-\frac{1}{2}$, so it has a slope of $-\frac{1}{2}$.

When lines are perpendicular, the product of their slopes is –1. Therefore, the slope of any line perpendicular to $y = -\frac{1}{2}x$ must have a slope of 2, since:

$$-\frac{1}{2} \times 2 = -1$$

If we browse the answers, it's clear that $\boxed{B}$ $x = \frac{1}{2}$ and $\boxed{D}$ $y = -2$ cannot be perpendicular to $-x = 2y$, since we saw in the preceding chapter that equations of the form $x = 2$ and $y = 3$ represent vertical and horizontal lines.

We can determine the slopes of the remaining answer choices by arranging them in the form $y = mx + b$:

$$\boxed{A} \quad -2x + y = 0 \quad \rightarrow \quad y = 2x$$
$$\boxed{C} \quad y + 2x = 0 \quad \rightarrow \quad y = -2x$$
$$\boxed{E} \quad -2x + y = 3 \quad \rightarrow \quad y = 2x + 3$$

Of these choices, (A) and (E) have slopes of 2 and (C) has a slope of –2. The correct answers are therefore (A) and (E).

Chapter 6: Coordinate Geometry

(8) Intersecting Lines – Every now and then, the GRE will ask test-takers to determine whether a point and line intersect or to find the coordinates where two lines cross.

- Both tasks are relatively simple.

  ➢ To determine whether a line and a point intersect, simply PLUG the coordinates of the point into the line.

- If the coordinates produce a TRUE statement, the line and the point INTERSECT, because any point that satisfies an equation lies on that line.

- Thus, the line $y = \frac{2}{3}x - 4$ intersects point (9, 2), since:

$$2 = \frac{2}{3}(9) - 4 \qquad \text{Insert } x = 9 \text{ and } y = 2.$$
$$2 = 6 - 4 \qquad\qquad \frac{2}{\cancel{3}}(\cancel{9}) = 2(3) = 6$$
$$2 = 2 \qquad\qquad \text{This is a true statement.}$$

  ➢ Likewise, if the coordinates produce a FALSE statement, the line and the point do NOT intersect.

- Thus, the line $y = \frac{1}{4}x + 3$ does NOT intersect the point (8, 7), since:

$$7 = \frac{1}{4}(8) + 3 \qquad \text{Insert } x = 8 \text{ and } y = 7.$$
$$7 = 2 + 3 \qquad\qquad \frac{1}{\cancel{4}}(\cancel{8}) = 2$$
$$7 = 5 \qquad\qquad \text{This is a false statement.}$$

  ➢ Determining the (x, y) coordinates where TWO lines INTERSECT is just as simple.

- When lines meet, the point of intersection represents the point that satisfies both equations.

- Thus, to find the point where two lines cross, you simply need to COMBINE the equations and SOLVE for the variables.

➢ In general, the easiest way to do so is to SET the two equations EQUAL to one another.

- Take the lines $y = 6x - 2$ and $y = -2x + 6$. Since $6x - 2$ and $-2x + 6$ <u>both</u> equal y, we know that $6x - 2 = -2x + 6$. If we simplify this statement, we get $x = 1$:

$$6x - 2 = -2x + 6 \;\;\rightarrow\;\; 8x = 8 \;\;\rightarrow\;\; x = 1$$

- Likewise, if we plug $x = 1$ into the equation for EITHER line, we get $y = 4$:

$$
\begin{array}{ll}
y = 6x - 2 & \qquad y = -2x + 6 \\
y = 6(1) - 2 & \qquad y = -2(1) + 6 \\
y = 4 & \qquad y = 4
\end{array}
$$

- Thus, the lines INTERSECT at point (1, 4), since setting their equations equal proves that $x = 1$ and $y = 4$.

➢ If the equations are not in the form $y = mx + b$, however, you may find it faster to use the ELIMINATION technique instead.

- Consider the following:

At what point in the xy-coordinate plane do lines $-3x + 7y = 8$ and $3x - 4y = 7$ intersect?

(A) 3, 4   (B) 5, 11   (C) 7, 8   (D) 8, 4   (E) 9, 5

Answer. E. To find the point where two lines intersect, you have to combine the equations. One way to do so would be to place each equation in the form $y = mx + b$ and to set the equations equal.

Here, it's faster to combine the two equations, since $-3x$ and $3x$ cancel when ADDED:

$$
\begin{array}{r}
-3x + 7y = 8 \\
+\;\; 3x - 4y = 7 \\
\hline
3y = 15
\end{array}
$$

If $3y = 15$, then $y = 5$. Plugging $y = 5$ into either equation proves that $x = 9$:

$$
\begin{array}{ll}
-3x + 7(5) = 8 & \qquad 3x - 4(5) = 7 \\
-3x + 35 = 8 & \qquad 3x - 20 = 7 \\
-3x = -27 & \qquad 3x = 27
\end{array}
$$

Thus, these lines intersect at point (9, 5), since adding the two equations proves that $x = 9$ and $y = 5$.

(9) Finding the Equation of a Graphed Line – To solve Coordinate Geometry problems, it's often necessary to determine the equation of a graphed line.

- Here's an example:

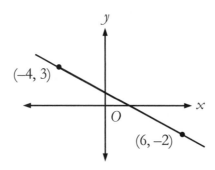

Line *l*, shown above, lies in the *xy*-coordinate system.

Quantity A	Quantity B
The *y*–intercept of line *l*	1

- To translate a graphed line into an equation, you first need to FIND the SLOPE.

  ➤ Because the slope of a line equals $\frac{y_2 - y_1}{x_2 - x_1}$, you can always determine a line's slope IF you know the coordinates of TWO points on that line.

- For example, the line above it connects points (–4, 3) and (6, –2), so its slope is $-\frac{1}{2}$:

$$\frac{y_2 - y_1}{x_2 - x_1} = \frac{(-2) - 3}{6 - (-4)} = \frac{-5}{10} = -\frac{1}{2}$$

- Next, SUBSTITUTE the slope for *m* in the equation $y = mx + b$ (remember, *m* = slope):

$$y = mx + b \quad \rightarrow \quad y = -\frac{1}{2}x + b$$

  ➤ Finally, PLUG in the coordinates of EITHER point to determine the line's *y*–INTERCEPT.

- Here, if we insert the point (–4, 3) into $y = -\frac{1}{2}x + b$, like so, we get:

$$3 = -\frac{1}{2}(-4) + b \quad \rightarrow \quad 3 = -(-2) + b \quad \rightarrow \quad 3 = 2 + b$$

- Since *b* = 1, the equation of the graphed line is $y = -\frac{1}{2}x + 1$. The answer to the question above, therefore, is (C), since the line has a *y*-intercept of 1.

> ➤ To HIDE information, the GRE often runs lines through the ORIGIN.

• In such cases, the exam does NOT indicate that the line intersects the origin, nor does it label the origin's coordinates.

• Here's a typical example:

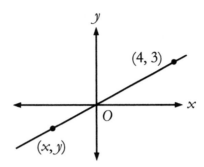

In the rectangular system above, if $x = -2.4$, then y equals

(A) –1.5 (B) –1.8 (C) – 2.1 (D) –2.7 (E) – 3

• If you encounter a line that's been DRAWN through the origin, you can TRUST that it does. The GRE will not try to mislead you with such diagrams.

> ➤ To solve problems like the one above, therefore, simply USE the coordinates of the ORIGIN to establish the equation of the line.

• Here, our line connects the points $(0, 0)$ and $(4, 3)$. Thus, its slope equals $\frac{3}{4}$, since $\frac{y_2 - y_1}{x_2 - x_1} = \frac{3-0}{4-0} = \frac{3}{4}$. If we INSERT this information into $y = mx + b$, we get:

$$y = \frac{3}{4}x + b$$

• To determine the line's y-intercept, we would normally plug in the coordinates of either $(0, 0)$ or $(4, 3)$ to solve for b.

> ➤ In this case, however, the line runs through the origin, so we know that $b = 0$. The equation of the line is therefore $y = \frac{3}{4}x$.

• Because point (x, y) lies on the line, we can PLUG its coordinates into $y = \frac{3}{4}x$ to solve for y. According to the problem, $x = -2.4$. Thus, the correct answer is (B), since:

$$y = \frac{3}{4}(-2.4) \quad \rightarrow \quad y = \frac{3}{\cancel{4}}(-\cancel{2.4}) \quad \rightarrow \quad y = 3(-0.6) = -1.8$$

Chapter 6: Coordinate Geometry

(10) Strategy Overview – You've now studied the fundamental properties of Coordinate Geometry.

• Almost every Coordinate Geometry question that you see on the GRE will test your understanding of one (or more) of these concepts.

➤ Some questions, however, require more than technical "know how". From time to time, you need a bit of strategy, too.

• What strategy to choose generally depends on what sort of information you have.

• Problems involving triangles, rectangles, and circles on the xy-plane tend to boil down to the basic properties associated with those shapes. The same goes for problems involving shaded areas or unusual shapes.

➤ For example, the SHADED region below is defined by a LARGE triangle with a height and base of 2 and a SMALL triangle with a height of 1 and base of 2.

• To determine the area of the shaded region, therefore, we simply need to subtract the area of the small triangle from that of the large triangle.

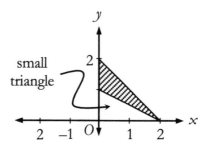

• The area of a triangle equals $\frac{1}{2}$(base × height), so the area of the large triangle equals $\frac{1}{2}(2 \times 2) = \frac{1}{2}(4) = 2$. Likewise, the area of the small triangle equals $\frac{1}{2}(2 \times 1) = \frac{1}{2}(2) = 1$. Thus, the shaded region has an area of 1, since 2 − 1 = 1.

➤ Questions involving points or lines generally come down to ordered pairs, distance, or working with $y = mx + b$.

• With such questions, if you're NOT SURE where to start, try to find TWO POINTS.

• As we saw in the last section, if you know the coordinates of two points, you can establish the equation of the line that runs between them.

➤ ESTABLISHING a line's EQUATION is almost always helpful because once you have an equation, you can PLUG in the COORDINATES of any point on that line.

- Take the question below:

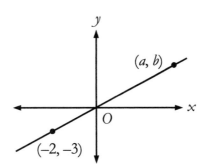

Quantity A

The ratio of b to a

Quantity B

$\frac{2}{3}$

- The line runs through points $(-2, -3)$ and $(0, 0)$, so we know that its slope equals $\frac{3}{2}$, since $\frac{y_2 - y_1}{x_2 - x_1} = \frac{0 - (-3)}{0 - (-2)} = \frac{3}{2}$.

➤ Likewise, we know that its y-intercept is 0, since it runs through the origin. The equation of the line is, therefore, $y = \frac{3}{2}x$.

- If we insert the coordinates of point (a, b) into this equation, we get:

$$y = \frac{3}{2}x \quad \rightarrow \quad b = \frac{3}{2}a$$

- The answer to this question is therefore (A), since dividing both sides of the equation by a proves that the ratio of b to a equals $\frac{3}{2}$:

$$b = \frac{3}{2}a \quad \rightarrow \quad \frac{b}{a} = \frac{3}{2}\frac{\cancel{a}}{\cancel{a}} \quad \rightarrow \quad \frac{b}{a} = \frac{3}{2}$$

➤ Finally, when solving problems WITHOUT diagrams, it never hurts to DRAW what you can.

- Like questions involving triangles, rectangles, and circles, questions involving Coordinate Geometry sometimes have VISUAL solutions.

- Sketching your own diagram can help you SEE RELATIONSHIPS that you might otherwise miss.

> ➤ This is particularly true for problems involving SPATIAL reasoning.

• Consider the following:

In the *xy*-plane, the point (1, 3) is on line *l*, and the point (3, 1) is on line *m*.
Each of the lines has a positive slope.

Quantity A

The slope of line *l*

Quantity B

The slope of line *m*

• If you suspect that you are working with INSUFFICIENT information, take a moment to imagine two scenarios that are as different as possible.

> ➤ Considering EXTREME possibilities can expose obvious solutions that technical approaches can miss.

• In the problem above, for example, we know that lines *l* and *m* are both positive. We also know one point of intersection for each. Given this information, however, we can envision several lines that meet such constraints:

Two Possible Slopes for Line *l*   Two Possible Slopes for Line *m*

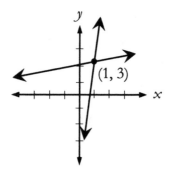
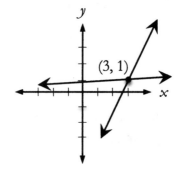

> ➤ As shown above, the slope of line *l* can be extremely steep or nearly flat. The same is true for the slope of line *m*.

• Since line *l* can have a slope that is greater or less than that of line *m*, the relationship between these quantities cannot be determined. The correct answer is therefore (D).

(11) Practice Drills – Solutions can be found on the pages that follow.

Points

1. Find the coordinates of each point in the diagram below:

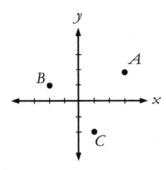

2. Plot the following ordered pairs in the xy-plane: (1, 3), (–3, 0), and (3, –2).

3. What is the distance between the points (–3, 2) and (5, –4)?

4. Find the midpoint between points (1, –5) and (5, 3).

Lines

5. Determine the slope, y-intercept, and x-intercept of the line $-2x + 4y = 12$.

6. What is the equation of the line graphed below?

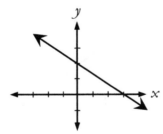

7. Graph the following equations on the xy-plane: $y = \frac{3}{2}x - 1$ and $y = -3$.

8. Are lines $y = \frac{3}{4}x - 2$ and $y = -\frac{4}{3}x + 1$ parallel, perpendicular, or neither?

9. What is the equation of the line that runs through the points (2, 3) and (4, 4)?

10. At what point do the lines $y = -4x + 2$ and $y = 2x - 4$ intersect?

11. Does the point (8, 7) lie on the line $y = \frac{3}{4}x + 1$?

Solutions

1. Points A, B, and C:

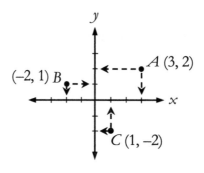

2. The ordered pairs $(1, 3)$, $(-3, 0)$, and $(3, -2)$:

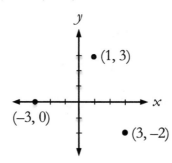

3. To determine the distance between two points, first SKETCH a RIGHT triangle. Then determine the lengths of the two legs. In the figure below, the vertical leg has a length of 6, since the y-coordinates shift from 2 to -4:

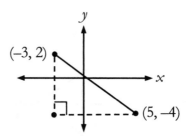

The horizontal leg has a length of 8, since the x-coordinates shift from -3 to 5. Thus, the distance between the points is 10, since the right triangle above is a 6–8–10 triangle.

4. To determine a midpoint, first AVERAGE the x-coordinates of the points. Then AVERAGE the y-coordinates. Thus, $(1, -5)$ and $(5, 3)$ have a midpoint at $(3, -1)$, since:

The average of the x-coordinates $\qquad\qquad$ The average of the y-coordinates

$$\frac{1+5}{2}=\frac{6}{2}=3 \qquad\qquad \frac{(-5)+3}{2}=\frac{-2}{2}=-1$$

5. To determine the slope and y-intercept of an equation, place it in the order $y = mx + b$. The m term will equal the slope and the b term will equal the y-intercept. Thus, this equation has a slope of $\frac{1}{2}$ and a y-intercept of 3, since:

$$4y = 2x + 12 \qquad \text{Add } 2x \text{ to both sides.}$$
$$y = \frac{1}{2}x + 3 \qquad \text{Divide both sides by 4.}$$

To determine the x-intercept of an equation, let $y = 0$ and solve for x. This line intercepts the x-axis at $x = -6$, since:

$$-2x + 4(0) = 12 \qquad \text{Let } y = 0.$$
$$x = -6 \qquad \text{Divide both sides by } -2.$$

6. This line intercepts the y-axis at 2, so its y-intercept is 2. It also intercepts the x-axis at 3. Between the points $(0, 2)$ and $(3, 0)$, the line FALLS two spaces and RUNS three spaces. Thus, its slope is $-\frac{2}{3}$:

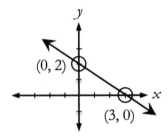

The equation of the line, therefore, is $y = -\frac{2}{3}x + 2$.

7. To graph an equation, first plot the y-intercept. Then use the slope to plot a second point. Finally, connect the two points with a straight line. The line $y = \frac{3}{2}x - 1$ has a y-intercept at -1 and "rises" 3 spaces for every 2 spaces that it "runs". Thus, we can graph it as follows:

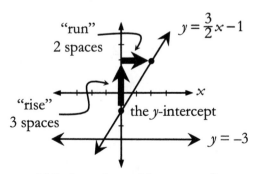

The equation $y = -3$ represents ALL the points with a y-coordinate of -3, so it forms the horizontal line at the bottom of the figure above.

8. The slopes of parallel lines are identical, and the slopes of perpendicular lines multiply to -1. $y = -\frac{4}{3}x + 1$ and $y = \frac{3}{4}x - 2$ are perpendicular, since the product of their slopes is -1:

$$-\frac{4}{3} \times \frac{3}{4} = -\frac{12}{12} = -1$$

9. To determine the equation of the line that runs through the points (2, 3) and (4, 4), first find the slope. Since slope $= \frac{y_2 - y_1}{x_2 - x_1}$, the slope of this line equals $\frac{1}{2}$:

$$\frac{y_2 - y_1}{x_2 - x_1} = \frac{4 - 3}{4 - 2} = \frac{1}{2}$$

Next, insert the slope into $y = mx + b$:

$$y = mx + b \;\rightarrow\; y = \frac{1}{2}x + b$$

Finally, determine the line's y-intercept, by inserting the coordinates of either (2, 3) or (4, 4) to solve for b. To keep the arithmetic as simple as possible, we've used (2, 3):

$$y = \frac{1}{2}x + b \;\rightarrow\; 3 = \frac{1}{2}(2) + b \;\rightarrow\; 3 = 1 + b \;\rightarrow\; b = 2$$

Thus, the equation of this line is $y = \frac{1}{2}x + 2$, since its slope $= \frac{1}{2}$ and its y-intercept $= 2$.

10. To determine the point at which two lines intersect, combine the equations to solve for the variables. Here, let's first set the equations equal:

$-4x + 2 = 2x - 4$	Set the equations equal to one another.
$6 = 6x$	Add $4x$ to both sides. Add 4 to both sides.
$x = 1$	Divide both sides by 6.

Next, let's plug $x = 1$ into either of the equations to solve for y:

$y = 2(1) - 4$	Plug $x = 1$ into $y = 2x - 4$
$y = -2$	Subtract.

Since $x = 1$ and $y = 2$, these lines cross at (1, –2).

11. To determine whether a point lies on a line, plug the point into the line.. If you get a true statement, the point lies on the line. Plugging (8, 7) into $y = \frac{3}{4}x + 1$ yields:

$7 = \frac{3}{4}(8) + 1$	Let $x = 8$ and $y = 7$.
$7 = 6 + 1$	$\frac{3}{\cancel{4}}(\cancel{8}) = 3(2) = 6$.

Thus, (8, 7) lies on $y = \frac{3}{4}x + 1$, since $7 = 6 + 1$ is a true statement.

Rare or Advanced Concepts

---

(12) Graphing Inequalities – If you can graph an equation, you know most of what you need to know to graph an inequality.

• Take the inequality $y \leq \frac{3}{2}x - 2$. We know that it has a slope of $\frac{3}{2}$ and a y-intercept of -2.

  ➤ We also know that every point (x, y) that satisfies it lies either AT or BELOW the line $y = \frac{3}{2}x - 2$, since y is either EQUAL to or LESS than $\frac{3}{2}x - 2$.

• Thus, the graph of $y \leq \frac{3}{2}x - 2$ consists of the line $y = \frac{3}{2}x - 2$ and the ENTIRE region BELOW it:

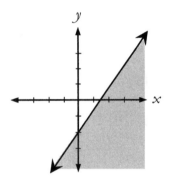

The graph of $y \leq \frac{3}{2}x - 2$

  ➤ Likewise, every point that satisfies the inequality $y > \frac{1}{2}x + 3$ is ABOVE the line $y = \frac{1}{2}x + 3$, since y is GREATER than $\frac{1}{2}x + 3$.

• The graph of $y > \frac{1}{2}x + 3$, therefore, consists of the region ABOVE $y = \frac{1}{2}x + 3$. The dotted line indicates that points on the line $y = \frac{1}{2}x + 3$ are NOT among the solutions:

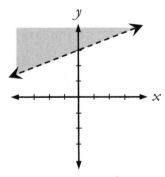

The graph of $y > \frac{1}{2}x + 3$

➤ To give you a sense of how the GRE might test your ability to graph inequalities, let's work through a practice problem together.

• Consider the following:

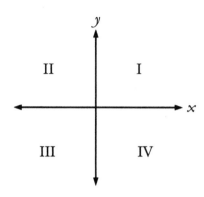

In the *xy*-coordinate system shown above, which of the following quadrants contain at least one solution to the inequality −5*x* + 3*y* < −6?

Indicate all such quadrants.

$\boxed{\text{A}}$ **I** $\boxed{\text{B}}$ **II** $\boxed{\text{C}}$ **III** $\boxed{\text{D}}$ **IV**

Answer: A, C, and D. According to the problem, −5*x* + 3*y* < −6. This inequality has a slope of $\frac{5}{3}$ and a *y*-intercept of −2, since:

$$3y < 5x - 6 \qquad \text{Add } 5x \text{ to both sides.}$$
$$y < \frac{5}{3}x - 2 \qquad \text{Divide both sides by 3.}$$

Further, *y* is LESS than $\frac{5}{3}x - 2$, so every point that satisfies the inequality lies BELOW the line $y = \frac{5}{3}x - 2$:

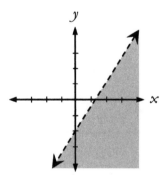

Because the shaded region of an inequality represents the set of all its solutions, the correct answer is A, C, and D, since only quadrant II lacks a point inside the shaded region.

(13) Reflections – In Coordinate Geometry, the term REFLECTION refers to the "mirror image" of a point or line across some line.

• That line is commonly known as the LINE of SYMMETRY.

> ➤ To understand the properties of reflection, consider the diagram below. Notice that points A and B are SYMMETRIC about the y-axis.

• Further, notice that point A is in the form (x, y), while point B is in the form $(-x, y)$:

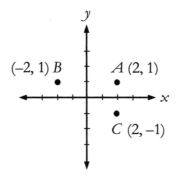

> ➤ Therefore, to reflect a line about the y-axis, you simply need to CHANGE the SIGN of its x-term.

• Thus, in the diagram below, lines $y = \frac{7}{3}x + 1$ and $y = -\frac{7}{3}x + 1$ are reflections about the y-axis, since their x-terms have OPPOSITE signs:

Reflection about the y-axis

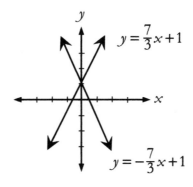

> ➤ Similarly, in the diagram at top, points A and C are symmetric about the x-axis. Point A is in the form (x, y), while point C is in the form $(x, -y)$.

• Therefore, to reflect a line about the x-axis, you simply need to CHANGE the SIGN of its y-term.

➤ In the diagram below, lines $y = \frac{2}{3}x + 1$ and $y = -\frac{2}{3}x - 1$ are reflections about the x-axis.

Reflection about the x-axis

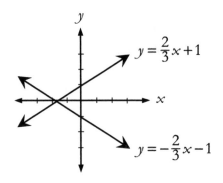

• By changing the sign of its y-term, $y = \frac{2}{3}x + 1$ becomes $-y = \frac{2}{3}x + 1$. This in turn becomes $y = -\frac{2}{3}x - 1$ when both sides of the equation are multiplied by –1:

$$-y = \frac{2}{3}x + 1 \quad \rightarrow \quad y = -(\frac{2}{3}x + 1) \quad \rightarrow \quad y = -\frac{2}{3}x - 1$$

➤ The GRE tests a FINAL sort of symmetry that occurs with respect to the line $y = x$.

• As we saw earlier, the line $y = x$ has a slope of 1 and passes through the origin. It also forms a 45° angle with both the x-axis and y-axis.

The graph of $y = x$

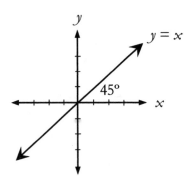

• Two lines are reflected about the line $y = x$ if their coordinates are REVERSED.

➤ For example, the points (4, 3) and (3, 4) REFLECT one another about $y = x$, as do the points (1, 5) and (5, 1).

• Therefore, to reflect a line about $y = x$, you simply need to INTERCHANGE the x- and y-terms. Below, lines $y = 2x + 1$ and $y = \frac{1}{2}x - \frac{1}{2}$ are reflections about the x-axis.

Reflection about $y = x$

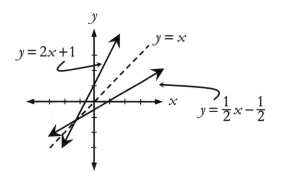

• By interchanging the x- and y-terms, $y = 2x + 1$ becomes $x = 2y + 1$. This in turn becomes $y = \frac{1}{2}x - \frac{1}{2}$ when you solve for y:

$$x = 2y + 1 \quad \rightarrow \quad x - 1 = 2y \quad \rightarrow \quad y = \frac{1}{2}x - \frac{1}{2}$$

➤ Questions about reflection are quite rare for the GRE. To get a sense of how you can be tested, consider the following:

If the line $y = 3x + 6$ is reflected about the line $y = x$, the x-intercept of the reflection equals

(A) 3 (B) 4 (C) 6 (D) 8 (E) 9

Answer. C. Two lines are reflected about the line $y = x$ if their coordinates are reversed. Thus, we can find the equation of a line reflected about $y = x$ by reversing its x and y terms.

Here, $y = 3x + 6$. If we switch the x and y terms, we get $x = 3y + 6$. In $y = mx + b$ form, this equation equals $y = \frac{1}{3}x - 2$, since:

$$x = 3y + 6 \quad \rightarrow \quad 3y = x - 6 \quad \rightarrow \quad y = \frac{1}{3}x - 2$$

To find the x-intercept of any equation, simply let $y = 0$ and solve for x. The x-intercept of the reflection is therefore 6, since:

$$0 = \frac{1}{3}x - 2 \quad \rightarrow \quad 2 = \frac{1}{3}x \quad \rightarrow \quad x = 6$$

Chapter 6: Coordinate Geometry

(14) Graphing Circles – Like points and lines, circles can be graphed on the *xy*-plane.

• The equation for doing so is $(x - a)^2 + (y - b)^2 = r^2$, where (a, b) is the center of the circle and *r* is the radius.

> ➤ Thus, the equation $(x - 3)^2 + (y - 4)^2 = 4$ represents a circle with a center at (3, 4) and a radius of 2.

• Likewise, the equation $x^2 + y^2 = 9$ represents a circle with a center at the origin and a radius of 3:

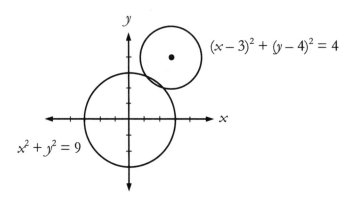

> ➤ Questions involving circles and the *xy*-plane are relatively rare for the GRE, particularly ones that make use of the equation above.

• Further, questions that involve the equation tend to be relatively easy—as long as you know the formula. Here's a typical example:

Which of the following equations represents circle with a center at (6, –2) and a radius of 3?

Select all such circles.

A $(x - 6)^2 + (y + 2)^2 = 9$ **B** $(x - 2)^2 + (y + 3)^2 = 6$ **C** $(x + 6)^2 + (y - 2)^2 = 3$

Answer. A. As discussed above, the equation for a circle is $(x - a)^2 + (y - b)^2 = r^2$, where (a, b) is the center of the circle and *r* is the radius.

Thus, if a circle has a center at (6, –2) and a radius of 3, the left half of its equation would be $(x - 6)^2 + (y - (-2))^2$, or $(x - 6) + (y + 2)^2$, and the right half of its equation would be $3^2 = 9$.

Of the equations above, only (A) has a left side that equals $(x - 6) + (y + 2)^2$ and a right side that equals 9. Therefore, the correct answer is (A) only.

Sherpa
Prep

➤ Just be careful not to assume that every Coordinate Geometry problem involving circles requires the equation for a circle.

• Most questions that combine circles and the *xy*-plane actually boil down to the DISTANCE between two points, as in the problem below:

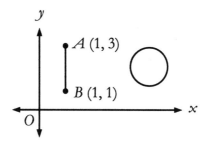

The circle above has a radius 2 and center (6, 2).

What is the greatest possible distance between a point on line segment *AB* and a point on the circle?

(A) 5   (B) 4√3   (C) 7   (D) 5√2   (E) 9

Answer. D. As shown below, the greatest possible distance between a point on line segment *AB* and a point on the circle is the distance between points *B* and *C* (or points *A* and *C*):

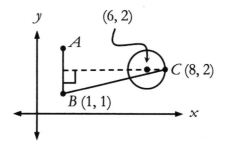

According to the problem, the circle has a radius of 2 and a center at (6, 2). Thus, point *C* lies 2 spaces to the right of the center, at point (8, 2).

To calculate the distance between points (1, 1) and (8, 2), we can sketch the right triangle shown above. Point *C* is 1 space **above** point *B* and 7 spaces to the **right**, so the triangle has legs of lengths 1 and 7. The triangle's hypotenuse, therefore, has a length of $5\sqrt{2}$, since:

$$1^2 + 7^2 = c^2 \quad \rightarrow \quad c^2 = 50 \quad \rightarrow \quad c = \sqrt{50} = \sqrt{5 \times 5 \times 2} = 5\sqrt{2}$$

Thus, the correct answer is (D), since line segment *BC* is the hypotenuse of the triangle.

(15) Functions & Parabolas – Every now and then, Coordinate Geometry questions involve functions.

• As you may recall from our book on <u>Number Properties & Algebra</u>, a function is a formula for which every "input" has a single "output".

➤ For example, the function $f(x) = 3x$ is a way of saying "every input x produces an output that is 3 times as large."

• Thus, an input such as $x = 4$ produces an output $f(x) = 12$, since $f(4) = 3(4) = 12$. Likewise, an input such as $x = -2$, produces an output $f(x) = -6$, since $f(-2) = 3(-2) = -6$.

• In Coordinate Geometry, the input and output of a function can be graphed as a point, where $x =$ the input and $y =$ the output $f(x)$.

➤ If one plots enough of these points, they form a LINE. Take the function $f(x) = |x|$.

• If you were to input the following values into the function, you would get the following outputs:

x	$f(x)$
−3	3
−2	2
−1	1
0	0
1	1
2	2
3	3

This pair represents the point (1, 1)

• Since each of these "input, output" pairs represents a point (x, y), where $y = f(x)$, the graph of $f(x) = |x|$ therefore looks like this:

The graph of $f(x) = |x|$

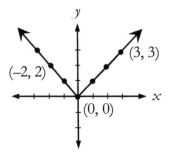

➢ Thus, EVERY function can be graphed by creating an "input, output" TABLE like the one on the previous page and then plotting the points.

• In many instances, however, it's faster to remember that for any function, $y = f(x)$.

• Because $y = f(x)$, a function such as $f(x) = \frac{5}{3}x - 2$ can be thought of as $y = \frac{5}{3}x - 2$, and thus having a slope of $\frac{5}{3}$ and a y-intercept of –2. Likewise, a function such as $g(x) = \frac{2}{3}x + 1$ can be thought of as $y = \frac{2}{3}x + 1$, and thus having a slope of $\frac{2}{3}$ and a y-intercept of 1.

➢ The functions $f(x) = \frac{5}{3}x - 2$ and $g(x) = \frac{2}{3}x + 1$ can therefore be graphed as follows:

The graph of $f(x) = \frac{5}{3}x - 2$ The graph of $g(x) = \frac{2}{3}x + 1$

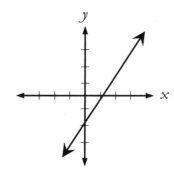
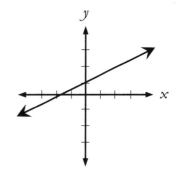

➢ In general, working with functions on the xy-plane is only tricky when QUADRATIC equations are involved.

• The graph of an equation in the form $y = ax^2 \pm bx \pm c$ produces a curved line known as a PARABOLA.

A vertical parabola with a y-intercept of –2

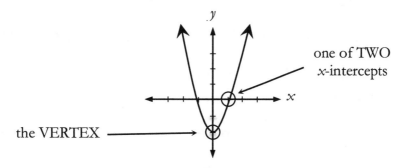

one of TWO
x-intercepts

the VERTEX

• Parabolas are symmetric about the line that passes through their vertex, and their x-intercepts are equidistant from this line, commonly known as the LINE of SYMMETRY.

➤ There are a couple of ways to GRAPH parabolas. The most exact way is to create an "input, output" table and to plot the points.

• For example, if we were to input the following values into the parabola $f(x) = x^2 - 1$ (in this function, the "bx term" = 0), we would get the following outputs:

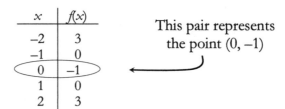

x	$f(x)$
–2	3
–1	0
0	–1
1	0
2	3

This pair represents the point (0, –1)

• Since each of these "input, output" pairs represents a point (x, y), the graph of $f(x) = x^2 - 1$ therefore looks like this:

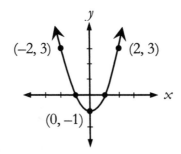

➤ Alternatively, if you just need a "rough idea" of what a parabola looks like, you can use the equation $y = ax^2 \pm bx \pm c$ to make some quick deductions.

• The "a term" determines whether the parabola opens up or down:

  $a > 0$, the parabola opens UP $a < 0$, the parabola opens DOWN

• Moreover, the further a is from 0, the steeper the parabola gets. The "c term" is the y-intercept, and the "b term", if there is one, shifts a parabola to the left or right of the y-axis. **If _a_ is positive**, the shifts work like this:

  $b > 0$, the parabola shifts LEFT $b < 0$, the parabola shifts RIGHT

➤ Thus, the function $f(x) = 3x^2 - 2x + 1$ would be steep ($a = 3$), open up ($a > 0$), and have a y-intercept of 1 ($c = 1$).

• It would also shift to the right of the y-axis ($b = -2$), since _a_ is positive and $b < 0$.

• Conversely, the function $f(x) = -x^2 + 3x - 2$ would be flat ($a = -1$), open down ($a < 0$), and have a y-intercept of –2 ($c = -2$). Although $b > 0$, this parabola would shift to the right of the y-axis ($b = 3$), since **the shifts above work in the opposite direction when _a_ is negative**.

➢ For any parabola, the x-INTERCEPTS are the SOLUTIONS to the equation $y = ax^2 + bx + c$.

• To find them, simply let $y = 0$ and solve for x, as you would for an equation in the form $y = mx + b$.

• For example, the equation $y = x^2 - 2x - 3$ has x-intercepts at $x = -1$ and $x = 3$, since:

$$x^2 - 2x - 3 = 0 \qquad \text{Let } y = 0.$$
$$(x + 1)(x - 3) = 0 \qquad \text{Factor the quadratic. } 1, -3 \text{ multiply to } -3 \text{ but add to } -2.$$
$$x = -1, 3 \qquad \text{Set each factor to 0 and solve for } x.$$

➢ Finding the x-intercepts of a parabola is often helpful, particularly if you need to determine the coordinates of its VERTEX.

• As we saw earlier, a parabola is symmetrical about the line that runs through its vertex, and its x-intercepts are equidistant from this line.

Graph of $y = x^2 - 2x - 3$

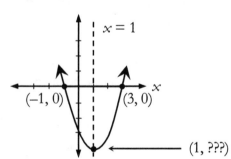

➢ Thus, an equation such as $y = x^2 - 2x - 3$ (shown above), has a line of symmetry at $x = 1$, since $x = 1$ is equidistant from the x-intercepts at $x = -1$ and $x = 3$.

• Likewise, the vertex of this equation also has an x-coordinate of 1, since the line of symmetry runs through the vertex.

• The y-coordinate of a vertex, therefore, can be determined by inserting its x-coordinate into the parabola. Here, the vertex lies at (1, –4), since plugging $x = 1$ into $y = x^2 - 2x - 3$ produces $y = -4$:

$$y = (1)^2 - 2(1) - 3 \qquad \text{Plug } x = 1 \text{ into } y = x^2 - 2x - 3.$$
$$y = -4 \qquad 1 - 2 - 3 = -4.$$

➤ On a final note, let's be sure that you can properly INTERPRET the graph of a function.

- On the GRE, you may encounter questions like the following:

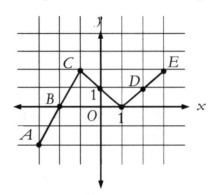

The figure above shows the graph of function _f_ in the _xy_-plane.

<u>**Quantity A**</u>   <u>**Quantity B**</u>

_f_(–1) + _f_(2)   _f_(_f_(3))

- To solve such questions, recall that the input and output of a function can be graphed as a point (x, y), where x = the input and y = the output $f(x)$.

➤ Thus, to find the OUTPUT of _f_(–1), we need to find a point on function _F_ with an _x_-coordinate of –1, since _f_(–1) has an INPUT of –1.

- In the figure above, point _C_ has an _x_-coordinate of –1. Therefore, the output of _f_(–1) is 2, since point _C_ lies at (–1, 2), which has a _y_-coordinate of 2.

- Likewise, to find the output of _f_(2), we need to find the point on function _F_ with an _x_-coordinate of 2. Because point _D_ lies at (2, 1), the output of _f_(2) is 1.

➤ Determining the output of _f_(_f_(3)) is a bit trickier, since we must apply the function twice: first to find the "inner" output of _f_(3) and then the "outer" output of _f_(_f_(3)).

- _f_(3) has an input of 3. The point on function _F_ with an _x_-coordinate of 3 is point _E_. Thus, the output of _f_(3) is 2, since point _E_ lies at (3, 2).

- Finally, to find the output of _f_(_f_(3)), we must REWRITE _f_(_f_(3)) as _f_(2) by plugging _f_(3) = 2 into the inside function. Thus, the output of _f_(_f_(3)) → _f_(2) is 1, since the point on function _f_ with an _x_-coordinate of 2 is point _D_, which lies at (2, 1). The correct answer is therefore (A), since _f_(–1) + _f_(2) = 2 + 1 = 3 and _f_(_f_(3)) = _f_(2) = 1.

(16) Problem Sets – The following questions have been arranged into three groups: fundamental, intermediate, and rare or advanced.

• Whether you're aiming for a perfect score or a score closer to average, mastery of the concepts in the FUNDAMENTAL questions is absolutely essential.

➤ As you might expect, the INTERMEDIATE questions are more difficult but are essential for test-takers who need an above-average score or higher.

• Finally, the RARE or ADVANCED questions test concepts that are very sophisticated or seldom encountered on the GRE.

• Mastery of such questions is required only if you need a math score above the 90th percentile.

➤ As always, if you find yourself confused, bogged down with busy work, or stuck, don't be afraid to fall back on your "Plan B" strategies!

Fundamental

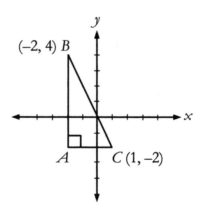

1. In the figure above, if AC and AB are parallel to the x and y axes, respectively, what is the area of triangle ABC?

    (A) 4   (B) 6   (C) 9   (D) 10.5   (E) 12

    Line L has the equation $-4x + 2y = 8$.

Quantity A	Quantity B
2. The x–intercept of line L	The y–intercept of line L

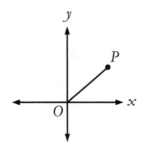

P is a point in the rectangular coordinate system and $OP = 4$.

Quantity A	Quantity B

3. The *x*-coordinate of point *P*   4

4. If line *l* has the slope $\frac{2}{5}$ and intersects the *x*–axis at $(-15, 0)$, where does line *l* intersect the *y*–axis?

(A) -3 (B) -2 (C) 3   (D) 6   (E) 12

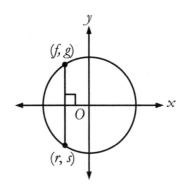

Point *O* is the center of the circle.

Quantity A	Quantity B

5. $f + g$ $r + s$

6. Line *g* in the *xy*–coordinate plane has the equation $y = mx + b$, where *m* and *b* are constants. What is the slope of line *g*, if *g* is parallel to the line $y = (2 - 3m)x + b + 4$?

(A) $-\frac{3}{2}$ (B) $-\frac{2}{3}$ (C) $\frac{1}{2}$ (D) $\frac{2}{3}$ (E) $\frac{3}{2}$

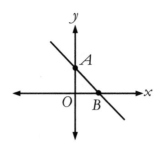

The equation of the line graphed above on the rectangular coordinate system is:

$$y = -\frac{5x}{6} + 2$$

Quantity A	Quantity B

7. The y-coordinate of point A The x-coordinate of point B

In the rectangular coordinate plane, points A, B, and C have coordinates (1, 4), (6, 9), and (6, 4), respectively.

Quantity A	Quantity B

8. AB BC

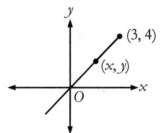

9. In the diagram drawn above, if $x = 2.4$, what is the value of y?

(A) 2.5   (B) 2.6   (C) 2.7   (D) 3.0   (E) 3.2

10. In the xy–plane, line p is perpendicular to the x–axis and passes through the point (–2, 5). Which of the following is the equation of line p?

(A) $y = 0$ (B) $y = 5$ (C) $x = -2$ (D) $y - 2 = x + 5$ (E) $y + 2 = x - 5$

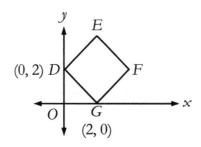

In the rectangular coordinate system above, *DEFG* is a square.

Quantity A	Quantity B

11.   The perimeter of *DEFG*   8

Triangle *ABC* lies in the *xy*-plane and points *A* and *C* have (x, y) coordinates $(0, 0)$ and $(4, 0)$, respectively. The area of triangle *ABC* is 12.

Quantity A	Quantity B

12.   The *x*-coordinate of *B*   The *y*-coordinate of *B*

13.   The graphs of $y = -3x + 4$ and $y = x^2$ intersect at which of the following points in the *xy*-plane?

Indicate all such points.

A (–4, 16)   B (–2, 0)   C (0, 9)   D (1, 1)   E (9, 16)

Intermediate

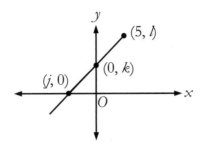

14.   In the *xy*–coordinate system above, if *j* has a value of –10 and *k* has a value of 8, what is the value of *l*?

15.   If *a* ≠ *b* and the slope of the line passing through points (–*a*, *a*) and (3*a*, *b*) is 2, what is the value of *a* in terms of *b*?

(A) $\frac{b}{9}$ (B) $\frac{b}{6}$ (C) $\frac{b}{3}$ (D) $\frac{2b}{3}$ (E) $\frac{3b}{2}$

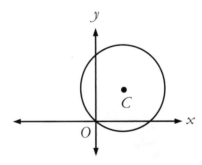

16.   If the circle above has center *C* at (4, 4), its area equals

(A) 8π   (B) 16π   (C) 24π   (D) 32π   (E) 36π

17.   In the *xy*–coordinate system, line *M* passes through the origin and point *F*. If point *F* is the midpoint of points *A* (2, 3) and *B* (6, 7), what is the slope of line *M*?

Enter you answer as a decimal.

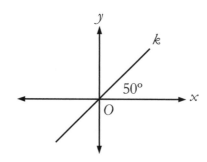

Point p (not shown) has rectangular coordinates (a, b) and lies
above line k.

	Quantity A	Quantity B

18. a b

19. In the xy–coordinate system, if (f, g) and $(f + 2, g + w)$ are two points on the line defined by the equation $x = 2y - 5$, what is the value of w?

        (A) 0 (B) 1 (C) 2 (D) 3 (E) 4

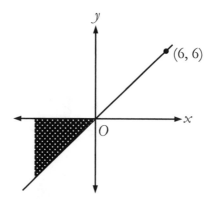

20.   Which of the following ordered pairs could represent a point in the shaded region of the graph shown above?

      (A) $(2, -4)$ (B) $(-2, -4)$ (C) $(-2, 4)$ (D) $(-4, 2)$ (E) $(-4, -4)$

21. What value of x will make the line containing points $(x, 9)$ and $(-3, 3)$ perpendicular to the line containing points $(6, x)$ and $(3, 0)$?

      (A) -9 (B) -6 (C) -3 (D) -2 (E) -1

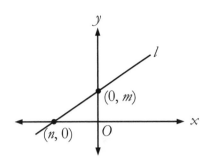

The line *l* is graphed on the rectangular coordinate axes.

Quantity A	Quantity B

22. n $\dfrac{-m}{n}$

23. In the xy–plane, line M passes through the origin and is perpendicular to the line $4x + y = k$, where k is a constant. If the two lines intersect at the point $(s, s + 1)$, what is the value of s?

Round your answer to the nearest <u>tenth</u>.

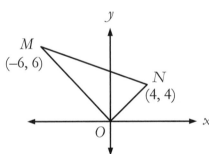

24. In the figure above, what is the perimeter of triangle *MNO*?

(A) $6+4\sqrt{2}$ (B) $12+8\sqrt{2}$ (C) $10+4\sqrt{5}$ (D) $10+10\sqrt{2}$ (E) $10\sqrt{2}+2\sqrt{26}$

Rare or Advanced

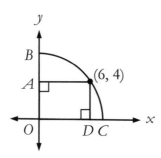

BC is the arc of a circle that has center O.

Quantity A	Quantity B

25. $AB - DC$ 2

26. Rectangle *WXYZ* lies in the *xy*–coordinate system so that its sides are NOT parallel to the axes. What is the product of the slopes of all four sides of rectangle *WXYZ*?

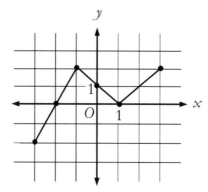

27. The figure above shows the graph of the function *f* in the *xy*–plane. What is the value of $f(f(-2))$?

         (A) –2   (B) –1   (C) 0   (D) 1   (E) 2

28. Which of the following is the graph of the equation $y = -x^2 + 2$ for all real values x? (<u>Note</u>: All graphs drawn to scale.)

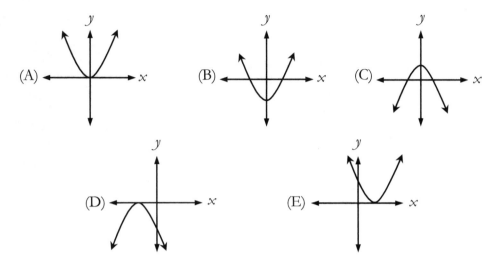

29. In the xy-plane, line l passes through the points (a, b) and (p, q), where $(a - p)(b - q) < 0$. If line l does <u>not</u> pass through the origin, which of the following could be the slope?

Indicate <u>all</u> such values.

$\boxed{A}$ −3 $\boxed{B}$ −1 $\boxed{C}$ 0 $\boxed{D}$ $\frac{2}{3}$ $\boxed{E}$ 2

30. In the xy–system, if a circle with center $(6, 0)$ is tangent to the line $y = x$, what is the area of the circle?

(A) 12π (B) 15π (C) 16π (D) 18π (E) 21π

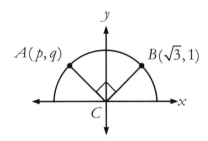

In the figure above, points $A (p, q)$ and $B (\sqrt{3}, 1)$ lie on the semicircle with center C.

Quantity A   Quantity B

31. p $-q$

32. If $y = \frac{1}{2}x - 3$ is reflected about the line $y = x$, which of the following statements are true about the reflection?

Select <u>all</u> such statements.

A The product of the slope and the y-intercept is positive.

B The x-intercept is 3.

C Any line to which the reflection is perpendicular has a slope of $-\frac{1}{2}$.

33. The vertex of $f(x) = x^2 + 4x - 5$ lies at the center of circle C. If circle C intersects point P $(1, -5)$, area of the circle equals

(A) π (B) 4π (C) 9π (D) 16π (E) 25π

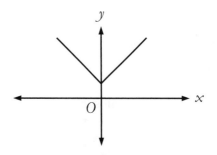

34. Function f, defined by $f(x) = |2x| + 1$ for all numbers x, is graphed above. For which of the following functions h defined for all numbers x does the graph of h intersect the graph of f?

Select <u>all</u> such functions.

A $h(x) = x + 3$ B $h(x) = 2x - 1$ C $h(x) = 3x + 1$ D $h(x) = 4x - 2$

35. In the xy–plane, the graph of $y = (x + c)(x + d)$ intersects the x-axis. If $c + d = 5$ and the graph intersects the y-axis at $(0, 6)$, which of the following could be the coordinates of a point of intersection?

(A) $(-6, 0)$ (B) $(-3, 0)$ (C) $(0, 5)$ (D) $(2, 3)$ (E) $(6, 0)$

(17) Solutions – Video solutions for each of the previous questions can be found on our website at **www.sherpaprep.com/masterkey**.

• BOOKMARK this address for future visits!

> ➤ To view the videos, you'll need to register your copy of <u>Master Key to the GRE</u>: <u>Geometry</u>.

• If you have yet to do so, please go to **www.sherpaprep.com/videos** and enter your email address.

• Be sure to provide the SAME email address that you used to purchase your copy of <u>Master Key to the GRE</u> or to enroll in your GRE course with Sherpa Prep!

> ➤ When checking your answers, we encourage you to watch the solution for any problem that you answered INCORRECTLY

• The same goes for any problem that took you MORE than TWO MINUTES to solve.

• After digesting the explanation, REVISIT your mistake a couple of days later to ensure that the problem no longer poses issues to you.

> ➤ If you struggle to solve the problem a SECOND time, add it to your "LOG of ERRORS" and redo it every few weeks.

• Solving tricky questions MORE THAN ONCE is the best way to learn from your mistakes and to avoid similar difficulties on your actual exam.

Fundamental		Intermediate	Rare or Advanced
1. C	12. D	14. 12	25. C
2. B	13. A, D	15. A	26. 1
3. B		16. D	27. D
4. D		17. 1.25	28. C
5. A		18. D	29. A, B
6. C		19. B	30. D
7. B		20. E	31. A
8. A		21. E	32. A, C
9. E		22. B	33. E
10. C		23. −1.3	34. A, C, D
11. A		24. E	35. B

Chapter 7

Summary

Summary

To be discussed:

Topic Review

- In the tables below, you'll find a summary of every Geometric concept tested by the GRE.

1	Lines & Angles
2	Triangles
3	Quadrilaterals & Rectangular Solids
4	Circles & Cylinders
5	Coordinate Geometry
6	Strategy Tips

- When surveying these tables, be sure to bear in mind that they are ONLY summaries. Used alone, they will not prepare you for the GRE.

  ➤ Rare or advanced concepts have been placed at the end of each section and are marked with an ASTERISK.

- These concepts are tested by the GRE very infrequently. If you don't need an exceptional math score, don't waste your time studying them!

Lines & Angles

1 The angle of ANY line is 180°.

2 OPPOSITE angles are EQUAL.

3 PERPENDICULAR lines meet at a 90° angle.

4 PARALLEL lines never touch.

5 A transversal cuts parallel lines into 4 "big" angles and 4 "small" angles.

6 In such cases, all "big" angles equal one another, as do all "small" angles.

7 BISECTORS cut angles and lines into two equal halves.

8 MIDPOINTS split a line segment into two equal halves.

9 The term POLYGON means "shape". A quadrilateral has 4 sides, a pentagon has 5 sides, a hexagon has 6 sides, and an octagon has 8 sides.

10 The sides of a REGULAR polygon have the same length, and the angles have the same measure.

11 The INTERIOR angles of any triangle add to 180°.

12 Those of any quadrilateral add to 360°.

13 For ANY polygon, the SUM of the interior angles equals $(n - 2)180°$, where $n =$ the number of sides of the polygon.

14 ALL polygons have one exterior angle for every interior angle.

15 The EXTERIOR angles of ANY polygon add to 360°.

16 An exterior angle of a TRIANGLE equals the SUM of the interior angles to which it is not adjacent.

Chapter 7: Summary

Triangles

1 The INTERIOR angles of a triangle add to 180°.

2 The EXTERIOR angles add to 360°.

3 ANY exterior angle equals the sum of the interior angles to which it is not adjacent.

4 An EQUILATERAL has 3 sides of equal length and 3 angles of 60°.

5 An ISOSCELES has 2 sides of equal length. The angles opposite the equal legs are also equal.

6 In any triangle, the largest leg is across from the largest angle. The smallest leg is across from the smallest angle.

7 A RIGHT triangle has one angle of 90°. The longest leg is called the hypotenuse.

8 The Pythagorean theorem ONLY applies to right triangles. It states $a^2 + b^2 = c^2$, where c = the hypotenuse.

9 There are four TRIPLES that you should memorize: 3–4–5, 5–12–13, 8–15–17, and 7–24–25. The last two are rare.

10 The sides of every 45°–45°–90° triangle have the RATIO $x : x : x\sqrt{2}$.

11 To get the leg lengths of a 45°–45°–90° whose hypotenuse LACKS a $\sqrt{2}$, cut the hypotenuse in half and multiply the result by $\sqrt{2}$.

12 The sides of every 30°–60°–90° triangle have the RATIO $x : x\sqrt{3} : 2x$.

13 For such triangles, the smallest leg is across from the 30° and the largest leg is across from the 90°.

14 Any RIGHT triangle in which the hypotenuse is twice as long as a leg is a 30°–60°–90°.

15 All equilaterals are composed of two 30°–60°–90° triangles.

16 The AREA of a triangle equals $\frac{1}{2}(\text{base} \times \text{height})$.

17 The height and the base are always PERPENDICULAR to one another.

18 An ALTITUDE extends from a vertex and intersects the opposing side at 90°.

19 For ALL triangles, each side must be LESS than the SUM of the other sides, but GREATER than the difference.

20 *SIMILAR triangles have identical angles and proportional side lengths.

21 *Two triangles are similar if (1) two angles are identical, (2) all three legs are proportional, or (3) two legs are proportional and the angle between them is identical.

22 *If a RIGHT triangle is composed of two SMALLER right triangles, all three are similar.

23 *A triangle is a RIGHT triangle if $c^2 = a^2 + b^2$, ACUTE if $c^2 < a^2 + b^2$, and OBTUSE if $c^2 > a^2 + b^2$.

24 *The Pythagorean theorem can be factored as the DIFFERENCE between SQUARES: $b^2 = c^2 - a^2$.

25 *REGULAR hexagons are composed of 6 identical triangles. Regular octagons are composed of 8 identical triangles.

Sherpa Prep

Quadrilaterals & Rectangular Solids

1 The INTERIOR angles of a quadrilateral add to 360°, as do the EXTERIOR angles.

2 A quadrilateral in which BOTH pairs of opposite sides are parallel is called a parallelogram.

3 In all parallelograms, opposite sides have the same length and opposite angles are equal.

4 Any two adjacent angles add to 180°.

5 The diagonals of a parallelogram BISECT one another and split the parallelogram into two equal triangles.

6 For all parallelograms, the AREA equals base × height and the PERIMETER equals the sum of the 4 sides.

7 As with triangles, the base and height of a parallelogram are always perpendicular.

8 Squares and rectangles are SPECIAL parallelograms. Both have four angles of 90°, while a square has 4 equal sides.

9 Since rectangles and squares are symmetrical, both have diagonals that bisect one another into 4 equal parts.

10 The diagonals of a square (when crossed) split a square into four 45°–45°–90° triangles.

11 A quadrilateral that has ONE pair of parallel sides is called a TRAPEZOID.

12 For all trapezoids, the AREA = the AVERAGE of the bases × the height.

13 In some cases, you have to SPLIT a trapezoid into a rectangle and one or more triangles to determine its area.

14 The area of a SHADED region = BIG area − SMALL area.

15 A RECTANGULAR SOLID is a three-dimensional rectangle. A CUBE is a three-dimensional square.

16 For a rectangular solid, VOLUME equals length × width × height. SURFACE AREA equals the SUM of the area of the 6 faces.

17 For a cube, VOLUME equals s^3, where s = side length, and SURFACE AREA equals the SUM of the area of the 6 faces.

18 The length of a DIAGONAL for any rectangular solid $= \sqrt{l^2 + w^2 + h^2}$. For a cube, the length of a diagonal $= s\sqrt{3}$.

19 *When working with volume, make sure you know the SPECIFIC dimensions of the shape. Otherwise, you can fall for the VOLUME TRAP.

20 *A RHOMBUS is a slanted square. Its diagonals are PERPENDICULAR to one another, and its AREA equals HALF the product of its diagonals.

21 *As a parallelogram becomes more SQUARE-like, its area increases, while its perimeter decreases.

22 *Given the area and perimeter of a rectangle, it's MUCH easier to "guess" the dimensions (i.e. the "guess trick") than to solve for them algebraically.

Chapter 7: Summary

Circles & Cylinders

1 The distance from any point on a circle to its center is known as the RADIUS.

2 A DIAMETER runs through the center of a circle and connects two points on the circle that lie directly across from one another.

3 For any circle, the diameter is TWICE the length of the radius.

4 The CIRCUMFERENCE of a circle equals $2\pi r$ (or πd), where $\pi \approx 3.14$ or 22/7.

5 The AREA of a circle = πr^2.

6 An ARC is a fraction of a circle's circumference. A SECTOR is a fraction of a circle's area.

7 The CENTRAL ANGLE of an arc or sector tells you what fraction of the circle an arc or sector represents.

8 Alternatively: $ARC = 2\pi r \cdot \frac{x}{360°}$ and $SECTOR = \pi r^2 \cdot \frac{x}{360°}$, where x equals the central angle and 360° equals the degrees within a circle.

9 An INSCRIBED ANGLE lies on the circle and is HALF the measure of its central angle.

10 Inscribed angles with equal measures have arcs of equal length, and arcs of equal length have inscribed angles of equal measure.

11 A shape is INSCRIBCED within a circle if all of its vertices lie on the circle.

12 A shape is CIRCUMSCRIBED about a circle if each of its sides touch the circle at exactly one point.

13 The diagonal of a circumscribed rectangle always intersects the CENTER of the circle.

14 If one side of an inscribed triangle is a DIAMETER of the circle, the triangle is a RIGHT triangle.

15 A CHORD is a straight line drawn from one end of a circle to another.

16 Chords get LONGER as they get CLOSER to the center of a circle, and a radius that is PERPENDICULAR to a chord BISECTS the chord.

17 A TANGENT is a straight line that touches a circle at exactly one point.

18 A radius drawn to the point of tangency is PERPENDICULAR to the tangent.

19 The VOLUME of a cylinder equals $\pi r^2 h$, where h is the height.

20 The SURFACE AREA of a cylinder equals $2(\pi r^2) + 2\pi r h$. $2(\pi r^2)$ represents the circles that comprise the top and bottom of a cylinder, and $2\pi r h$ represents the rectangular wrap that connects the circles.

21 When working with circles, always FIND the CENTER of the circle before assuming that something is a radius or a diameter and LABEL every RADIUS that's been drawn.

Coordinate Geometry

1 The *xy*-plane is composed of a vertical number line (the *y*-AXIS) and a horizontal number line (*x*-AXIS).

2 The point where the two axes meet is known as the ORIGIN.

3 Every point on the *xy*-plane can be represented by an ORDERED PAIR (*a*, *b*), where *a* = the *x*-coordinate of the point and *b* = the *y*-coordinate.

4 To get the distance between two points, sketch a RIGHT triangle in which the hypotenuse represents the distance. Then use the Pythagorean theorem.

5 To find the MIDPOINT between two points, first average the *x*-coordinates. Then average the *y*-coordinates.

6 The SLOPE of a line measures how steep it is. A line with a positive slope rises, and a line with a negative slope falls.

7 Given two points (x_1, y_1) and (x_2, y_2), the slope of the line that connects them can be determined with the SLOPE formula:

$$\text{slope} = \frac{y_2 - y_1}{x_2 - x_1}$$

8 This formula is also known as "RISE" over "RUN", where "RISE" = vertical change and "RUN" = horizontal change.

9 To express an equation as a line, arrange it in the form $y = mx + b$. In this order, m = the slope and b = the *y*-intercept.

10 To GRAPH an equation, plot two points using the *y*-intercept and slope. Then connect the points with a straight line.

11 To find the *x*-INTERCEPT of a line, let $y = 0$ and solve for *x*.

12 HORIZONTAL lines have the form y = "number" and a slope of 0. VERTICAL lines have the form x = "number" and an undefined slope.

13 Lines are PARALLEL if their slopes are equal. Lines are PERPENDICULAR if the PRODUCT of the slopes equals –1.

14 To determine whether a point and a line INTERSECT, plug the point into the equation. A true statement proves that they do.

15 To find the point at which TWO lines intersect, combine the equations to solve for *x* and *y*. (*x*, *y*) will be the point of intersection.

16 To get the equation of a graphed line, find TWO points. Use the points to get the line's slope. Then plug <u>either</u> of the points into $y = mx + b$ to determine *b*.

Coordinate Geometry (Rare or Advanced)

17 *To graph an inequality, express it in the form $y = mx + b$. If $y > mx + b$, shade all points above the line. If $y < mx + b$, shade all points BELOW the line.

18 *Use a DOTTED line to represent the inequality if the line itself is NOT included among the solutions.

19 *A reflection is a mirror image across a line of symmetry. Points (x, y) and (y, x) are reflections about the line $y = x$. Thus, to reflect a line about $y = x$, switch its x and y terms.

20 *Likewise, points (x, y) and $(x, -y)$ are reflections about the x-axis. Thus, to reflect a line about the x-axis, make its y-term negative.

21 *The equation for a CIRCLE is $(x - a)^2 + (y - b)^2 = r^2$, where (a, b) is the center of the circle and r is the radius.

22 *To plot a FUNCTION on the xy-plane, let $f(x) = y$. For more complicated functions, create an "input, output" table and plot the points.

23 *An equation in the form $y = ax^2 \pm bx \pm c$ produces a PARABOLA. The "a term" is the slope, the "b-term" shifts the parabola left or right, and the "c term" is the y-intercept.

24 *If $a > 0$, the parabola opens upwards. If $a < 0$, the parabola opens downwards.

25 *If $b > 0$, the parabola shifts left, and if $b < 0$, the parabola shifts right — as long as a is positive. If a is negative, the shift occurs in the OPPOSITE direction.

26 *Parabolas are SYMMETRICAL, so the x-coordinate of a vertex lies between its x-intercepts. To find a vertex's y-coordinate, plug the x-coordinate into the parabola's equation.

27 *To INTERPRET the graph of a function, recall that x = the input of a function and y = the output. E.g., if $f(2) = 3$, the function has a point at $(2, 3)$, since the input 2 produces the output 3.

Strategy Tips

1   When solving Geometry problems, first DRAW what you can and then LABEL everything. Geometry is a visual subject. Adding new insights atop the original problem can help you SEE relationships that are easy to miss.

2   For problems involving LINES and ANGLES, look ACTIVELY for relationships that you know (e.g. do any angles form a line?).

3   For such problems, it can also be helpful to ignore some lines temporarily, since exam makers often disguise basic relationships with unnecessary lines.

4   The "$180° - x$" trick can come in handy with tricky problems involving interior angles.

5   When working with shapes WITHIN shapes, be sure to identify ALL the possible shapes.

6   Watch out for VISUAL TRAPS. Although many figures are roughly drawn to scale, some diagrams are intentionally misleading.

7   Picking numbers is a GREAT way to solve problems that lack concrete values. Choose numbers that are easy to work with and respect any constraints within the problem.

8   Geometry problems are often ASSWHOLES (i.e. they have variables in their answer choices.) Picking numbers is also a GREAT way to solve such problems. When picking for ASSWHOLES, avoid 0, 1, and 100, and choose numbers that are unique.

9   Geometry problems often involve SPATIAL reasoning. Considering scenarios that are as DIFFERENT as possible often exposes simple solutions for such problems.

10   On the GRE, UNUSUAL shapes or figures can always be SPLIT into simple shapes such as rectangles, triangles and semicircles.

11   When working with circles, always FIND the CENTER of the circle before assuming that something is a radius or a diameter and LABEL every RADIUS that's been drawn.

12   To solve Coordinate Geometry questions, it's often necessary to establish a line's equation so that you can plug points into that equation.

Sherpa Prep

Master Key to the GRE

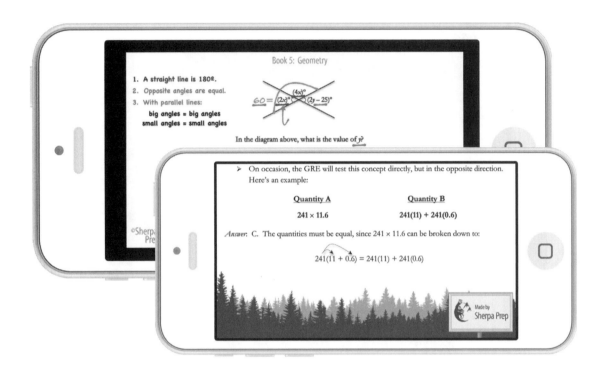

GOLDEN STATES OF GRACE